Chopin's Piano

PAUL KILDEA

Chopin's Piano

A Journey Through Romanticism

ALLEN LANE
an imprint of
PENGUIN BOOKS

ALLEN LANE

UK | USA | Canada | Ireland | Australia
India | New Zealand | South Africa

Allen Lane is part of the Penguin Random House group of companies
whose addresses can be found at global.penguinrandomhouse.com

First published 2018
001

Copyright © Paul Kildea, 2018

The moral right of the author has been asserted

Set in 10.5/14 pt Sabon LT Std
Typeset by Jouve (UK), Milton Keynes
Printed in Great Britain by Clays Ltd, St Ives plc

A CIP catalogue record for this book is available from the British Library

ISBN: 978–0–241–18794–4

Contents

CONTENTS

List of Illustrations

Excerpt from T. S. Eliot, *Prufock and Other Observations*, reproduced by kind permission of Faber & Faber Ltd

Excerpts from George Sand, trans. Dan Hofstadter, *The Story of my Life*, reproduced by kind permission of The Folio Society

Excerpts from Jean-Jacques Eigeldinger, *Chopin: Pianist and Teacher, As Seen by his Pupils*, trans. Naomi Shohet, Krysia Osotowicz, Roy Howat, reproduced by kind permission of Cambridge University Press

Preface

I began thinking about the history of pianism as a doctoral student, working under the supervision of the brilliant social and economic historian Cyril Ehrlich. In the mid-1970s Cyril had written a terrific book, *The Piano: A History*, an exploration of the impact of the pianoforte on society, industry and entertainment, from Mozart's time onwards, which he had revised and republished two years before I came to work with him. His focus was not so much on how these instruments were played, or how knowledge of nineteenth-century pianos would add ballast to historically informed performance, a movement then in full swing. As a fine amateur pianist, who had educated himself musically on the family piano and his father's 78s, Cyril was instead intrigued by the social phenomenon the instrument represented.

Chopin's Piano: A Journey Through Romanticism is the opposite of Cyril's book; its thread is a single instrument, not an entire industry, one made in Palma in the 1830s and which had a most eventful life. When initially I began tracing the history of the piano – who owned it, what was composed and played on it, what it came to mean to different people over time – I realized that to do the subject justice I also had to write about how pianism changed following Chopin's encounter with the instrument, how audiences, society, taste and programming changed alongside it, and how musical Romanticism forged such interesting and unexpected paths during the nineteenth and twentieth centuries as different performing styles and political and cultural ideologies staked their claim. Many other ideas and historical events were subsequently caught up in the narrative. In twenty-four chapters divided into two parts (a nod to the twenty-four pieces, originally published in two books, that constitute the astonishing collection Chopin finished on this instrument), I use the history of the piano to write about the arc of musical Romanticism, including our complex relationship with it today.

Cyril and I talked about many things in marathon supervisions involving beer and frankfurters, though I cannot recall ever discussing the musical *Salad Days*, which opened in London in 1954 just as he was writing his PhD thesis (on cotton marketing in Uganda), and which enjoyed a record-breaking run of over 2,200 performances. It tells the story of an old piano that has an almost intoxicating effect on anyone who hears it played. At one point the instrument vanishes, which causes great consternation among those who have come to rely on its hypnotic properties, and which prompts the full company to sing 'We're Looking for a Piano'. This is more or less what I get up to in this book.

Apart from the conversations I had with Cyril all those years ago, for which I remain ever grateful, many people were generous with their expertise, friendship and hospitality as I researched and wrote this book. Those involved in the construction, restoration or collecting of pianos and who were of immense help include Jean-Claude Battault (Musée de la Musique, Paris); Alec Cobbe and Alison Hoskyns (The Cobbe Collection); Olivier Fadini; Uli Gerhartz (Steinway & Sons); Solomon Haileselassie (Coolidge Auditorium, the Library of Congress); Chris Maene and his team, including Tine Mannaerts and Wolf Leye; Donald Manildi (International Piano Archives at Maryland); and Christophe Nebout (Pianos Nebout).

Museums and archives were a rich resource and I would like to thank Christopher Hartten and his colleagues – in particular Cait Miller and Walter Zvonchenko – at the Performing Arts Reading Room of the Library of Congress, Washington D.C., who steered me through the Landowska/Restout collection; Maciej Janicki and Grażyna Michniewicz (Muzeum Fryderyka Chopina); Jayson Dobney and Ken Moore (Metropolitan Museum, New York City), along with a very helpful security guard with a master's degree in guitar, whose name I stupidly failed to ask; Martin Elste (Musikinstrumenten-Museum, Berlin); Lilia Franqui (Probate Court, Coral Gables); Jochende Schwarz (Felicia Blumenthal Music Center in Tel Aviv); and Gérard Tardif (L'Association pour la Sauvegarde de l'Auditorium de Wanda Landowska).

A number of musicians had fascinating and diverse thoughts about Chopin and pianism, including two old friends, Dejan Lazic and Cedric Tiberghien. Jeremy Filsell (Artist in Residence at Washington National Cathedral and Music Director of Washington's Church of the Epiphany) was generous with his time and his ideas on improvisation. Michael Black and Simon Kenway, two outstanding musicians, were, as ever, stimulating friends and generous hosts, as was Simon's mother Carmel. Genevieve Lacey had inspiring thoughts on just about everything. Christopher D. Lewis had some great tales to tell about Landowska and Pleyel, and kindly sent my way a number of photographs I had not seen before. Linda Kouvaras not only plays the piano beautifully but talks about it and music with equal skill. Helen Moody gave me late-night help with homework. Skip Sempé is a passionate and erudite Wanda Landowska advocate and I greatly benefited from my time with him. Peter Roennfeldt shared his knowledge of early pianos and generously allowed me to sit in on a trio rehearsal with his fellow musicians Margaret Connolly and Daniel Curro. Jill Stoll, apart from being a really fine pianist, told me about a viola in Vienna. Finn Downie Dear and Laurence Matheson play beautifully and had interesting things to say about Chopin, as did Chiyan Wong about Busoni. Keith Radford introduced the adolescent me to Szymanowski, though never managed to convince me then of Chopin's brilliance (my fault entirely). Anita Lasker-Wallfisch was kind enough to revisit in my company the harrowing events of 1939–45.

Scholars who generously shared their expertise include Malcolm Gillies, who also read the book in manuscript and had his usual array of whip-smart comments and criticisms; the superb critic and sideways-thinking John Allison; the continually inspiring Jennifer Doctor; Jean-Jacques Eigeldinger (whose treasure-trove book, edited by the creative and original pianist and musicologist Roy Howat – whom I also thank – was an invaluable resource); and Alain Koehler, Jennifer Bailey, Mackenzie Pierce and Caroline Gill, all of whom had valuable comments to make. I am grateful for the support of Professor Barry Conyngham and Professor Gary McPherson at the University of Melbourne, where I am an Honorary Principal Fellow at the Conservatorium of Music. Carla Shapreau, who is currently working on what will become the standard text on the looting of musical instruments and collections during the Second World War, was extremely generous with her thoughts and time, as was Willem de Vries, whose research into Nazi looting was both pioneering and invaluable. Teri Noel Towe shared his knowledge of Landowska and memories of Denise Restout.

I thank Sue Hackett for inspiring conversations, friendship and French translations, along with Nicole Dorigo, Oscar Strasnoy and Peter Kraus, who also provided translations.

I am grateful to friends and family in different countries who hosted me while I was researching and writing, or told me stories that have become part of the text, including Warwick Anderson, Merryn Anstee, Alex Biernacki, Penny Bradfield, Maxime Burzlaff, Michael Cooney, Trish Dearn, Arjun Devanesan, Amanda Douge, Tim Dunlop, Paul Fitzsimon, Kate Forster, Olivia Gesini, Lavinia Greenlaw, Tom Hamilton, Andrew Higgie, Jennifer Higgie, Lindy Hume, Ruth Kraus, John Lawrence, David Oldham, Breandáin O'Shea, Deborah Phillips, Lee Primmer, Jonathan Reekie, James Rondeau, Peter and Pam Rowe, Paul Ryan, Paul Schutz, Tanya Smith, Joey Swanchara, Lindy Tennent-Brown, Peter and Catharina Tinniswood (who introduced me to Christopher Pike, who told me about his uncle Roland Weisshuhn), Benjamin Waters, Andrew Watts, David Wroe, my amazing sisters Susan, Margaret, Elizabeth and Catherine, their partners, and my father Paul. Dennis Stevenson gave me a private viewing of the Tate's Turner exhibition, which got me thinking about ships, while Graeme Honner and Andrew Comben read parts or all of the manuscript and had helpful things to say (though I add the usual disclaimer that any errors are of my own devising).

I am blessed with a fabulous agent, David Godwin, who has around him a great team, including Heather Godwin, Amy Mitchell, Kirsty McLachlan and Philippa Sitters.

This is my second book for Penguin/Allen Lane and I could not be more grateful for Stuart Proffitt's incisive mind, clear eye and passionate interest in this project, which began the moment I first mentioned it to him, and will no doubt continue long past publication. Both Ben Sinyor and his predecessor Donald Futers were of enormous help in getting the book to press, Ben more or less adopting it, lavishing it with a degree of care and affection I could not have anticipated. I thank Richard Mason for his expert copy-editing and incisive queries, Jim Stoddart and Isabelle De Cat for the exquisite cover, and Richard Duguid, Francisca Monteiro and Penelope Vogler at Penguin for their clear-eyed and imaginative attentions to the book, which are greatly appreciated.

Paul Kildea, February 2018

BOOK ONE

The Lodestar of Musical Romanticism

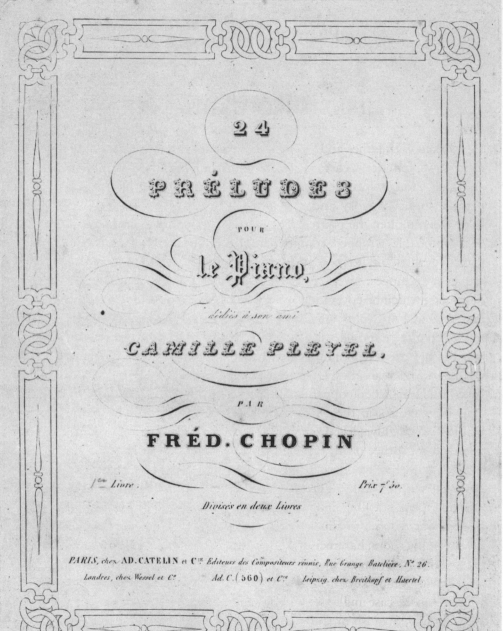

24

PRÉLUDES

POUR

Le Piano,

dédiés à son ami

CAMILLE PLEYEL,

PAR

FRÉD. CHOPIN

1.er Livre.　　　　　　　　　　　　　　Prix 7.^f 5o.

Divisés en deux Livres

PARIS, chez AD. CATELIN et Cie Editeurs des Compositeurs réunis, Rue Grange Batelière, N.° 26.

Londres, chez Wessel et C.°　　Ad. C. (560) et Cie　　Leipzig, chez Breitkopf et Haertel.

Gravé par A. Vialon.

I

Palma, 1830s

He worked with lathes and wooden mallets, adzes and gougers, fine-tooth saws, mandrels, casting moulds and kiln, pliers, pots of lacquer and glue. He cut spruce and local softwood, hardwood blocks and planks, sheets of ivory and mahogany veneer. He heated pig iron that, when molten, he poured into moulds, which he then slaked in cold water. He wrapped copper windings around iron strings and threaded them on to a reinforced frame. He created a complex sequence of hinges, levers, long metal rods, wrest pins and wooden hammers, which he covered in spun wool, felt or deerskin. He lathed and planed hardwood into two delicate, ornamental legs, which bulbed in five or six places, like exquisite gnarly roots. Above ivory-wafered keys he fixed an intricately carved lacework panel, a strip of a dozen or so square tiles. On to the mahogany casing over this Moorish frieze he attached copper candle paws.

In big factories in the 1830s – Broadwood, say, or Pleyel – piano making was highly specialized. There were belly-men crafting sound-boards from spruce or fir, tensing it slightly, holding the subtle curves in place with great wooden ribs, as if filleted from a large animal; wood seasoners taking planks of beech, sycamore and deal from the saw pit, labelling them, stacking and airing them outdoors until their moisture content was reduced to almost nothing, and only then moving them to the seasoning room; hammer makers crafting dowelling and felt in progressively smaller sizes, like Russian nesting dolls; cutters and ivory workers fashioning keys from limewood, ebony and fat fingers of ivory veneer; square-case makers building external carpentry; veneer men working with Spanish or Cuban mahogany an eighth of an inch thick and costing five guineas per cubic foot; fret cutters carving ornamental latticework; cleaners-off and polishers readying the instrument for sale.

Each artisan had his own task, his own area of the factory (with its own climate), the sequence of production understood by three or four hundred men magicking a thousand pianos a year from an intricate formulation of beefwood, birch, cedar, lime, fir, zebrawood, sycamore, satinwood, and iron, brass, copper, steel, black lead, baize, felt, vellum, ivory, linseed oil, emery paper, putty powder and beeswax.

A double-page spread in *L'Illustration* in June 1855 shows how all these pieces fitted together. Pleyel's headquarters, showroom, workshops and concert hall are handsomely depicted (an imposing edifice in Paris's second *arrondissement*), while its mill and factory in the rue des Portes-Blanches, Saint-Denis, north of the city, dominates the surrounding landscape, its grounds dotted with tall chimneys and towering stacks of planed wood. Inside there are well-staffed factory lines and all sorts of industrial tools, which create instruments for *grandes maisons parisiennes*. By mid-century there were specialist firms capable of supplying strings and hammer rails, felts and pins, though Pleyel cut no such corners. Every step in production was recorded in the company's ledger: *Caissier, Clavier, Échappement, Finisseur, Couvercles, Vernisseur, Égaliseur* – a date marking the completion of each stage of each instrument, along with the name of the workman responsible.

The piano maker working alone twenty years earlier, some distance from Paris, had no such facilities, no such procedures and records, precious few materials: he must have had to improvise relentlessly. Yet in such unpromising circumstances he built an instrument no more than four feet high, with six and a half octaves of ivory keys and ebony accidentals. He incorporated a folding keyboard (as on a ship's piano) and affixed a small, finely written label to the front board, which he then varnished over:

'Manufactured by Juan Bauza, Mission Street, Palma'.

Bauza had no inkling of his piano's remarkable destiny: no conception of the astonishing music that would be composed and performed on it, or its sequence of owners – some distinguished, others not – or its uncanny ability to survive the most improbable, unfortunate circumstances. Nor could he have predicted what the piano would come to symbolize as the music composed on it changed in sound and meaning, as performers, audiences and political ideologies fought over the unique cultural value and historical significance it eventually acquired.

2

Palma, Paris, 1838

Her party disembarked in Palma late morning, a port official listing its arrival as he might the *dramatis personæ* of an unpromising play:

> First Class:
> > Madame Dudevant, married.
> > M. Maurice, her son, minor.
> > Mlle Solange, her daughter, minor.
> > M. Frédéric Chopin, artist.
> Second Class:
> > Mme Amelia, chambermaid.

Madame Dudevant and her retinue had left Barcelona aboard *El Mallorquin* at sunset on 7 November 1838, sailing the 160 miles south in eighteen hours. The *Mallorquin* had criss-crossed this route since its launch in 1830, the moment when the island began exporting citrus fruits and fattened pigs, and importing on return voyages the spare, early shoots of tourism. The paddle-steamer's beds were best suited for penance, a later passenger would write, seasickness and the stench of burning coal reaching every corner of below decks. First-class passengers ate with silver cutlery off china plates; Madame Amelia was not so fortunate. Well before the *Mallorquin* slipped into the harbour, signal operators in a chain of watchtowers transmitted to Palma her passage past Dragonera, the sentry island off Majorca's west coast.

The steamer's passenger tickets mid-century featured an etching of *El Mallorquin*, which was later the source of an undated boxwood print: it illustrates a sturdy 45-metre craft with three masts and black copper plating sheathing its wooden hull against weeds and ship-worm; large paddles on port and starboard sides; hatted sailors working ropes and pulleys at the bow, a Spanish flag flapping on a pole at the stern; and stiff-backed passengers sitting on deck as though in church, protected from the salt spray and poor weather by a modest canopy. 'Printed with the world's oldest functioning press', the engraving boasts, though this claim to antiquity cannot disguise the fact that it is a modern-eyed, nostalgic view of steamship travel: the ship's name is too prominent; there are eel-like waves chopping against the paddle; and from a fleur-de-lys collar around the funnel mouth dark plumes of fine-lined coal smoke belch into the sky. It is a little like the work of Norfolk fisherman–artist John Craske, who in the early decades of the following century lent a handcrafted, old-fashioned air to the exquisite nautical images he created in swirls of oil and plump rice-grain embroidery stitches. History needs relics, and Monsieur Frédéric Chopin's steamer now has a mast, a paddle wheel, a funnel, a flag – a face.

Prints of the island are more reliable, not least Lorenzo Muntaner's illustrated map (1831), which shows a port town entirely walled in by accordion-bellow ramparts, with two hundred streets and plazas, divided into four *cuarteles* (quarters), inside the fortification. Muntaner includes a striking silhouette profile of the Gothic church in the Convent of Santo Domingo, which was reduced to a rubble of columns and cornices a year before Chopin and Dudevant's visit – a consequence of Spain's suppression and confiscation of monasteries, as ordered by Prime Minister Juan Álvarez Mendizábal in October 1835 – and lists Palma's population as 36,008 residents occupying 5,437 homes.

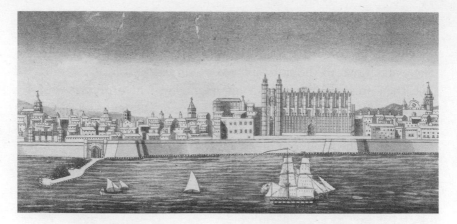

Not quite a year after Dudevant, her children Maurice (fifteen) and Solange (eight), her maid Amelia, and Chopin arrived in Palma, the artist and musician Jean-Joseph Bonaventure Laurens travelled to the island, also on *El Mallorquin*. He was escaping the strong winds and morning frosts of Languedoc, inspired by Beethoven's setting of 'Kennst du das Land?', a poem (about Italy) in Goethe's *Wilhelm Meisters Lehrjahre* (*Wilhelm Meister's Apprenticeship*), which the adolescent Mignon sings to Wilhelm as a wistful folk song, the cold German countryside crushing her spirit:

> Do you know the land where the lemon trees blossom,
> Where amid dark leaves golden oranges glow,
> Where a gentle breeze blows from the blue sky,
> Where the myrtle stands silent and the laurel high?
> Do you know it well?
> It is there I would travel with you, my beloved.

Laurens knew Majorca only through the botanist Jacques Cambessèdes's *Excursions dans les îles Baléares* of 1826; before arriving he could therefore not conjure up the terrain and buildings beyond Palma, nor the food and customs, religious feasts and local dress, the island's rhythm and the brilliance of its light. In two weeks he made sketches for the fifty-five lithographs he published the following year in *Souvenirs d'un voyage d'art à l'île de Majorque*.

Lithography is really too fussy a medium for a travelling artist. Laurens had to create an image on smooth limestone using wax crayons, coat it with a weak mix of acid and gum arabic, wait while the solution sank into the pores of the unmarked parts of the stone and created a salt crust, wet the limestone just enough that the solution was drawn to the salty surface, roll on a thin sheen of oil-based ink, then press thick paper against the stone. The process requires a decent workshop, imagination, and good source material in either a sketchpad or memory – all of which Laurens had in abundance back home. There he produced prints of exceptional warmth and detail.

Laurens re-created the turrets above Palma's busy market (stocked with hares, fresh fish and vegetables, apples, oranges, lemons, beans, walnuts, pomegranates, capsicums and rice); rows of fixed-cap tower mills grinding cereals and pumping water; villagers with baskets on their heads walking to town or sitting in the square, large hats shielding them from the strong autumn sun and heat; a cowled monk from one of the monasteries suppressed in 1835, politely begging in the streets; fishermen navigating their boats into Porto Pi, an old Moorish lighthouse behind them. In one print, of a scene not far from where fishing boats are secured, a man and woman chat while going about their work, framed by the port, thick ramparts hugging the bay, vessels of all sizes and functions on the water, palm trees tall against the distant buildings, and the Cathedral of Santa Maria of Palma (La Seu), steeples high in the air, dominating the landscape.

Each of Laurens's lithographs looks back to an exotic seaport world of peasants dressed in calfskin, of knife grinders, of night watchmen on sing-song patrols, of Moorish houses with whitewashed walls and flat roofs stacked with pigeon cages; and of the once splendid Silk Exchange, a marvel of Valencian Gothic architecture, its gold-lettered motto, running along the walls in the Hall of Columns, counselling merchants to act truthfully so that they might prosper on earth and thereafter *vita fructur aeterna* – enjoy eternal life. Not for Laurens the recent gasworks and coal trade of a port slowly awakening to the industrial age.

It was immediately evident in Palma that thirty-four-year-old Madame Dudevant cut a most unusual figure. Dressed entirely in black – usually a redingote or a sentry-box coat with matching breeches, waistcoat and boots – her shiny plaits pinned by a silver dagger, a velvet ribbon around her neck securing a large diamond crucifix, Dudevant walked through the port, cigar in hand. The French caricaturist Alcide Joseph Lorentz captured her well ten years later, standing with page-boy hair as though a religious apparition, within clouds of her own making, fingers holding a white cigar, her right elbow on a pile of manuscripts. In his inscription Lorentz uses the name she had carried by then for nearly twenty years: *If this portrait of George Sand leaves the mind a little perplexed, it is because, as we know, genius has no gender.*

Sand was the writer Flaubert admired and the woman Baudelaire boorishly derided as heavy and garrulous, her morals those of a janitress or courtesan. ('The fact that there are men who could become enamoured of this slut is indeed a proof of the abasement of the men of this generation.') Matthew Arnold, Sand's junior by eighteen years, was more generous and accurate, identifying a woman not weighed down by the past or the conventions of her day, but rather an artist searching for a freer conception of humanity. Some commentators were preoccupied with her appearance, Auguste Barbier deciding she was a boy dressed as a woman. Others (besides Baudelaire) were fascinated by her moral reputation, the young poet (and Sand's future lover) Alfred de Musset saying of her silver dagger that 'a woman of such slight virtue hardly required so immoderate a weapon'.

Alexis de Tocqueville, meeting her at dinner a few months after the February Revolution of 1848, was astonished by Sand's forensic description of the political climate – the number and resolve of the

Parisian working class and the signs of the catastrophic explosion to come in the Paris Commune of 1870–71. Later, when Flaubert wrote to her in despair about the slaughter and capitulation of the French during the Franco–Prussian War and the overthrow of yet another government ('France is sinking slowly, like a rotten hulk'), Sand responded with optimism about humanity's continued advance. Franz Liszt said that 'although she had the arm of a sculptor, her hand was delicate enough to trace the most delicate reliefs that leave only the lightest trace in the stone'. Oscar Wilde thought she first had to have love affairs so she could write about them, while Henry James admired the many liberties her work took with memory: 'Madame Sand remembers to the point of gratefully – gratefully as an artist – reconstituting.' Even Cole Porter, a hundred years after Sand's trip to Majorca, had a view: 'When, in Venice, Georgia Sand with Chopin romped,/Her libido had the Lido simply swamped.'

There was never a consensus about her, which did not concern Sand for one moment. In her masculine clothing she passed unnoticed in the capital's narrow, dirty streets, and gained entrée to the quarters of society conventionally denied to women – the balcony at the Opéra, for example – without spending hours tonging her hair into corkscrew curls, slipping into corsets and *chemises*, day dresses or evening gowns, applying scent and make-up, finding pins and shawls, cloaks and cards, overshoes and umbrella, and all the other requirements of bourgeois and aristocratic Parisian life. She lived beyond the restrictions and expectations of her gender, writing with verve from the privileged position of an intelligent insider and outsider about love, marriage, affairs, family, women, class, beauty, culture, Paris, politics and poverty.

All this was controversial enough in Paris; in Palma in 1838 it was inconceivable. Robert Graves, who lived in the tiny Majorcan village of Deyá from the late 1920s until his death in 1985, translated Sand's memoir of her time on the island, *Un hiver à Majorque* (*A Winter in Majorca*), annotating it with rare animosity ('Her memory is at fault ... The Mediterranean has no tides ... They are an extremely clean people', et cetera). Graves thought her and Chopin's visit represented 'a personal clash between the pre-Revolutionary Classical world and the world of post-Revolutionary Romanticism': Sand had come to show the backward Majorcans they could free themselves of their moral and intellectual manacles if only they put their minds to it.

Yet she had no such aim. She had simply chosen to opt out of what Walter Benjamin would label the 'Capital of the Nineteenth Century', to remove her family for a short time from the routines, expectations and complications of Parisian life, to experience instead a slower pace and warmer climate, to alleviate her son's poor health, and to give her new relationship with Chopin a chance to grow, away from the public gaze. They would be gone for a year, perhaps two, living cheaply on the island, writing (Sand), composing (Chopin), painting (Maurice), doing lessons (Solange). They were in Majorca, its population only 160,000, in search of the images and experiences that would shortly entrance Laurens, visitors to an island hoping for another world and with no especial wish to bring their old one with them.

The passport on which Chopin travelled described him as five feet seven inches tall, with an oval face, round chin, medium-sized mouth, and French parentage, this last detail only half true. He was worryingly slight: two years after Majorca, he weighed just ninety-seven pounds (forty-four kilos).

In her memoir Sand writes that if public curiosity demands biographies, 'the portrait should be limited to the description on one's passport, drawn up by the local police chief in an unemphatic, uncompromising style'. Chopin's first biographer Frederick Niecks took her disingenuous cue, detailing his medium height and slim frame, small feet and delicate hands, pale, almost transparent countenance, chestnut hair (parted on one side), aquiline nose and intelligent eyes, sweet smile and graceful gestures.

Chopin, then twenty-eight, was six years Sand's junior. They had met at the end of October 1836 in the Hôtel de France, in the apartment Liszt had taken with his mistress, the Countess Marie d'Agoult. It was not a promising encounter, Liszt observing that 'Chopin at first seemed to dread Mme Sand more than other women since, like the Sibyl, she said things that others knew not how to say.' Chopin himself said to the German conductor and composer Ferdinand Hiller, 'What an unattractive person La Sand is. Is she really a woman?' Yet by late summer 1838 it was acknowledged within their overlapping circles that the two were lovers. Not all approved. On the eve of their departure for Spain the Marquis de Custine wrote vindictively to the French author Sophie Gay about Sand's impact on his friend. 'Consumption has taken possession of that face, making it a soul without a body. The unfortunate creature cannot see that the woman has the love of a vampire!' Yet Custine had written to Chopin about his health over a year earlier ('You are ill: what is worse, your illness might become really serious'), so he could not truthfully lay his condition at Sand's door. Besides, Custine could never quite manage to separate his friendly concern for Chopin from more amorous feelings: in his eyes, Sand had no chance.

To their friends, Chopin and Sand seemed happy enough. Not long before their travels Eugène Delacroix invited them to sit for him in his large studio in the rue Notre-Dame de Lorette. It was an entrancing space: a double-height ceiling with a full-length skylight adjusted by blinds; artworks on easels and every available surface; clean squirrel-tail paintbrushes looking like tulips in vases; a small brazier (surely not up to the task of heating the atelier in winter), its long stovepipe

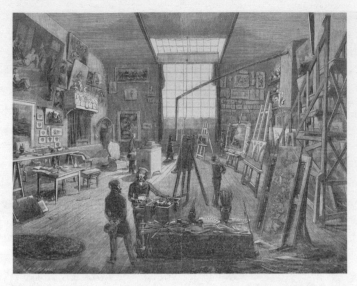

reaching high over the working area like a thick branch; desks with papers, books, decanter, inkwell, maulstick; a *chaise longue* and various armchairs. For the double-portrait session Delacroix had installed a *pianino* – the small piano then popular in Paris – that he instructed Chopin to play while he sketched, angling himself and his subjects so that Chopin's hands were hidden and not a distraction. (Chopin in any case kept his body still when playing, as he instructed his pupils to do.)

Delacroix captured something genuine and moving in Sand, who sits to Chopin's right, cigar in hand, absorbing the music around her. The two are detached from each other, but their affinity is palpable.

But it was in his depiction of Chopin that Delacroix really succeeded, for he caught something unguarded in his expression and pose – his steely concentration and noble bearing, but also his sense of isolation in company. Delacroix painted Chopin the distinguished Romantic artist, the composer of polonaises and waltzes; a *Marche funèbre* he would soon stitch into his Sonata in B flat minor; a startling, complex collection of twelve Études; the Nocturne in C minor, which opens out like a rare orchid, but only for an instant, closing again just as quickly without notice. Chopin has earned the bearing Delacroix gives him, though at the expense of his humour and curiosity, his wonderment and inventiveness, his warmth and generosity, his child-like imagination, his youthful misfortunes in love too. 'No soul was more brilliant, delicate or unselfish,' Sand would much later write of her former lover, 'no wit more brilliant in its moments of gaiety, no intelligence more serious and complete in its domain.' Illness changed his good nature, she added, as if to balance the scales, darkened his imagination, increased his sensitivity.

Seven years earlier, soon after he had arrived in Paris, Chopin had written to his friend Tytus Woyciechowski:

> So far as my feelings are concerned, I am always out of step with other people. It depresses me horribly and I would give anything for a breathing-space, a whole day during which no one would look at me or say a word. If I'm in the middle of a letter I can't bear it when the bell rings and in strides a huge, fully grown, powerful, bewhiskered creature who sits down at the piano, improvises God knows what, storms, bangs like a madman, writhes about, crosses his hands and hammers on one note for fully five minutes with one enormous finger which Heaven intended for holding the whip and reins of some farm steward away in the Ukraine . . .

All the qualities Sand identified in him – and a few of those Delacroix caught in his portrait – were already in place: the sensitivity and solitariness, the humour and intelligence. In time Chopin would become the lodestar of musical Romanticism.

3

Palma, Valldemossa, 1838

It was an odd time to visit Majorca. Civil war had flashed throughout Spain since the death five years earlier of King Ferdinand VII, which ignited familial disagreement over whether his successor would be his brother, Carlos, or his infant daughter, Isabella, whose interests were looked after by her mother, Maria Christina, Ferdinand's widow and Regent of Spain. Refugees and émigrés descended on the island seeking sanctuary, finding instead Carlists and Christinos as partisan there as they were on the mainland. The commander-in-chief issued a dramatic order just three days before Chopin and Sand's arrival:

> The district of the island of Majorca is declared to be in a state of war. Henceforth everybody will be subject to military authority, without prejudice to other constituted authorities who will continue in the legal exercise of their respective functions, albeit with the obligations of obeying and complying with whatever may be required of them in the interest of public security.

In Palma they took the only habitable accommodation available, semi-furnished rooms in a former military barracks on Calle de la Marina, close to the old Arab Quarter, its name now rendered in Catalan, the root of the local dialect Mallorquí, which is, with Spanish, the official language of the island. Carrer de la Mar is only five or six metres wide and is entered at the city end through a narrow Moorish arch. On the east side are shuttered five-storey apartment buildings in every shade, on the west the former barracks, whose walls are made of large blocks of sandstone hewn from local quarries, hastily piled on top of each other. A modern plaque – high up on the stone, its names and dates in perfect order – verifies the street's most famous inhabitants: *The Polish musician Frederic Chopin*

(1810–1849) and the French writer George Sand (1804–1876) lodged in this street on 8 November 1838, the day they arrived in Mallorca, a visit to the island that ended on 13 February 1839.

Chopin's health and mood in these initial days were promising. To his Polish friend and copyist Julian Fontana in Paris he wrote of turquoise skies and lapis lazuli seas, emerald mountains and clear, clean air, palms and cedars, olive and orange trees, figs and pomegranates – everything to be found in the hothouses of Paris's Jardin des Plantes. He described the sunshine and moderate temperatures, the summer clothes worn by the townsfolk, the guitars at night playing for hours at a time. 'Oh, my dear fellow, I am really beginning to live. I am close to all that is most beautiful. I am a better man.'

Sand thought the climate as warm as a French June, perfect for exploring the port's mix of High Gothic splendour and Moorish remnants: ramparts and stone peasant houses; thermal baths; unfamiliar street names; carved lintels and arabesque scrolls; tall windows divided by slender pillars; ornamental staircases leading up to enormous dark, bare rooms; and, beyond the city, the Jardines de Alfabia, nestled into terraced hills and irrigated by waterwheels.

The Majorcan king James I's great monument to the port and the faith he imposed on the inhabitants when he reconquered and Christianized the island in the thirteenth century is the Cathedral of Santa Maria, a building of stunning proportions and impact, pieced together over centuries from great slabs of ashlar. In the mornings, at the time of year when the sun hits the rose window on the east facade, the interior is bathed in soft, warm light. It is not, however, the same quality of light that Chopin and Sand encountered: most of the needle windows were then filled with mortar, apertures at the top allowing in only small fingers of illumination, while others – including the cathedral's additional exquisite rose windows – were considerably altered following an earthquake in 1851, then by Antoni Gaudí early in the twentieth century, and once more to repair damage caused during the Spanish Civil War.

Yet even in the glum light of 1838 there was plenty to admire: solid stone trunks reaching up and spreading into a fine-branch canopied ceiling; a cavernous nave uncluttered by either chairs or pews, where people moved about freely or sat with backs stiff against columns; an

altar pointing the penitent towards Mecca, not Jerusalem, its pos-
itioning a leftover from the original mosque whose grounds the
cathedral had colonized; full-size apostles and prophets serving as
sentinels at the Mirador portal; marble figures in the Flemish style
enacting blurry biblical scenes; ornate reliquaries, often outshining
their contents; side chapels containing the tombs of long-dead bish-
ops; the remains of two kings, James II and James III of Majorca,
dressed in fine robes and appearing extremely well preserved. Sand
admired the limestone and the marble sarcophagus holding James II,
yet found the interior too austere, the November light too weak to
illuminate the cathedral's features to any advantage; she quickly dismissed 'this huge, majestic pile'.

She was dismissive too of Palma's rude levels of service, of mattresses as hard as slate, vermin in the beds, scorpions in the soup, and
monotonous, uncommon dishes. Most Majorcans were understand-
ably distracted and in any case had no use for the letters of introduction
Sand brought from Paris. It was all so unsettling for the visitors: civil
war, the blunt responses of put-upon locals, the poor condition of
their lodgings, the thrumming and wailing through the night. Even
worse was the incessant racket from the cooperage below their rooms:
the deliveries of wood and coal and hammering of metal on anvil,
the noisy dispatch of barrels to Majorca's millers and wine makers,
farmers and blacksmiths.

There was something even more debilitating for Chopin. 'I dream
of music,' he wrote to Camille Pleyel, his French publisher, soon after
arriving, 'but I can't write any because there are no pianos to be had
here – in that respect it is a barbarous country.' It was the complaint
of an artist thrown from his routine, a composer who habitually
wrote his exceptionally original works at the piano and who now
found himself without the one tool he needed. So after a week of
industry at full tilt below stairs but little of it above, Chopin, Sand,
her children and the maid moved to a house in Establiments, off the
Palma road, a small enclave north-west of the port, a property found
for them by the French consul, Monsieur Fleury.

Son Vent – the summer house in Establiments, which translates from
Mallorquí as House of the Wind – cost Chopin and Sand fifty francs

a month and was kitted out with wooden camp beds padded with paper-thin mattresses, straw-bottomed chairs, and rough-cut wooden tables. There were glazed windows in most rooms, though there were neither fireplaces nor chimneys, just a small brazier that filled the house with noxious fumes but little heat, and left the occupants with dry throats and charcoal-smoked eyes.

Yet the surrounding countryside felt to them like a beautifully kept orchard, divided by colour as though on an artist's palette: amber (maize), red (tomatoes and peppers), yellow (lemons), white (myrtle) and green (moss). Bells around the necks of asses and mules at pasture clanked away during the night, but little else disturbed them. 'In Majorca, the silence is deeper than anywhere else,' Sand later wrote. She was intending to revise *Lélia*, her radical book of 1833 about male and female desire, parts of which she now found gauche, and to begin what would become her religious novel *Spiridion*; but, as she wrote to Chopin's great friend Wojciech Grzymała, with 'neither donkey, servant, water, fire nor safe means of dispatching manuscripts', they were finding it difficult to settle. 'In such circumstances I am cooking instead of writing,' she told Grzymała, despondently doing her best with local ingredients ('in a country where geese are regarded as beings from another world, and chickens still itch when they descend from the spit'), which she fried in pork grease or rancid oil – the unripe olives that year having been attacked by fruit fly and left to rot on the ground before harvesting.

Chopin, weakened by the stench and suffocating effect of the charcoal smoke, was by no means well in Establiments. And despite temperatures of eighteen degrees and air outside scented with roses, oranges and figs, he caught a feverish cold. A succession of doctors (the grandest charging forty-five francs for his advice) prodded him and made dire pronouncements. 'It is all having a bad effect on the Preludes,' he told Fontana in early December, referring to the collection of piano pieces that had occupied his imagination for some time, the thread of which he was attempting to pick up in Majorca. 'God knows when you will receive them.'

Before leaving Paris, Chopin had ordered from Pleyel a *pianino*, but it reached Marseilles only as he was writing to Fontana at the beginning of December, where it was loaded on to a merchant ship, destined, Chopin feared, to spend the next months in one or other port, hostage to rains and customs bottlenecks, to the lethargy that accompanies the onset of winter. 'The lack of a piano is a source of great distress to me on the boy's account,' Sand told Grzymała on 3 December, just as Chopin's health returned. 'He has hired a local one which gives him more vexation than consolation. All the same he is working.' The instrument was the one made by Juan Bauza of MissionStreet, Palma.

Majorca was indeed then a musical backwater, insulated from the pianoforte's sudden and immense popularity throughout mainland Europe in the 1820s and 1830s, sparked by the achievements of Pleyel (Paris), Conrad Graf (Vienna), John Broadwood and Sons (London), Sébastien Erard and his nephew Pierre (Paris), each firm lodging new patents with a regularity that challenged the others. Hélène Choussat de Canut, whose husband Bazile acted as Sand's banker while she was in Majorca, had bought from a previous French consul a Pape piano – a model Chopin almost certainly knew from his visits to Pape's showroom and concert hall on the rue des Bons-Enfants in Paris – though an instrument of this quality was a rarity on the island.

In Palma, Bauza was completely isolated from these European developments. He lived less than a kilometre from the artillery barracks, only a couple of hundred metres from the theatre Sand attended one evening with Madame Canut, where eyeglasses 'stabbed at her all night'. Apart from his address and this piano, nothing is known of him – not even whether he was responsible for a number of instruments or was merely a hobbyist, a single project on his mind, inspired by something he had seen or read about. Perhaps he was one of Majorca's famously slow carpenters, about whom Sand is so rude in *Un hiver à Majorque* (on this earning Graves's hard-won corroboration): a good furniture maker would have the skills and tools to build a piano. Or a clock maker, schooled in fine machinery and intricate mechanics, self-taught if necessary (as was the horologist John Harrison): a clock maker too would know how to make a piano if he put his mind to it.

There was then no one single way to build one: it was much like the automobile industry at the end of the century, inventors and keen-eyed engineers advancing their own ideas, often their own patents, consensus following only later. Consolidation of sorts came only in the 1860s and subsequently, thanks largely to the craft and innovation of Henry Engelhard Steinway and his five sons in their loft on Varick Street, Manhattan. Before Steinway, piano makers simply responded as best they could to the challenges laid down by great composers: Beethoven in his final five sonatas (1816–22); Liszt in his Sonata in B minor (1853, the year Steinway, Blüthner and Bechstein were founded); Brahms in his first concerto (1858).

So the nascent revolution of the 1830s and 1840s – which saw instruments gradually increase in size, and strings and frame in tension – was not solely concerned with the pianos being made: what also now mattered was the way they were played (and by whom), and the music being written for them. Liszt exploited the possibilities of Sébastien Erard's double escapement action – whereby a note could be re-struck before the hammer had returned to its resting position, a technique that aped Paganini on the violin and which sounded startling on a keyboard – and changed the physicality of piano playing: a pianist's arms, shoulders and back were now pressed into service to add weight and heft to the attack. Pianos and pianists were suddenly required to do far more, as Liszt acknowledged in the late 1830s, writing about instruments that ran from four As below middle C (A0) to four Gs above (G7). 'In its span of seven octaves [the piano] embraces the range of an orchestra; the ten fingers of a single man suffice to render the harmonies produced by the combined forces of more than 100 concerted instruments . . . We make arpeggios like the harp, prolonged notes like wind instruments, staccatos and a thousand other effects which once seemed the special prerogative of such and such an instrument.' (Saint-Saëns was hardly the only pianist to observe that initially Liszt alone could play his own works.) Such ready innovation ensured the piano's quick passage into popular culture. A year before Chopin and Sand's trip to Majorca, Charles Dickens plotted Mr Pickwick's escape inside one, removing the innards to make room: consumerism, not solely the advocacy of progressive musicians, was helping drive both industrial and cultural shifts.

By the very circumstances of its construction and its place in the not always linear evolution of the modern piano, Bauza's instrument was out of date before it was completed. It possessed no technological pretensions: it was unable to support thicker or longer strings, greater tension or a larger compass, its wooden frame and iron bracing a hostage to the island's fierce climate. Yet it had its own beauty, and was in any case a rare artefact: a *pianino* in Majorca in the 1830s.

The winter of 1838 closed in on Chopin and Sand too quickly. The rains arrived early and leaked through into Son Vent, the villa's walls, pargeted with lime, swelling with moisture. Sand wrote that the damp settled on their shoulders like a cloak of ice. She also told of superstitious townsfolk interpreting Chopin's hacking cough and visiting doctors as signs of consumption, and of the 'boorish Gómez', the rich businessman in Palma who owned the house and who, according to Sand, evicted them after an indiscreet doctor in the port speculated widely on Chopin's health. Yet even on the day he moved to Establiments, Chopin mentioned to Fontana the prospect of staying in 'a wonderful monastery on the most fabulous site in the world: sea, mountains, palm-trees, a cemetery, a crusaders' church, ruins of a mosque, olive-trees a thousand years old'. For as Sand scrambled in Palma to find accommodation far from the cooperage, she heard about an apartment in a former Charterhouse in Valldemossa (Valley of Moses), promptly paid a desultory thirty-five francs as rent for the year, and waited for it to become available. ('It is a huge, old, deserted Carthusian monastery whose monks seem to have been cleared out by Mendizabel [sic] especially for me,' Chopin told Fontana.) When Son Vent proved debilitating for poor Chopin and left Sand with no time to write, and when the apartment was finally ready for them, they broke whatever understanding they had with Gómez, who demanded recompense for the loss of income and the contaminated bedding that he insisted be bought and burned.

This was mid-December, a month after they had made their escape from Calle de la Marina. 'Tomorrow I am going to that marvellous monastery at Valldemossa,' Chopin wrote to Fontana from Palma, where they had fled during the worst of the rains, 'to write in the cell of some old monk who perhaps had more fire in his soul than I have but stifled it, stifled it and put it out, for it was of no use to him. I expect to send you my Preludes and Ballade shortly.' Bauza's *pianino* was transported the sixteen kilometres up the mountains to its new home in a *birlocho* – an open-sided mule-drawn cart – navigating a spider's web of terrible dirt tracks ('roads are made by the torrents and repaired by landslides', Chopin observed dryly), none offering any more obvious or logical a route than the next.

The village of Valldemossa is high in the Majorcan mountains, 425 metres above the sea, the final approach then made almost impenetrable by a thicket of holm oak, carob trees, poplars, pines, and dense woods of olive trees. The temperature is noticeably cooler than in Palma, bitter winds soughing through narrow streets that today host a string of businesses and attractions associated with the village's famous visitors: a tapas bar called Preludios; souvenir shops stocked with familiar images; tended gardens; and, in the square outside the monastery entrance, a bronze bust of a solemn-looking Chopin.

In 1838 it was a sparsely populated hill town. Even so, the monastery and their three-room cell, once inhabited by Chopin's imagined old monk with stifled soul, lifted their mood. Chopin thought the local villagers rogues to a man – peddling a barrow load of oranges for a mere *maravedí* or two, yet charging vast sums for a trouser button – but was captivated by the eagles high in the skies above the monastery, surfing the thermals rising from the valleys, or swooping down to carry off sparrows from the pomegranate tree in the courtyard. He was captivated too by the glorious moon and the ever-changing colours of the landscape at sunset – not the alluring pinks, bright purples, silvery mauves and pure transparent blues of Establiments, but a whole other sequence of shades, which cut across the valley, blue-tinged and darker, more menacing, shorter-lived, shaped by the altitude and surrounding mountains.

Sand too was enraptured by the landscape, its wildness and unpredictability, pockmarked randomly by twisted, bent trees. She loved the thorns guarding beautiful flowers, the velvet moss and rush carpeting the ground, the stone-studded paths that slipped without notice into a ravine, the woods scattered with large rocks, as if from the sky, the fast streams running by dense bushes of myrtle and woodbine, and the solitary farmhouse, an oasis in such wilderness.

Chopin wrote to Fontana:

Palma. 28 December 1838

or rather Valldemossa, a few miles away; between the cliffs and the sea a huge deserted Carthusian monastery where in a cell with doors larger than any carriage-gateway in Paris you may imagine me with my hair unkempt, without white gloves and pale as ever. The cell is shaped like a tall coffin, the enormous vaulting covered with dust, the window small. In front of the window are orange-trees, palms, cypresses; opposite the window is my camp-bed under a Moorish filigree rose-window. Close to the bed is an old square grubby box which I can scarcely use for writing on, with a leaden candlestick (a great luxury here) and a little candle. Bach, my scrawls and someone else's old papers . . . silence . . . you can yell . . . still silence. In short, I am writing to you from a queer place.

He was sleeping and working in a room a little under four metres wide, a little over six metres long, with doors to an adjoining area of identical size with access to the courtyard, which in turn led to a smaller room with a large hearth that Sand found perfectly useless for cooking, the chimney unable to draw smoke; she would labour instead outside over a portable charcoal stove. The barrel-vault ceiling in Chopin's room does indeed look like the inside of a coffin lid (though the filigree rose vent wears its Moorish influences lightly).

The small window is only a metre off the ground, slightly recessed in a niche, and looks out on to a courtyard filled with orange and cypress trees and, over a waist-high wall, to steep terracing on the hill beyond, which Sand likened to a moonlit amphitheatre in which gods fought over their grievances. By the door to the courtyard from the kitchen room is a plaque celebrating the distinguished Chopin scholar Édouard Ganche, who first visited Valldemossa in 1928 (a year before Graves) and, until his death in 1945, remained a level-headed and sceptical arbiter of the claims and counterclaims about Chopin's stay in the monastery.

The original buildings of the Cartuja de Valldemossa date from the fourteenth century, though various additions were made as the order's prosperity increased and the old structures deteriorated; most of what survives was constructed in the eighteenth century. The monks lived a life of simple prayer and contemplation, allowed only thirty minutes of communal conversation a week, left to eat alone in their cells each night the food passed anonymously through the hatch opening on to the cloister. Their diet consisted of fish, vegetables, the milk of goats and sheep, a little bread, some wine made from vines on the mountain, diluted with water. They were allowed meat only when ill: turtle soup, rich in protein, made from amniotes they kept in the gardens (the meat of the few cows on Majorca was lean and tough). 'Doomed to eat alone, work alone, suffer and pray alone,' Sand wrote of a monk's life in Valldemossa, 'he must surely have had only one need left, namely, to escape from this dreadful confinement.'

A sketch-plan of the monastery from 1845 shows nine cells the size of Chopin and Sand's in a row along the building's southernmost flank, finished by a double-sized apartment for the prior at the eastern end. Each had its own chapel, individually decorated with gilt and pictures – in the most vulgar taste, Sand thought, the plaster saints so frightful she would not have cared to meet them after dark. The courtyard houses a large square cemetery the width of five apartments, each monk having dug his own grave. The whole patch is separated from the cells by a long corridor almost four metres wide, which runs the length of the monastery. Opposite the prior's apartment is the Patio de los Mirtos (Courtyard of the Myrtles) and behind that the Iglesia Nueva (New Church). Other terraces and gardens are detailed – at the time of Chopin's visit they were already running wild – as are other buildings, which were then falling into ruin, infusing the atmosphere with a desolate, melancholic air. The plan also includes the names of the various Spaniards who took the opportunity of the suppression of the monasteries to rent apartments there cheaply from the government.

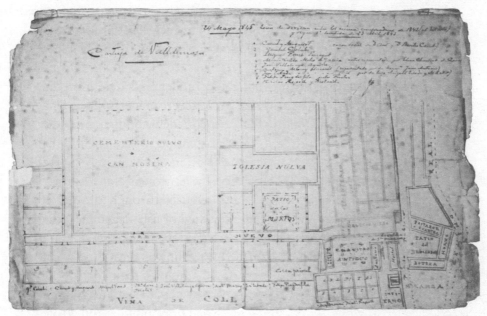

The reception room in the prior's cell is now grandly appointed in gorgeous crimson wallpaper, terracotta floor tiles, gilded mirrors, frames and clocks, rococo furniture with gold detail, brocaded cushions, various ecclesiastical items, and a fine collection of books and illustrated manuscripts. None of it seems to belong here. Furnishings this fine would have been looted after 1835; what was originally in these rooms would have been much more modest.

Cell number four is now a museum, which contains facsimiles of Chopin's letters to Pleyel and Fontana, and a fine-scrawled manuscript page of Sand's *Un hiver à Majorque*; Sand's accounts with the banker Canut; a lock of Chopin's hair, which Sand kept even after their relationship had ended; one of Chopin's smart waistcoats, with five buttons and an ink-blue floral pattern against the black; sketches of the cell and garden by young Maurice; a replica of the cast of

Chopin's elegant hand made immediately after his death by the sculptor Auguste Clésinger; the scene immediately before Chopin's death, re-created in Teofil Kwiatkowski's sombre painting of 1849, *Chopin on his Deathbed*, a copy of which hangs nearby; steamer tickets and minutes regarding the formation of the company Empresa del vapor Mallorquin and the purchase (from 'Sres. Duffres y compañía de Aberdeen') of *El Mallorquin*; etchings, cartoons (Lorentz's caricature of Sand among them), and paintings, including one of Chopin's funerary monument in Paris's Père Lachaise Cemetery – more of Clésinger's work. In the corridor outside the cell giant effigies of Chopin and Sand inspect the comings and goings, she in an improbable Majorcan festival dress with a lace *rebozillo en volant* over her left shoulder, hair parted fiercely in the middle in the local style, great smudges of blue eye shadow high on each cheek; he in a green jacket and altogether too much rouge.

Sand kitted out the apartment modestly. She paid 1,000 francs for leather chairs with wooden frames and Moorish patterns pressed into the hide, a tall dresser, trestle-beds, straw-bottomed chairs, a couch, cushions, a few longhaired sheepskins, and quilted coverlets, which she bought from a Jewish merchant in Palma. She convinced a visiting sacristan to lend them a splendidly carved oak chair, which was slowly falling prey to worms and rats, and which cast Gothic shadows over the walls, successfully re-creating the atmosphere of the original monastery, so she thought. Bits and pieces of this furniture remain today, though there is no sign of the stove Sand commissioned from a Palma blacksmith for Chopin's room, which cost a hundred francs, took a month to make and an hour to light, its chimney thrust ignobly through the small window (as recorded in Maurice's sketch).

This 'queer place' was not quite deserted of monks when Chopin and Sand moved in. As elsewhere throughout Spain, the religious community in Valldemossa had been broken up by the events and edicts of 1835, though the apothecary, Brother Gabriel Oliver, remained at the Cartuja's pharmacy and continued to serve the villagers searching for couch grass for fever, or marshmallow for abscesses and ulcers. (He hid his habit under his bed when they arrived; in his breeches, stockings and waistcoat he looked like one of Molière's characters, Sand thought.) The shelves of the pharmacy are

today lined with original Catalan pottery jars and flasks made of Majorcan glass in bright greens and yellows, which once stored *cassia* or *calamo aromático* or *adormidera blanca* or *cantáridas*, the emerald-green beetle known as Spanish Fly, which induced poison or passion depending on its application. Sand was dismissive of those drugs with obscure names and forgotten virtues – 'the Nail Parings of the Great Beast' and the like – though this did not prevent her from buying the apothecary's couch grass ('for its weight in gold') when Chopin's health deteriorated, or quantities of gum-benzoin when the smell from the stove, whose cement lining had been bulked out with dried cow manure, overpowered the cell.

At last they fell into a routine built on the sun and the shadows. Two years later England's Great Western Railway would initiate the slow crawl throughout Europe towards Standard Time, yet in Majorca then, as everywhere else, time was still local. In the mountains it was even more local than down at the port: in the low December sun a ridge of Serra de Tramontana to one side kept them in shadow until noon, as did another on the other side from 3 p.m. The afternoon shadows drew deep mists behind them, and the temperature in the shady garden never rose above ten degrees Celsius. This winter in Majorca was particularly harsh: Sand writes of severe nights in Valldemossa ('one of the coldest parts of the island'), with two inches of snow.

Sand gave her children lessons until lunchtime, after which they played in and around the Cartuja while she read and wrote, often under a tree in the cemetery. Or the children went off on walks far from the monastery grounds, enjoying whatever sunshine they could find, Maurice a liberated hare (Sand's description), soaked to the waist, his health now restored. Even when alone she was not left undisturbed. Amelia's indolence became apparent, and though María Antonia, their pious neighbour in the cloisters, helped prepare their meals, she stole food in the process. Village children brought to the cell door a churn of tart goats' milk, which was fuller and thinner than when they set off (the children having added water to offset the milk they had drunk en route), and the melancholy goat that Sand bought to avoid this daily routine wandered through the cloisters bleating pitifully, producing very little milk, anticipating the defeated mood that would take hold of them in the New Year. She nonetheless wrote swiftly, her eye on passing deadlines and their dwindling finances. Chopin also composed quickly, working throughout the day and much of the night, making up for lost time. Even so, at the end of December he wrote to Fontana, 'I can't send you the Preludes for they are not finished: I feel better and will hurry up.'

Various events fell outside this routine. Once her work was done for the day (but not the night), Sand would go exploring with her children, on the mountainside in good weather, within the cloisters in bad – Solange on the hunt for a fairy palace in an undiscovered attic, Maurice determined to find instead the relics of some awful tragedy he sensed deliciously close at hand. In the cloisters they discovered a small chapel beautifully preserved, religious exercises still pinned to a wooden frame, portrait cards of saints on the backs of chairs for the monks to face and venerate when kneeling, withered flowers in vases on the altar, half-used candles in sconces, the smell of incense lingering in the air. It was like a ghost ship, an elegant craft without a crew in sight, riddles at every turn.

On a walk to the coast a villager appeared from nowhere and appointed herself their guide, leading Sand along a narrowing path around a sugarloaf rock until she suddenly found herself looking through a craggy void to the sea far below, waves dashing out strange music from an unknown world, she thought. (Gustav Doré encountered exactly this scene on a later visit, which he re-created in his otherworldly illustrations for Dante's *Inferno*.) Maurice pulled her back, roughly, worried child with errant parent.

On another occasion villagers, farmers and tradesmen clutching torches marched up the hill, led by a horned devil all in black, his face blood-red, accompanied by bird-headed imps with horse tails, their way paved by singers wailing Moorish melodies with full-throated vigour and instrumentalists clacking wooden castanets, strumming guitars and mandolins, striking violins with bows or fingers. It could have been straight from *The Town Musicians of Bremen*, or a nightmarish *Walpurgisnacht*. In fact it was just Shrove Tuesday and there was a dance in honour of a local tenant-farmer who had married, which would have kept Sand's party enthralled had it not been for the rancid oil and garlic the villagers wore like cologne. On another day, in celebration of the island's patron saint, the whole village gathered at the Town Hall while a priest sprinkled holy water on the procession of black pigs and mules passing by a statue of Saint Anthony, before retiring to the inn to dance the *fandango mallorquín*.

Religion was the source of much of Sand's amusement and wonder. But religion was also at the heart of the misunderstanding and disapproval that thrummed between her and the village, and of the menacing atmosphere whirling around the Cartuja. 'Why attempt to deny that sinister abodes like these, dedicated to an even more sinister religious cult, have some effect on the imagination?' She made no effort to disguise her distaste for the beliefs of the villagers and the ghosts of monastic life. No one from their apartment went to church; instead each was merely a curious bystander at the *festes* crowding Valldemossa's liturgical calendar. When on the feast day of Saint Anthony a visitor returned to the village inn after dinner with Chopin and Sand at the monastery, he was accosted by the priest (who had earlier blessed the procession of mules), who asked about the strange French lady who made her own cigarettes, drank coffee at all hours, slept during the day and wrote at night.

Whether or not Graves was right about their visit encapsulating the clash of pre- and post-Revolutionary eras, it was certainly one of a primitive agrarian economy against secular urbanity. In Valldemossa only the mayor, notary and a few others would have spoken Spanish, and Sand picked up nothing of the local Mallorquí; this only added to the villagers' incomprehension at the strangers in their midst. The lack of understanding went beyond language into an essential distrust of Sand's cavalier attitude to her immortal soul. Solange emulating her mother in the colour and shape of her dress, the hang of her hair, Maurice running wild through the cloisters, or sketching incessantly when boys of his age were generally in lessons or working, was one thing; the disdain that Chopin and Sand held for the religion of the locals – the Catholic religion of both their homelands, after all – was something altogether more serious. Chopin's illness was further proof of their immorality, a divine punishment meted out by a vengeful God. 'That consumptive,' María Antonia told her friends, 'will go to Hell, first for being a consumptive, and next for not going to confession.'

Many have shared Graves's animosity towards Sand and *Un hiver à Majorque* since its serialization in 1841 and publication a year later. (Laurens's *Souvenirs d'un voyage* was the immediate inspiration to write it.) Sand's hostility in the book towards Majorca's peasantry (inaccurately interpreted afterwards as a general dislike of the working class), her refusal to play the grand author in Palma society and her owlish response to the disappointment of well-heeled locals, her nocturnal wanderings in the monastery's cemetery, and her antagonism towards the religion of the island were all rehearsed in an article in *La Palma* in 1841 following the publication of *Un hiver à Majorque*, as was the way (according to *La Palma*) in which she dismissed the islanders as 'cowards, hypocrites, pickpockets, Indian monkeys, Polynesian savages'.

As the days turned bleaker, as the winds and Chopin's health grew worse, Sand found it difficult to put up any front. 'We nicknamed Majorca "Monkey Island" because, when surrounded by these crafty, thieving and yet innocent creatures, we grew accustomed to defending ourselves against them, but felt no more resentment or scorn than Indians feel towards chimpanzees or mischievous, timid orangutangs.' Sand was trying half-heartedly to understand the customs of the culture she encountered, but was instead struck by invidious comparisons with the one she had left behind, half surprised not to find dragons on the lip of the world. 'George Sand is the most immoral of writers,' the refutation in *La Palma* concludes, 'and Mme Dudevant the most obscene of women!' Nonetheless, her eye was keen, her tongue wickedly sharp, and between laughs and blows *Un hiver à Majorque* does something indispensable for anyone interested in the history of Romanticism: it gives us a seat close to Frédéric Chopin as he completed the Preludes.

4

Valldemossa, Marseilles, Nohant, 1838–9

It is a seat with only a partial view, though, for Chopin barely exists in *Un hiver à Majorque*. Throughout Sand refers to him as 'a member of my family', 'our invalid', 'one of us', or 'the sufferer'. There was an element of nineteenth-century literary convention to all this – Jane Austen's 'Earl of ——', '——shire Militia', and the like. But mostly it was Sand, for all her admirable social insouciance, protecting Chopin's privacy and propriety. (Her own propriety or otherwise – her many affairs and her legal separation from Casimir Dudevant – was by then a matter of public record.) There was also a touch of what Graves wrote about his lover Laura Riding in the preface to his own blistering memoir, *Good-Bye to All That*, that were she to appear as a character in his story she would be robbed of her autonomy. In *Un hiver à Majorque* Chopin is a ghost at the feast. We read of climate and food and character and illness and livestock and religion, but not actually how Chopin wrote the nineteenth century's greatest collection of piano miniatures. Only in her letters and, later, in *Histoire de ma vie* – the memoir she serialized for *La Presse* in 1854 and published as a book a year later – did Sand flesh out her slight contemporaneous references.

Admittedly, by the time she wrote *Histoire de ma vie* there was precious little to hide. In 1846, with a year left to run in their relationship, Sand published *Lucrezia Floriani*, a novel about the fraught affair between the fearless Lucrezia and a sickly German prince with a Polish name six years her junior, 'delicate both in body and mind . . . with neither age nor sex . . . a beautiful angel, with a face like a sorrowing woman'. Chopin was at first ignorant of the overlaps between his story and Prince Karol's – or at least feigned indifference, which often appears the same thing – and Sand denied any connection. Parisian society was less blinkered: Delacroix's discomfort one evening as

Sand read excerpts to the gathered salon and Heinrich Heine's brutal assessment ('She has treated my friend Chopin outrageously in a divinely written novel') were more representative of how the literary set viewed it. In his biography of Chopin published in 1852, Liszt leapt on the correlation between prince and composer, freely quoting chunks from *Lucrezia* as though they were from an official record. Sand's correspondence and memoir are therefore better biographical allies for Chopin than either *Lucrezia Floriani* or *Un hiver à Majorque*.

In January 1839 Sand wrote to her friend Countess Carlotta Marliani from the cell table, 'Chopin is playing on a poor Mallorquin piano which reminds me of Bouffé's piano in "Pauvre Jacques".' She was referring to a *comédie-vaudeville* she had seen a few years earlier at the Théâtre du Gymnase in Paris, written by Théodore and Hippolyte Cogniard and featuring as the hapless title character Jacques Bouffé, a huge star of the French stage. Jacques is an old, impoverished musician (his frock coat 'much worn', according to the stage directions) whose mind wanders so much that he has lost his pupils, but whose lucidity returns whenever he discusses music, at which point he rushes to his antiquated keyboard to execute 'the most difficult extemporaneous pieces in so inspired a manner'.

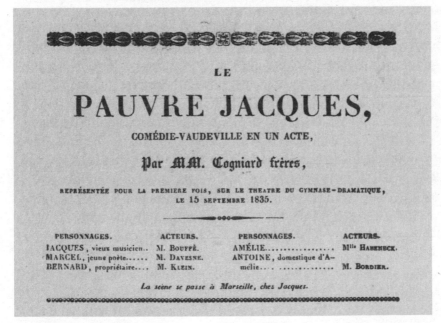

In *Histoire de ma vie* Sand writes about the singular pieces Chopin composed on this 'poor Mallorquin piano'. She first sets the scene: the insistent, grim winter; Chopin's sickness (pulmonary congestion); the phantoms and terror he sensed in the cloisters; the feverish despair he felt when composing. She then singles out the most significant of his achievements on the island. 'It was there he composed the loveliest of those few pages which he modestly called Preludes':

> They are master works. Several of them offer to our thoughts visions of long-departed monks, and the sound of those snatches of funereal plainsong that so oppressed him; some are melancholic and mild; they came to him at hours of sun and health, with the children's laughter floating over the window sill, with the distant thrum of guitars, with the pale roses abloom in the snow. Others are sad and mournful, and while beguiling your ear they rend your heart.

Sand's descriptions of Chopin's works were always too literal, in a way that would come to dominate their presentation and scholarship in the decades that followed, audiences, publishers and musicians grappling as best they could with the confounding works in their heads or hands. Yet here she contented herself with the broadest possible brush and used it deftly.

Chopin had been thinking about a collection of twenty-four Preludes since autumn 1835 at the latest, the point at which he completed his two Nocturnes, Op. 27. (When two years later he published his giddy Impromptu in A flat, Op. 29, he skipped the opus number he had reserved for the Preludes.) Completion dates of individual Preludes are, for the most part, impossible to pin down, though there are a few scraps to work from. In 1837 Chopin asked Fontana to make a copy of Prelude No. 17 so that he might present it to Count Perthuis, aide-de-camp to King Louis-Philippe. He drafted nos. 2 and 4 on manuscript paper containing the fair copy, in his own hand, of the Mazurka in E minor, Op. 41, No. 1, which is dated 28 November 1838. (This was when Chopin and Sand were battling the wind, damp and despondency of Son Vent.) And on the same sheets he sketched then discarded ideas for a prelude in C sharp minor, which suggests the completed Prelude postdated the Mazurka.

The best determination of when he wrote the individual pieces is by musicologist Jean-Jacques Eigeldinger. For his 2004 edition of the Preludes and in other writings, Eigeldinger examined drafts, correspondence, stylistic tics and additional works by Chopin, weighed up the probable limitations of the piano to hand (with Sand's verdict on it in mind), and judiciously concluded that in Palma, Establiments and Valldemossa, Chopin probably composed nos. 2, 4, 5, 7, 9, 10, 14, 15, 16 and 18.

Chopin was writing his collection in the shadow of Bach's forty-eight Preludes and Fugues, two in each major and minor key, though he made immediate structural distinctions. Rather than ape Bach's slow chromatic progression through the keys, Chopin followed each major key with its relative minor, before advancing the set a fifth and repeating the process. This was the design of Johann Hummel, who had used it in his own collection of twenty-four Preludes, composed in Vienna in 1814–15 in no great burst of inspiration.

It was the intrepid Jean-Joseph Laurens, in *La France Musicale* in 1843, who first identified *Das Wohltemperierte Klavier* as the only score Chopin had with him in Majorca; he most likely squirrelled out this information from the French consul Fleury, who hosted Chopin and Sand for the days after they fled Sol Vent and waited for their new apartment to be made ready. This would have surprised none of Chopin's pupils. Friederike Müller, who studied with him from October 1839 until spring 1841 and whose promising European career was halted only by her marriage to the Viennese piano maker Johann Baptist Streicher, wrote of a lesson in which Chopin played from memory fourteen of Bach's Preludes and Fugues, responding to her admiration with the quick deflection, 'It is never forgotten.' Perhaps not, but it was unusual for the time. Volumes of Bach's music were by no means commonplace, and those in existence were not always accurate or complete. (In his 1829 performance of the *St Matthew Passion* in Leipzig, a concert credited with initiating Bach's revival in the nineteenth century, Mendelssohn used his own hugely truncated edition.) In the first decade of the century, following publication in 1801 of a Peters edition of *Das Wohltemperierte Klavier*, a number of alternative printings were released. Yet in 1838 Carl Czerny, embarking on a complete edition of Bach's 'ancient' keyboard works, could still acknowledge the scarcity of the great musician's published scores. He was determined to rectify this lacuna, writing in his preface about music beyond mere fashion and taste, about a composer who knew 'how to unite all the secrets of the most abstract and subtle harmonic combinations with true beauty and sublimity, and who became thereby the Teacher and Lawgiver to all future times'.

Teacher and Lawgiver: this was the Bach of Chopin's imagination, the composer whose works he invariably played when preparing for his own infrequent public recitals. It was the Bach too of Chopin's teaching studio, where pupils learned his music – the Suites, individual fugues, and, later, the occasional Prelude – before Chopin's own works or those of Beethoven. Bach was also the musician on Chopin's mind at the end of his life when he told Delacroix of his conviction that Beethoven was obsessed with Bach: by his stature, of course, but also by the construction of the music itself, which bled into Beethoven's own scores, he thought, and gave him his foundations. Chopin was not interested in the large-scale Romantic orchestra that came after Beethoven, nor in the stout works and genres that both enabled and demanded its steady growth. In Majorca he had with him none of Beethoven's or Schubert's sonatas, nothing by his contemporaries Schumann and Liszt. Instead he had with him the collection that would later be recognized as perhaps the greatest monument of eighteenth-century music. From *Das Wohltemperierte Klavier* Chopin took both rule and precedent, distilling the intricacy and beauty of Bach's contrapuntal writing into his own music, along the way creating something wholly unique.

A single image offers a snapshot of the strange, inventive brilliance of the Preludes: a page of incipits, which publishers at the end of the century began to include in their editions of the collection – a musical *aide-mémoire* as much as an index. Although this mechanism had a fairly long history and distinguished application – a publisher advertising a composer's scores, say, printing on a flyer the opening bars of the works he wished to promote; another publisher identifying on a composer's contract the piece he was taking on – this way of thinking about music only became commonplace in the wake of Ludwig Ritter von Köchel's magisterial thematic catalogue of Mozart's scores, which

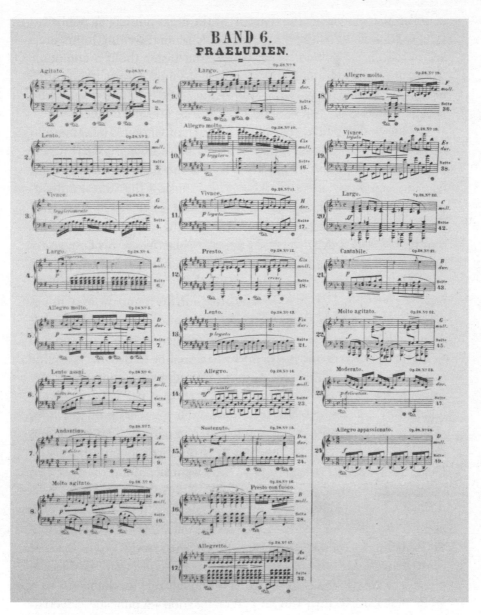

Breitkopf & Härtel published in 1862. Although Breitkopf had produced a specialist thematic catalogue of Chopin's works ten years earlier, it was 1879 before a volume of the Preludes included incipits.

It is not simply that this single page juxtaposes the contrasting textural and harmonic ideas Chopin explored in these twenty-four pieces;

it is also that the incipits manage to capture so quintessentially what follows (though of course they cannot prefigure the improbable flourish or mad, tacked-on coda that bring a number of the Preludes home from chromatic hinterlands). In this collection of miniatures there is no throat clearing, no padding, no waste, no time to spare: the entire genetic make-up of each Prelude is present in the opening bars.

The incipits do one further thing: in their variety and intensely idiomatic character they underline just how much Chopin in the Preludes exploited every aspect of the pianos of the day, squeezed out every last drop of their capacity. Debussy understood this about Chopin when later in the century he told his pupils, 'Chopin is the greatest of them all, for through the piano alone he discovered everything.' No tricks, no large-scale orchestras, no grand operas or other narrative devices: this is music in its purest expression, without a single wasted note or misplaced gesture. It is what makes the Preludes so thrilling to play: they form Debussy's 'everything' – different essences of music orbiting around each other, unrelated but overlapping, insistent that a familial bond is there if only we look.

The Majorcan Preludes are spread out fairly evenly through the collection. In No. 2 (A minor) unmoored harmonies underpin a melody no more sophisticated than something in a medieval psalter (a handful of notes artlessly stretched out), harmonies that ebb with alluring disregard for convention and key, which Chopin defines only in the final cadence when, midstream, he casually drops anchor. No. 4 (E minor) is a brittle piece in which a bland chain of harmonies slips down a note at a time, glueing together as best it can the melody Chopin places above, which he extends almost to breaking point. No. 5 (D) is built around a lumpy spinning-wheel figuration that sets off immediately and does not let up until the end, its character that of an étude, its tempo and intricacy suggesting that the Bauza's action was spry enough. No. 7 (A) is a gentle music-box waltz that Chopin does not let run down (though he shuts the box's lid immediately and without warning after the sixteenth bar). No. 9 (E) is a gruelling, insistent funeral march in the middle of the keyboard, under which the bass lumbers like organ pedals, the harmonies lurching from one point to the next in double-dotted Baroque figurations. In No. 10 (C sharp minor) scale patterns from high in the piano alternate with chorale fragments at its centre, an improbable duel that proves surprisingly well matched. No. 14 (E flat minor) is like a fabulous Bach toccata, with the skeleton of a nursery rhyme or folk song wired into the last three bars, out of place amid such fine, lace-like finger work – out of place too in the dark key of E flat minor. (It is a little like Mahler's grim excursions into the same nostalgic territory sixty years later, where nursery tunes are given the bleakest harmonic backdrops.) The hypnotic ostinato of No. 15 (D flat) works its magic from the outset and establishes the melodic material of the growling, chromatic storm to come. (This was Schubert's device in one of the most exquisite songs he ever wrote, 'Die liebe Farbe' in *Die schöne Müllerin* of 1823, which Chopin must have known, and in which a repeated note runs throughout.) No. 16 (B flat minor) is another right-hand étude that fills out the upper octaves of the piano with chromatic meanderings while the left hand does its best to stake a claim to the piece's core tonality. No. 18 (F minor) is like someone arguing with

himself – interrupting, stuttering, slowly gaining in confidence and fluency, prone to wild coloratura declamations.

The Paris Preludes, composed between autumn 1835 and November 1838, are, on the whole, no more fleet-footed than those composed on the inferior Bauza piano, no less concentrated in structure and gesture. No. 1 (C) so persistently stakes its claim on both its tonality and Bach's own first Prelude that it leaves us completely unprepared for the wild excursions that separate it from the rhapsodic final piece, No. 24 (D minor), with its tempo marking (Allegro appassionato) and opening motif almost certainly a veiled tribute to Beethoven's Sonata, Op. 57 'Appassionata'. No. 3 (G) behaves like an étude for the left hand, the disjointed right-hand melody sketched in as an afterthought. No. 6 (B minor) was probably written with Chopin's friend Auguste Franchomme in mind, whose cello playing inspired him during his time in Paris and here shaped a left-hand melodic line that would sit and sound well on a cello's open strings. No. 8 (F sharp minor) spells out a drone melody in the right-hand thumb, which Chopin fills out with an increasingly chromatic patina, the left hand providing arpeggiated slices of whichever key it finds itself in – almost in compensation for what is going on above. No. 11 (B) sets up a beautiful dance melody as though on a solo violin, which Chopin plays with for a short time before seeming to lose interest, quickly drawing to a close with a very plain cadence. No. 12 (G sharp minor) is a chase: monotonous, careering, with a sense of breathless danger to it, as though it could unwind at any moment, though it lasts only a minute.

No. 13 (F sharp) is the only Prelude in the collection whose incipit does not do it justice: halfway through, the opening barcarolle gives way to a stand-alone section of sublime beauty. (Chopin would take genre and key to even greater heights in his Barcarolle, Op. 60 in F sharp of 1845–6.) No. 17 (A flat) is one of the most rhapsodic of the Preludes: small melodic arcs in the right hand filled out with widespread chords in the left, all presented in the *stile brillante* of Chopin's youth. No. 19 (E flat) takes simple triplet arpeggios, jumbles the letter order, and from this conjures up a sweet tune well above the fray. No. 20 (C minor) is another funeral march, its chords as thick and close as a blazing Gabrieli brass canzona, underpinned by a thudding bass drum. No. 21 (B flat) is a simple bel canto aria above a tangled left hand, with elegant turns and polite chromatic asides, the finger leaps aping the virtuosic gestures of Paris's fashionable Théâtre Italien. No. 22 (G minor) has the character of a Chopin ballade – double octave melody in the left hand with see-saw harmonies in the right – though one in miniature, for it is over in less than a minute. And No. 23 (F) could just as easily be a virtuosic violin and cello duet, its texture spare, its mood genial.

It is possible to identify in Chopin's youthful works the influence of Weber and a few other masters of post-Classical pianism, just as it is possible to find traces of Buxtehude in Bach. But by the early 1830s all the elements of his mature language were in place: a chasm had opened up between Chopin and his musical ancestry. His originality lent all these works a distinctive core and character. Schumann identified this quality in 1838: 'Chopin can hardly write anything now but that we feel like calling out in the seventh or eight measure, "It is by him!"' The same could not be said of so many of his contemporaries. Partly this distinctiveness was because Chopin loosed his music from its vertical alignment. He spells out melodies in ornate language that at times seems at odds with the unconventional harmonic syntax holding them in place; either one could stand alone quite happily, but Chopin's originality lay in the way he imagined the two together, the quality Paul Dukas a century later would regard as Chopin's great legacy: unprecedented harmonic freedom and mobility. Partly it was that he fused this radical outlook with a conservative temperament: Mendelssohn aside, Beethoven at times, no one else was then consciously looking to the eighteenth century for musical inspiration. But mostly, as Schumann said, it was that it was impossible to confuse him with anyone else: the music's originality was its primary identifying feature.

In the Preludes, the confidence with which Chopin navigated the gap between precedents and originality is doubly absorbing because such brevity scarcely gave him space or time to set out his musical arguments. Yet it is precisely the evanescent quality of each Prelude that was so risky and radical. It is almost as if in this collection Chopin, who had no palpable interest in the music of his contemporaries, nor for that matter in appearing modern, was impatient for the music of the future: the music of *fin de siècle* Poland and France, of Karol Szymanowski and Claude Debussy in their own sets of Preludes (1899–1900 and 1909–13), which are at every turn a homage to Chopin. He built a bridge between the eighteenth and twentieth centuries, between Bach and the Impressionists, between the recognized harmonic and performance conventions of his time and those that would follow only later. Chopin's undertaking is all so alluring and unexpected: a collection of twenty-four improvised thoughts yoked together in an overarching harmonic scheme, yet with each 'idea' (Sand's rather good term for each Prelude) independent of the next, all of them removed from the Romantic masterpieces composed in the same years: Schumann's *Études symphoniques* (1834–7) and *Kreisleriana* (1838), Liszt's pot pourri *Album d'un voyageur* (1837–8). Chopin put down each 'idea' as a challenge to himself as much as to his contemporaries. Inside his cell in Valldemossa he sidestepped the disparate worlds of his contemporaries and predecessors. There he wrote these short, almost surreal works that broke from all logic about what a piano piece was meant to be and were completely distinct from anything else composed at the time. The Preludes transgressed musically further than any other work. Through their individuality and originality, through their extreme distillation of Romantic ideas, the Preludes first defied the artistic aesthetic of the mid-nineteenth century and then came to define it.

A definitive list of the works Chopin composed or completed in Majorca will never be known, but it would include as many as ten Preludes; the Ballade in F, Op. 38; early sketches for the Scherzo in C sharp minor, Op. 39; two Polonaises, Op. 40; and the Mazurka, Op. 41, No. 1. For all Chopin's isolation and illness, for all the implicit uncertainty as he and Sand tended their nascent relationship, for all the limitations of Juan Bauza's piano, these were months of exceptional achievement, handsomely repaying Chopin's decision to join her in Majorca.

In *Histoire de ma vie* Sand writes not just about what Chopin composed, but also how. She describes his unrestrained improvising, how the music was seemingly plucked from the air, which he then notated and polished, playing it through on the piano to check whether his script matched the sounds in his head, often painfully unsure it did.

She records his miraculous spontaneity on walks, humming away to himself, quickly returning home to try out a new idea, the piece then sounding to Sand complete, sublime. But then came 'the most crushing labour I have ever witnessed':

> It was a train of efforts, waverings, frustrated stabs at recapturing certain details of the theme that he had heard; what he had conceived as a unity he now over-analysed in his desire to get it down, and his chagrin at not being able to rediscover it whole and clear plunged him into a sort of despair. He withdrew into his room for days, weeping, pacing up and down, breaking his pens, playing a measure a hundred times over, changing it each time, then writing it out and erasing it as many times, and beginning all over again on the morrow with painstaking and desperate perseverance. He would spend six weeks on a page, only to hark back to what he had first roughed out.

It is the process also described by the Hungarian Joseph Filtsch, in Paris in 1842 as chaperon to his brother Károly (Karl), Chopin's greatest pupil. Joseph was struck by the difference between the ease and beauty of Chopin as improviser and Chopin as composer, how when he attempted to write down his inspired original thoughts he spent days of nervous strain and desperation. 'He alters and re-touches the same phrases incessantly and walks up and down like a madman' – able to capture the essence, but not the substance.

Grzymała thought Chopin's improvisations were often more daring than the works they became. Delacroix, defending his friend, likened them to preparatory sketches for a painting, though later decided his analogy was not quite right, that Grzymała might have a point, that the miraculous improvisations were somehow better than the finished works – less guarded, more inspired. In his journal Delacroix argued with himself about whether Chopin's brilliant flashes of inspiration were tempered by the process of writing them down. 'No! one does not spoil a painting by finishing!' Not spoil it, but was there somehow less room for imagination once musical ideas were committed to paper? Did the need for foundations overwhelm the beguiling decorations? Perhaps, Delacroix thought, for 'a finished building encloses the imagination within a circle and prevents it from straying beyond its limits'. This is surely what Chopin did, Delacroix decided: he contained his brilliance and fancy within an architectural framework of his own devising. Inevitably this sometimes left the improvisations more daring than the works they became.

Grzymała and Delacroix were noticing what neurologists would much later analyse: a musician's brain does unusual things when he or she improvises. It switches off personal and musical inhibitions to allow virtuosic experimentation without the creative process being shut down by the very human instinct to control and formalize. In this regard it is similar to speaking a foreign language: if in the early months too much attention is paid to grammar or structure or cases, nothing will ever be said out loud. Without the brain's override mechanism, it seems impossible that the shy, modest Chopin would have been able to entertain those gathered in Paris's most fashionable salons and intimate parties with his musical flights of fancy. At the piano, in the company of friends and admirers, all inhibition, personal or musical, completely disappeared. Only afterwards, in small talk, or alone as he laboured with pencil and paper, did it return, and was he menaced by doubt and self-criticism.

Sand does not say specifically how closely Chopin's inspired meanderings in the slightly boozed company of friends compared to his finished work; the process was no more interesting to her than the number of drafts she wrote of a novel. The closest she comes to it is in her passage on the genesis of Prelude No. 15, the so-called 'Raindrop'. It was the first or second week of January 1839 and she travelled with Maurice by *birlocho* to Palma, a journey of around three hours, to obtain the release of the newly arrived Pleyel piano. (They negotiated an import tax of 300 francs, against the 700 francs demanded.) The return trip, in sudden, dramatic winter rain, taken against the wishes of the ill-tempered driver, lasted seven hours, the coach lurching and sliding over fast-disappearing tracks, the stubborn mule repeatedly sitting defiantly on its haunches, the driver cursing roads and rain, refusing Sand's peace offering of a cigar. They arrived back at the monastery, soaked and despondent, only to hear Chopin at the Bauza piano playing a new piece, reacting with a start as they came into the cell, almost certain they must have perished on their journey. Sand writes of how Chopin had seen the fated trip in a dream, so he told her, which he found impossible to separate from reality. In this

dreamlike state he sat at the piano, picturing himself also dead, floating in a lake, fat drops of water plopping rhythmically on his chest.

After Chopin played them however much of the new work he had
retained, Sand drew his attention to the sound of raindrops on the
monastery roof or terrace tiles, a sound replicated in the ostinato
quavers throughout the Prelude, so she said, as monotonous as steady
rainfall. Chopin responded angrily, Sand recorded, dismissing such a
childish correlation between the rain and his dream, the storm and
his music, and Sand backed down. Later she decided his 'genius was
filled with the mysterious sounds of nature, but transformed into
sublime equivalents in musical thought, and not through slavish imitation of the actual external sounds. His composition of that evening
certainly echoed the drops of water which were drumming on the
resonant tiles of the charterhouse; but they had been rendered in his
imagination, and in his song, by tears falling from heaven on his heart.'

Perhaps this was a moment of what Henry James labelled her fanciful recall. Yet Solange at the end of the century, remembering a man who could make a piano sound like an army, an orchestra, an archangel, and a composer who could conjure up funeral marches as easily as triumphal ones, also wrote about the Prelude in such terms. 'What rays of sunlight on flowers in full bloom, on the glittering river, on the valley of scented lemon trees! What tears from the depths of the damp cloister! . . . And what melancholy raindrops falling one by one on the tiles in the cell garden!' At the very least, Sand's description of Chopin's imagination and creative process – *mysterious sounds of nature . . . transformed into sublime equivalents in musical thought* – encapsulates Chopin the alchemist.

There is a good reason why Chopin would so fiercely resist Sand's suggestion of mimicry in this genre above all others. Czerny, a former pupil of Beethoven's and one of the chief architects of Romantic pianism, wrote in 1836 that a pianist earned his greatest distinction in a concert or soirée by beginning not with the intended work but with a prelude: it settled both pianist and audience into the mood and tonality of the work to come, all the while hinting at the musician's virtuosity, which he would soon display. (They were mostly men: women – apart from Clara Schumann in later decades – tended not to improvise at all, surely one of the more aesthetically complex demarcations between genders in the nineteenth century.) It was understood that such preludes were to be improvised or at the very least, if some preparation had been undertaken before the performance, the original work of the pianist. As the handful of published collections attests, the resulting preludes tended to be fairly unsophisticated, most of them little more than extended cadential progressions in the key required, knitted together or embellished with flashy passagework over the full compass of the ever-growing instrument – signposts not destinations.

In his own Preludes, Chopin was far more ambitious. He was toying with understood conventions and composed intricately crafted, complex works that seemed to be improvised but which could only be captured on paper. Of course the pieces were changed by that, as both Grzymała and Delacroix observed; it is simply what happens when oral communication is written down. But Chopin rejected Sand's attempt to connect the heavy rain and the Prelude because in this collection he was reinventing the genre, seeking out the porous stretches of the border between improvisation and composition, and there letting the notes spill from one side of each tradition to the other. He did not appreciate Sand's mundane observation.

In Venice in the winter of 1874–5, twenty years or so before Solange recorded her reminiscences of Chopin, Édouard Manet encountered Charles Toche in Café Florian and told him how difficult it was to portray in a painting a hat sitting correctly on a model's head, or create the impression that a boat on water was constructed from real wooden planks, assembled by a craftsman according to the rules of geometry and carpentry. In the Preludes, Chopin shows how little he cared about such rules: this hat, that boat, these planks of wood. He did not believe his job was to capture a physical phenomenon in music – this at a time when composers were beginning to grapple with the same challenges of representation Manet would later articulate – let alone show he knew how objects were put together. In the Preludes he sought to comprehend his audiences' explicit, almost sensuous, expectations, and then confound them – all the while he kept them sitting round his piano. It was exactly as Sand much later wrote about music's power to take hold of the heart without ever having to explain itself, her views having evolved over time. 'It maintains itself in an ideal sphere where the listener who is not musically educated still delights in the vagueness, while the musician savours this great logic that presides over the masters' magnificent issue of thought.'

Improvisation would lose its cachet in the following decades. In its place a new culture of interpretation emerged, as pianists tried to come to grips with the enormous challenges set them by difficult published works: Beethoven's final great sonatas; Schubert's intricate piano works; Liszt's virtuosic keyboard essays. Liszt, a brilliant improviser, was in part responsible for this change. In early middle age he drew a line between improvisation and composition, first by making a big play of performing other people's music – establishing himself as the century's great interpreter – then by withdrawing from public concerts to concentrate on composing, writing down and knocking into shape his best (and sometimes less than best) extemporizations. But for a short time in the history of the modern piano – a span of a few decades, no more, before international copyright lent musical works a suit of armour against improvisatory breaches of law – and involving just a handful of exceptional composer-executants, these two distinct but overlapping traditions spoke to each other. And then the one was occluded by the other.

When Sand wrote to Marliani about the poor Majorcan piano, Pleyel's instrument had not yet been carried out of customs and up the precarious mountain trails to the monastery. But then Sand, Maurice and the muleteer brought it to Chopin's room where it 'filled the lofty, echoing vault of the cell with a glorious sound'. Even the villagers were caught up in the excitement, as Maurice recorded.

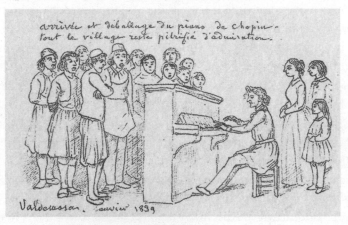

His mother responded similarly. 'I write to you from my hermitage in Valldemossa,' she told Marliani. 'In this no quarter is given me by the warbling piano of Chopin working in his normal, beautiful, way, to the astonishment of the eavesdropping walls of the cell.' Bauza's instrument was pushed ignominiously to one side, where it would remain for a very long time.

On 22 January 1839 Chopin wrote to Pleyel, 'Dear friend, I am sending you the Preludes. I finished them on your cottage piano, which arrived in perfect condition in spite of the sea-crossing, the bad weather and the Palma customs. I have instructed Fontana to hand over my manuscript.' He mentioned other works: the Ballade (French and English rights only); two Polonaises; a third Scherzo. 'If you like, the whole lot will descend upon you, month by month, until the arrival of the composer himself who will tell you more than he can write.' His relief is palpable: after months of ill health and domestic uncertainty, of poor weather and working conditions, the collection he had been thinking about for three years or more was completed.

Only a week separates Sand's letter to Marliani about the Bauza piano and Chopin's letter to Pleyel, seven days during which Chopin toiled away in his room, the children leaving him to his work, Sand providing food and succour. In that week Chopin would have played the Preludes through on the finer instrument – as he would the other works he listed – making minor adjustments where necessary, probably writing in pedal markings, after which he dispatched his manuscripts to Fontana. Given the time it took him to refine his ideas from initial inspiration to fair copy, given also the sheer number of works he completed in these months, the Preludes were obviously more or less finished by the time the French piano arrived. In his letter to Pleyel, Chopin was being courteous but extremely literal: he did indeed finish the Preludes on the newly arrived piano, though most of the work in Majorca had been done on the other.

Chopin instructed Fontana to copy the Preludes for Breitkopf & Härtel and hand the original manuscript to Pleyel. He asked him also to sort out his finances, including payment of 425 francs for three months' rent to January on his Paris apartment ('and then politely give notice of quitting'). And in closing, 'I embrace you. I am living in my cell and sometimes have Arabian dances and African sunshine. Then there is the Mediterranean . . . I'm not sure, but I think I shan't come back before May or even later.'

Three weeks later they were gone. From Barcelona on 15 February, Sand wrote to Marliani a letter in fraught contrast to those Chopin sent Pleyel and Fontana. She described a climate increasingly deadly to Chopin, and told of their flight from the monastery to Palma in a hired cart without springs, which induced in Chopin a blood-spitting fit and marked him, once more, as a consumptive. 'We were treated like outcasts at Majorca – because of Chopin's cough and also because we did not go to church. My children were stoned in the streets . . . I should have to write ten volumes to give you an idea of the cowardice, deceit, selfishness, stupidity and spite of this stupid, thieving and big-oted race.'

One sufficed. Much later Sand said Chopin detested everything under the Spanish sun, though none of Chopin's letters from their months on the island gives this impression. Such things can turn on a coin. Perhaps as the winter advanced Chopin and Sand were worn down by the villagers' distrust and hostility. Perhaps, too, the sheer relief at finishing such a substantial body of work made Chopin rest-less, and the future more enticing than the present. Whichever (as Sand told Marliani in late February), 'Another month in Spain and we should have perished there, Chopin and I; he of melancholy and disgust, I of fury and indignation.'

They had intended to ship the Pleyel back to Paris but, again, had not reckoned with Palma's port officials. Advised of the prohibitive export tax and the unlikelihood that a Majorcan would buy a con-sumptive's piano, Sand arranged instead to sell it to Madame Canut, who sold her own treasured Pape to pay and make room for it. The Bauza piano was simply left in their rooms in the Cartuja.

They boarded *El Mallorquin* once more, sharing it this time with a hundred fattened pigs intended for the mainland, the crew treating the animals better than it did her party, Sand thought. In the harbour in Barcelona they transferred directly to a French brig and there, in the elegant drawing-room atmosphere of the below-deck quarters, they were attended to by the commandant and the ship's doctor, before going ashore to an inn.

A week later they travelled to Marseilles where they stayed for almost three months, Chopin's health only slowly improving, his diet consisting mainly of milk (food later added to fatten him), his slight frame warmly wrapped as though he was a young lady. 'I have gone awfully thin and I look wretched,' he told Grzymała, 'but I am now eating to gain strength.' Bit by bit he resumed a version of the life he had led in Paris, though with no pupil in sight. He began to play again and went on walks through town with Sand, where they talked about mutual friends and plans and the port – both familiar and foreign – in which they found themselves holed up.

Although his health improved, his finances remained grim. From Marseilles he implored Ernest Canut to settle his debt with Pleyel of twelve hundred francs for the piano, which Canut duly paid. In a later photograph of the Canut drawing room the Pleyel is positioned beneath a gauche oil painting far outshone by its extravagant frame, various trinkets along the lid, its fallboard open: it is clearly a working instrument, not a revered historical artefact. (It was later returned to the monastery and authenticated by Pleyel: 'In response to your request, we can confirm the authenticity of piano no. 6,668.')

Chopin's correspondence from Marseilles is full of real and imagined financial slights and wranglings at the hands of his various publishers over the Preludes, and quick negotiations regarding the sale of the other Majorcan works. His glove maker and tailor wanted him to settle his account ('let them wait, the idiots!'), and rent and sub-lettings in Paris needed fixing. He could not now remember the opus number he had reserved for the Preludes, which would lead to the collection being published in France without one, an omission left unrectified for some time. Chopin wrote to Fontana that the Preludes were to be dedicated to Pleyel and the Ballade to 'Robert Schumann' – whom he had first met in Leipzig four years earlier and liked, or at least admired *just* enough, to contemplate such a dedication – crossing out the endearment 'my friend' upon consideration (though retaining the redundant 'h'). He went on to tell Fontana, 'If Pleyel insists on having the Ballade, then dedicate the Preludes to Schumann.' His instruction arrived too late for the German edition of the Preludes, which carried the name Chopin had written on the fair copy and forgotten about: Joseph Christoph Kessler, whom Chopin had known and liked in Warsaw. (Kessler had dedicated his own collection of twenty-four Preludes to Chopin.) In such erratic circumstances were Chopin's Preludes prepared for publication.

Sand's correspondence in these months singles out Chopin's kindness, his tenderness and patience, but fears 'his whole being is too delicate, too exquisite and too perfect to exist long in our coarse and heavy earthly life'. ('But I am so used to seeing him away in the skies that it does not seem to signify whether he is alive or dead.') This is the main reason why the music he composed in Majorca was 'full of the scent of Paradise', she thought. In early May they travelled by boat to Genoa, hugging the coast, their return to Marseilles two weeks later blighted by a rough passage. Finally they set off for Sand's grand house and estate at Nohant, with its woods and gardens (later beautifully painted by Delacroix), its farmlands and little church, three hundred kilometres south of Paris.

In subsequent years Chopin repeatedly told Liszt that this short visit to Majorca was one of the happiest periods in his life, and that he was afraid 'he would never again find a time suffused with such female tenderness and musical inspiration. It was as if, like Linnaeus' clock, the time of day was told by the blossoming of flowers, each with a different perfume and each disclosing other beauties as they opened outwards.' These sentences are more revealing than the

misogyny and incomprehension ingrained in almost every account of Chopin's time with Sand in Majorca. Whatever the hardships, in the shadows of the mountains, battered by winds, ill health and local hostility, Chopin composed with rare concentration, producing a body of singular, great works, all the while being nourished by the remarkable Madame Dudevant.

5

Paris, 1831–9

On his return to Paris and good health Chopin moved into a small apartment at 5, rue Tronchet, just behind the Madeleine, Napoleon's Corinthian temple in the first *arrondissement* (today's eighth). His directions to Fontana in late September 1839 about the preparation and furnishing of the apartment were precise, even fussy. For the bedroom and sitting room, dove-grey wallpaper in a glossy finish, with narrow dark-green strips at the border – 'quiet and neat rather than commonplace, vulgar and petty-bourgeois'; his bed and desk from the old apartment to be cleaned and repaired by a good cabinet maker, his mattress by a bed maker; the chairs and rugs to be beaten; an 'honest steady Pole' to be hired as valet on eighty francs a month (without food), though self-evidently sixty would be better.

He asked that Fontana also find Sand a place with some urgency: her ill-fated play *Cosima* was soon to go into production and she needed to be settled once more in Paris. Her apartment, Chopin instructed, should be detached, if possible, with a garden or courtyard, three bedrooms (two of them joined and away from the third), two servant rooms, a dining room, a drawing room (which need not be grand, Sand told another friend, since she never entertained more than twelve people at a time), a study, cellar, parquet flooring, and fireplaces in most rooms. Crucially, it needed to face south and catch the sun ('for the boy and for my rheumatism too', she told Grzymała separately, her eye on Chopin), and be quiet, 'with no blacksmiths in the neighbourhood, no ladies of the streets'.

On these instructions Fontana produced for Sand a mews flat in the gardens of 16, rue Pigalle, on the northernmost border of the second *arrondissement* (today's ninth), the outermost reaches of old-walled Paris. Sand filled the apartments with oak furniture, Chinese vases, stands of fresh flowers, paintings by her friends Delacroix and Maurice's future father-in-law Luigi Calamatta (a rather austere portrait of Sand as some kind of oracle, completed the year before she travelled to Majorca), green furnishings, a rosewood square piano, and two mattresses on the floor in her bedroom – Turkish style – whose walls were painted brown. Balzac observed all this with a mixture of bemusement and admiration, noting too his friend's tiny hands, her incessant smoking, and her late-afternoon rising, as though she were an exotic nocturnal creature, perfectly timing her day around Chopin's teaching.

Chopin would spend two years travelling the one and a half kilometres between the rue Tronchet and the rue Pigalle before giving up his apartment and settling into the smaller part of Sand's residence, telling his well-heeled pupils that they must venture out there from their comfortable and fashionable *quartiers* for the privilege of his instruction. Some sent a carriage instead, collecting him from Sand's home and returning him there after the lesson. It cost them an extra ten francs.

Chopin's return to the capital was also a re-entry into Parisian society. He instructed Fontana to visit his tailor Dautrement and order a pair of dark-grey winter trousers and a black waistcoat with a discreet, elegant pattern (much like the vest in Valldemossa). From Dupont on the rue du Mont-Blanc he was to order him a new hat,

using the measurements on the hatter's books, made in that year's fashion, though, since he had no idea of exactly what this was, it had best not be too exaggerated. Chopin was not the type of dandy that Balzac makes the tragic Lucien in *Lost Illusions*, who visits Staub the celebrated tailor, Verdier the cane maker, Madame Irlande for gloves and shirt studs, a reputable shoemaker, and a respected draper to replace his coarse holland shirts and cheap jaconet cravats, emptying his small purse along the way. Nor was he that of Baudelaire's definition – the 'man who is rich and idle, and who, even if blasé, has no other occupation than the perpetual pursuit of happiness'. He simply worked too hard. Yet with his hatter, tailor and glove maker, with the cologne he bought from Houbigant-Chardin (a famous *parfumerie* on the rue Saint-Honoré), with the particular soap he sourced from merchants off the boulevards, and with his fastidious attention to clothing and grooming, Chopin certainly dressed as one.

His return was also acknowledgement that his relationship with Sand was no mere summer liaison. To Fontana he touched on the unhappy affairs and poor health that had hitherto marked his time in Paris, poignantly asking that his friend 'see to it that all black thoughts and exhausting coughs are kept from me in my new abode. Try to keep me well, and wipe out for me, if you can, many an episode of the past. It would be no bad thing if I could achieve a few years of great and perfect labour.'

Although his new apartment was in the first *arrondissement*, most of Chopin's Parisian life – from his arrival in October 1831 until his death in October 1849 – played out in the second. The *deuxième* ran from just north of the Jardin des Tuileries to the foot of Montmartre and was populated by a lively mix of the *ancien régime* and the new industrial-capitalist Parisians. In the years Chopin lived on the rue Tronchet the capital's population would reach one million, a twentieth of France's total. Paris was bursting through the girdle-wall ringing the city, its circumference twenty-four kilometres, its height not quite four metres, its sixty-odd toll barriers controlled by *Fermiers généraux*, who accumulated immense wealth from the duty they collected on wine, beer, cider, vinegar, meat, coal, firewood and gypsum, all of it brought into the capital in carriages and carts.

Smugglers devised ever more ingenious methods of avoiding these heavy taxes, camping out in some comfort among the debtors and merchants living just beyond the walls and Parisian law.

When Chopin first arrived in Paris in September 1831 the city bursting through this wall was quickly changing in character as well as size. Charles X had been exiled the previous year in a popular uprising, the subject of Delacroix's most famous painting, *La Liberté guidant le peuple* (1830), his call to arms and thrilling piece of myth-making. The barefoot, bare-breasted figure of Liberty (Marianne), *Tricolore* in hand, steps through gunpowder smoke and over the king's slain soldiers, leading on a disparate collection of gentleman revolutionaries, peasants, brigands and buccaneers, while a youth by her side wields two pistols – surely Delacroix's evocation of the republican drummer boy Joseph Bara, who had died valiantly in the French Révolution, his own mythology carefully tended. The painting has come to encapsulate the July Revolution, which installed Louis-Philippe as King of the French, all the while sowing the seeds of the revolutions to come. It perfectly bears out Julian Barnes's description of Delacroix as 'some great fiery explosion happening at the same time as Romanticism' – a fair description of Chopin too.

From 1833 until his departure for Majorca in late 1838, Chopin lived on the rue de la Chaussée-d'Antin, first at number five, then at thirty-eight. Galignani's popular guide to Paris (1830) describes the typical resident of this *quartier*, the polished Parisian so different from the 'pensive inhabitant' of the Marais, different again from the coarse tenants of the northern *faubourgs*. Chopin's new friend Heine – whose poetry was much admired in Germany but whose radical politics made him unwelcome there – wrote witheringly about the bankers and stockbrokers who made their home on the Chaussée-d'Antin, these venal occupants of the Bourse (another of Napoleon's neoclassical temples). 'Here, in the vast space of the high-arched hall, here it is that the swindlers, with all their repulsive faces and disagreeable screams, sweep here and there, like the tossing of a sea of egotistic greed, and where, amid the wild billows of human beings, the great bankers dart up, snapping and devouring like sharks – one monster preying on another . . .'

It is to his mansion on the Chaussée-d'Antin, to the sumptuous drawing room furnished in brilliant whites and golds, that the unscrupulous banker Baron Danglars invites Dumas's Count of Monte Cristo. Facilitating a crucial step in the count's slow, elegant dance of vengeance with those who had years earlier framed him for treason, Danglars grants the count unlimited credit, which he also has with the bankers Laffitte and Rothschild. In real life the Baron de Rothschild lived close by, on a street named after Laffitte. After meeting Rothschild through the Polish Prince Czartoryski, it took Chopin no time at all to be welcomed into the high society propping up Louis-Philippe's July Monarchy. (Dumas's novel, first serialized in 1844–5, begins in 1815 and ends ten years or so into Louis-Philippe's reign.) Rothschild's wife and daughter became Chopin's pupils, which gave Chopin both social and professional cachet. 'I have found my way into the very best society,' he could tell a friend in Poland in January 1833, with an endearing mixture of pride and comedy (he was only twenty-three). 'I have my place among ambassadors, princes, ministers.' He had arrived in Paris almost by accident and with no firm plans to stay: this was an unexpected if welcome elevation that would effectively keep him in the city for the remainder of his life.

Balzac writes of the boulevards between the rue de la Chaussée-d'Antin and the rue de Richelieu, of their strange, marvellous apartments and houses, palaces and piles. 'Once you have set foot here, your day is lost if you are a man of thought. It is a gilded dream and an unbeatable distraction. The engravings of the print sellers, the daily entertainments, the tidbits of the cafés, the gems in the jewellers' shops, all is set to intoxicate and overexcite you.' This was the domain of the *flâneur*, who could afford its gilded dreams and had the leisure to savour them, the creature who epitomized Balzac's witty assertion that '*Flânerie* is a science; it is the gastronomy of the eye.'

Rich tradesmen and shopkeepers populate the Palais-Royal, Galignani writes, all selling the latest fashions. But move away from this strip, towards the rue Saint-Denis or down to the Pont-Neuf, and you will discover warehouses full of wool, silk, stuff, linen and, on the *quais*, gold- and silversmiths, opticians, makers of mathematical instruments. Tanners and dyers, brewers and spinners, potters and prostitutes are a little further east, or down on the riverbanks, the prostitutes less obtrusive in Paris than in London because they must register with municipal authorities and submit to regular police inspections. Galignani underlines the politeness of the lower orders, how the narrow streets sing out with the cordial *Monsieur*, *Madame* and *Mademoiselle* as workers pass each other.

The *deuxième* was also home to the Opéra and Opéra-Comique, the Palais-Royal, the theatres Français, Variétés, Nouveautés, and M. Comte, along with the gas-lit and tree-lined Boulevard des Italiens, the cemetery of Montmartre, the renowned Chinese Baths and Frascati's gaming house. The Café de Paris served boned larks, the Café Tortini delicious ices. (The future George Sand met Casimir Dudevant in Café Tortini in 1821 and married him the following year.) A young Henry Wadsworth Longfellow gleefully described to his father the musicians and jugglers along the Boulevard des Italiens, the lame beggars, the men with monkeys, the Turks in oriental costume, the Frenchmen with curled whiskers and wrinkled (nankeen) trousers, the booksellers and cobblers. 'You cannot conceive what "carryings on" there are there at all hours of the day and evening!'

Given the concentration of important historical buildings, the *deuxième* was unexpectedly progressive. The Opéra-Comique boasted horse-powered air-conditioning – a system of gears, axels and cogs, all turned by a draught horse on a circular walkway in the theatre's basement (as though in the bowels of a horse ferry), which pumped air over large blocks of ice and then out through vents into the auditorium. And the *arrondissement* remained progressive for the remainder of the century:

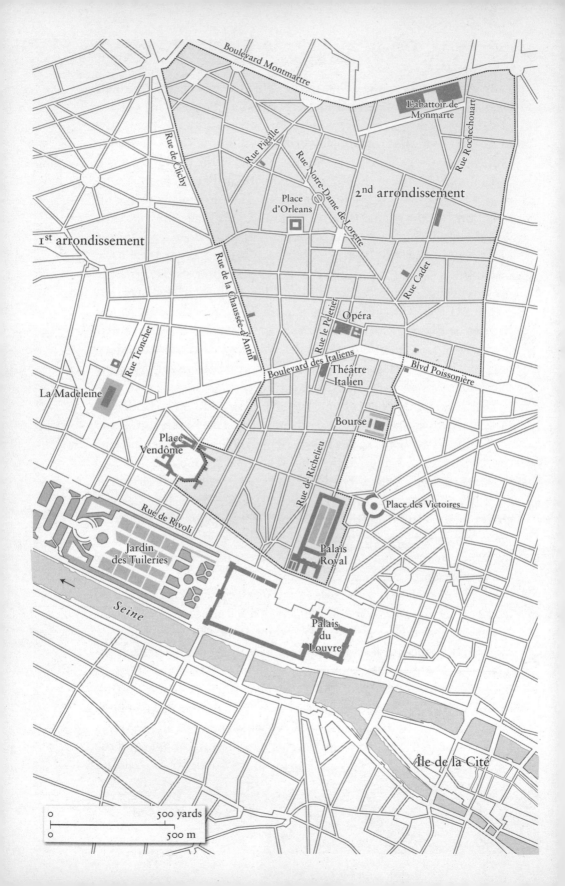

in 1880 Émile Zola wrote of the modernized arcades near the Théâtre des Variétés, in which a 'perfect stream of brilliancy emanated from white globes, red lanterns, blue transparencies, lines of gas jets'.

The arcades were part of capitalist Paris long before gas lighting, their marble floors and glass roofing offering a gilded refuge from the dirty streets, tiny pavements (where they existed at all), and the chaos caused by teeming carriages containing slim young men and women dressed in what Baudelaire dismissed as the eccentric costumes of the season. 'The carriage drives off at a brisk trot along a pathway zebra'd with light and shade, carrying its freight of beauties couched as though in a gondola, lying back idly, only half listening to the gallantries which are being whispered in their ears . . .'

At the end of the 1830s the district contained a further emblem of modern Paris. Embarcadère des Batignolles, a short walk from Chopin's apartment on the rue de la Chaussée-d'Antin, opened in 1837 and joined Paris with Saint-Germain-en-Laye twenty kilometres west of the capital. It was the country's first public railway line, twelve years after England's, its Paris terminal conceived with Palladian rigour, as caught in a lithograph early in its operations: a mix of arches and pillars and sharp geometric lines overseeing steam engines pulling small passenger cars, against a tree-studded backdrop of Montmartre.

This one rail route presaged a France easily connected to the rest of the Continent, its landscape dotted with grand stations like the one that grew out of Embarcadère des Batignolles in the 1840s, Gare Saint-Lazare, which Monet later painted as a glass temple full of billowing smoke and uniformed railway workers, bridge buttresses and hazy gas lighting, the arriving trains and embarking passengers often little more than smudges of paint.

Thirty years before Monet, Hugo, the great chronicler of nineteenth-century France, signalled the impact that railways would have on French art. In 1841 he described the unbelievable speed of his first train journey, the flowers along the tracks turning into blotches or stripes, the corn transforming itself into a mess of yellow hair, the steeples and trees dancing in the distance. 'Now and then, a shadow, a shape, the upright figure of a ghost appears and disappears in a flash besides the door . . . Inside the carriage, people say, "It's three leagues from here; we'll be there in ten minutes."' Industry was changing the shape and substance of French art, as ever more tonnes of coal were mined – in the Loire basin or from deep seams in Pas-de-Calais near Belgium – and distributed throughout the country to keep the trains moving, the gaslights glowing.

Images of these changes would fast accumulate, for in 1838 Louis Daguerre successfully photographed the Boulevard du Temple, the theatre strip in the sixth *arrondissement*, capturing in mirror image a collection of chimneys and poplars, long shadows cast by the morning sun, tiled roofs and cobbled road, and higgledy-piggledy facades as flat as the backdrops inside the boulevard's theatres. Yet Daguerre also caught the first ever photographic image of a person: a man standing entirely alone in front of a near-invisible shoeshine boy, perfectly still in the five minutes or so his boot is spat on, polished, shined, spat on again, shined once more, those around him moving too quickly to leave on the glass plate anything but a ghostly trail. In this moment, in the same year in which Delacroix painted Chopin and Sand, portraiture was changed for ever.

When Georges-Eugène Haussmann began his wholesale consolidation and renovation of the capital soon after Chopin's death – cutting great swathes through the slums, opening the city to the light and air and the social control that Louis-Napoleon Bonaparte craved – he was simply tapping into a modernizing vision for the country that had originated in the First Republic and was enshrined in the short-lived Second (1848–52). Yet even as Haussmann transformed streets into avenues, avenues into boulevards – great arteries pumping the life of the city beyond the boundaries marked by the old wall of the

Ferme générale, which helped increase the number of *arrondisse-ments* from twelve to twenty – it was still possible late in the century to read the *ancien* patchwork society in the former *deuxième*. In his novel *L'Assommoir* (1877), Zola at one point places his doomed pro-tagonist Gervaise Macquart in a hotel on the Boulevard de la Chapelle, looking 'to the right, towards Boulevard de Rochechouart, where groups of butchers, in aprons smeared with blood, were hang-ing about in front of the slaughterhouses', the breeze carrying the smell of blood and offal and the hanging carcasses of the butchered animals. This was the *arrondissement* that Chopin knew. It gentri-fied as the Second French Empire found its feet, without completely losing the sights and smells of the 1840s and the revolutionary fire that produced them.

The fire was lit in the early 1830s, Cherubini thought, and turned Paris into a city of cholera and revolution. The two conditions were linked: the disease fermented in the poorest neighbourhoods, the epi-demic in 1832 killing more than 18,000 inside the city walls, the vast majority in slums riddled with poor sanitation, dirty water and politi-cal discontent, and populated by the casualties of industrialization: craftsmen and craftswomen of rural France, thrown out of work by the introduction of spinning-looms and steam machinery, trying their luck in the capital. Thus Heine could write despairingly of the city's shoemakers and spinners, rag-pickers and beggars, and how 'the mul-titude murmured bitterly when it saw how the rich fled away, and, well packed with doctors and drugs, took refuge in healthier climes'. Chopin's friend Antoni Orlowski watched rich patrons abandon the city, leaving behind impoverished musicians ('as numerous as dogs') who were frustratingly immune to the disease; there was no more mutual sympathy between them during the epidemic than before. In his drawings Honoré Daumier turned to this scene again and again: the panicked, aproned maid walking quickly over her threshold, past the dead body in the street, a handkerchief clasped impotently over her mouth, the dead man's stick-thin dog wandering forlornly nearby, masked workers carting off corpses in rough-planked coffins.

It is the scene, too, that Sand observed from her vantage point above the Quai Saint-Michel – the small flat she took at the end of 1831 when she separated from Dudevant – cholera gaining ground by

SOUVENIRS DU CHOLÉRA-MORBUS.   69

the day. 'It stole rapidly towards us and mounted our house floor by floor. It carried off six people, stopping at the door of our garret as if disdaining so meagre a prey.' Below her the corpses of the city's poor were piled high in improvised hearses, no kin behind them, drivers urging on their horses out of the desperate *quartiers*, passers-by fleeing the cortèges, residents certain they were being poisoned by their social superiors, their despondency and apathy overwhelming. 'I remember that two little boys stood by me with sad faces,' Heine later wrote, 'and one asked me if I could tell him in which sack his father was. The stillness of death reigns over all Paris, a stony expression, serious, is on all faces.'

From his own vantage point on the fourth floor of the Bazar de l'Industrie on the Boulevard Poissonière – where merchants bought and sold linen, velvet, blond lace and twisted cotton ('the passersby here are no longer elegant, fine dresses would be out of place, the artist and the literary lion no longer venture into these parts', Balzac writes in his 1845 history of the boulevards) – Chopin watched the social unrest that follows contagion and heard both the weak thrums of disaffection and louder shouts of revolution. On Christmas Day 1831, his first in the city, he wrote to his friend Woyciechowski in Poturzyn of the social mix on the streets and squares below him: vendors hawking penny-pamphlets (*Priests in Love*, say, or *Romance of the Archbishop of Paris and the Duchesse de Berry*); bearded Republicans and Bonapartists in red waistcoats, Carlists in green, Saint-Simonians in blue, each group gathering under its own manifesto and banner; noisy street demonstrations and protests, the national guard dispersing and arresting citizens, hussars and mounted gendarmes ineffectually shepherding the crowds; loud whistles and chants giving way, late at night, to the *Marseillaise*. 'The lower classes are completely exasperated and ready at any time to break out of their poverty-stricken situation,' he wrote to Woyciechowski, 'but unfortunately for them the Government is extremely severe on such movements and the slightest gathering in the streets is dispersed by mounted police.' All this would culminate in the terrible reprisals of 6 June 1832, which Hugo later mined for the climax of *Les Misérables*: the cannons and slaughter; the tumbrels carting bodies to the morgue where they were stacked high into a wall of gruesome masonry (Sand's description in *Histoire de ma vie*); the sickening stench and stain of blood everywhere.

Chopin negotiated quite another battle-worn constituency in this decade. From November 1830, en route to Paris from Warsaw, he had spent eight months in Vienna, practising daily at Graff's piano shop (as he spelled it), taking his meals each evening in *Der wilde Mann* (The Wild Man), carrying his newly acquired strudel-weight well, so he thought, wondering what he should perform in his big concert in that city, flattered that his F minor concerto was being talked about around town and ranked above Hummel's most recent piano concerto. While all this made up Chopin's fishbowl life, Warsaw was host to a bold political uprising of Polish soldiers and subjects against their country's partition under Russian, Austrian and Prussian rule – confirmed in 1815 at the Congress of Vienna – and suffered the inevitable savage recriminations of the Imperial Russian Army.

The Russo-Polish War would last until October 1831, at which point the vastly superior Russian Army crushed the dissenters and deposed the government, placing the entire Kingdom of Poland under Russian rule, adding yet more tinder to an already bursting box. Polish dissidents and malcontents, artists and aristocrats, landowners and Romantics made their way in large numbers to Paris, settling in the

Faubourg-du-Roule *quartier* if they had managed to liquidate their assets before fleeing, or in the second *arrondissement* and the slums of 'little Poland' behind Notre-Dame if they had not. They were the familiars of Chopin's childhood: pupils and parents he had met at the upper-middle-class Lyceum where his father taught; Polish academics and intellectuals from the University of Warsaw next door, with whom his parents had socialized; fellow students of Józef Elsner at Warsaw's main school of music; aristocrats, industrialists and landowners in whose houses Chopin was first noticed as a fine pianist and composer.

These same people haunted him in Paris – regardless of his well-deserved reputation for political apathy, the suspicion among friends being that he was untouched by revolution and its ferments. Yet in September 1831, with the last, terrible push of the Imperial Army still to come, Chopin wrote of the Warsaw terrors. It reads as powerfully as Hugo, Chopin imagining suburbs stormed and burned, young Polish men captured or killed on the barricades, graveyards defiled by Muscovite scum, soldiers seizing and killing womenfolk, children starving. 'Oh, God, God! Make the earth to tremble and let this generation be engulfed! May the most frightful torments seize the French for not coming to our aid!'

The following year he performed in fund-raising concerts for Polish immigrants (though he declined to write a nationalist hymn or anthem for use by dissidents), sharing their mad nostalgia for the homeland – especially when it rained, or when visitors played him the latest airs from home, or when certain foods were served, certain scents smelled. He was honest and miserable in his early letters to Woyciechowski, writing of feigned cheerfulness, especially with his countrymen. 'Among Poles I see Kunasik, Morawski, Niemojowski, Lelewel and Plichta, besides a vast number of imbeciles,' he wrote in December 1831; and he was still seeking out their company or companionship ten years later, any thought of returning to Warsaw having long passed.

Joseph Filtsch described him in 1842 at a sad little soirée attended by 'people who used to fill the highest places in the kingdom and who, after their unhappy revolution, have taken refuge in Paris, where they have met with a cordial reception' – like some grim parade of émigrés in a novel by Turgenev (himself a later exile in both Germany and France). 'I am tortured by all sorts of forebodings, anxieties, dreams or insomnia, the impulse to live, followed by a wish to die – a kind of delicious trance or unconsciousness,' he wrote to Woyciechowski in the aftermath of the brutal Russian victory. 'Everything seems sour, bitter, salty – a ghastly mix-up of feelings agitates my mind.'

His anxiety in these early years in Paris was not about language or the alienation that can come from not knowing it. He spoke and wrote French perfectly well, though with an accent in his speech and less wit than we can read in his Polish letters (and bad handwriting in both languages). He was not marked by the usual problems of living in a second language – speaking in a voice too loud or too whiny, too precise or too cadenced, too slow or, in those happy days, too fluent. Yet he still loved the opportunity to talk in Polish, whether with his valet or his friend Delfina Potocka (whose looks Proust described as 'at once delicate, majestic and malicious'), or the city's many émigrés. Liszt thought Chopin viewed the French language through a prism of frustration and condescension, immediately dismissive of its lack of nuance, too quick to reply 'Oh, it's untranslatable!' when asked the meaning of a Polish expression, or the words, in French, of a Polish slogan or song. Yet regardless of the strains and conflicts, in French Chopin was scrupulously polite, funny, sensitive – qualities that characterized his new friendships in Paris, his dealings with counts and courtiers, with the financiers who overnight changed his fortunes, and later, of course, with his lover George Sand.

There was one final constituency in Chopin's milieu, almost more febrile than any other, populated by the musicians and entrepreneurs, orchestras and instrument makers, teachers and pupils who in the 1830s turned Paris into the musical capital of the world. Chopin wrote home describing three excellent orchestras, Rossini directing his own operas, and about the great singers of his day – Luigi Lablache, Giuditta Pasta, Maria Malibran and Giovanni Rubini – on stage at the Théâtre Italien, creating roles that remain in the repertory today, and about Adolphe Nourrit, Henri-Étienne Dérivis, Julie Dorus-Gras and Nicolas Levasseur at the Opéra. There were concerts at the Conservatoire where, in this decade and after, the city's sudden hunger for Beethoven was fed. Berlioz wrote mischievously of this phenomenon, describing a concert in 1841 in a small, dirty hall, oil lamps flicking light into the shadows to reveal pale ladies with eyes raised towards heaven, their beefy consorts trying to remain awake, each having first asked the other what was in any case so heroic about the symphony they were about to hear.

Sophie Gay thought the habitués of the Théâtre Italien were even more superficial, mired in old audience traditions, interested only in gossiping about Lablache or Malibran, Rossini and *raouts*, the grand balls at the Apponyi Palace. According to Alexandre Dumas *père*, the fashion in the capital was for the curtain to rise on an almost empty house, the audience arriving in dribs and drabs throughout the first act in a mêlée of box-door banging, loudly shared greetings and scrappy conversations – about horse races, unknown beauties, improbable liaisons. Even so, Chopin, who had been startled by the range and quality on display in Vienna – so different from provincial Warsaw – was hugely impressed.

On the eve of the July Monarchy the pianist Wilhelm von Lenz, who would later write intimately about Chopin and his circle, painted a picture of a modish, blinkered musical world in Paris, of audiences dismissing Beethoven's last sonatas as 'the monstrous abortions of a German idealist who did not know how to write for the piano', of Mozart never reaching the heights of Friedrich Kalkbrenner, of audiences in thrall to that 'bland master-joiner Hummel'. Yet it all changed remarkably quickly – and not simply in the sudden public appreciation of light music that Louis-Philippe either inspired or demanded. Louis Véron, who made his money peddling medicaments up and down the country (and who could easily have been Donizetti's inspiration for the character Dulcamara in *L'elisir d'amore*), bought the franchise of the Opéra in 1831 from a government determined to rid itself of the trouble and expense, and set about changing Parisian taste, notably and immediately with Meyerbeer's *Robert le diable*, which opened just before Chopin arrived in the capital and which was talked about everywhere, from the salons to the shops.

Chopin attended a performance at the end of 1831 and marvelled at the chorus of devils singing through megaphones as spirits rose from their graves; the processions of monks and clergy swinging censers; the overpowering sound of the grand organ from the stage; the dramatic gas lighting, which had transformed the visual aesthetics of the Opéra on its introduction nine years earlier (though divas continued to drop belladonna into their eyes to make them shine more brightly, as they had when lit by candles).

Véron assembled precisely this kind of mad circus for Halévy's *La Juive* four years later ('Emperor's trumpeters, preceded by three mounted guards richly armed and equipped . . . One hundred soldiers richly armed and dressed in coats of mail and armour', read the stage directions), which in 1852 Berlioz parodied with a wicked eye in *Evenings with the Orchestra*. Grand Opera, he wrote, looking back on the 1830s with a mixture of fondness and middle-age disdain, consisted of

> high Cs from every type of chest, bass drums, snare drums, organs, military bands, antique trumpets, tubas as big as locomotive smokestacks, bells, cannon, horses, cardinals under a canopy, emperors covered with gold, queens wearing tiaras, funerals, fêtes, weddings, and again the canopy, the canopy beplumed and splendiferous, borne by four officers as in *Malbrouck*, jugglers, skaters, choirboys, censers, monstrances, crosses, banners, processions, orgies of priests and naked women, the bull Apis, and masses of oxen, screech-owls, bats, the five-hundred fiends of hell, and what have you – the rocking of the heavens and the end of the world, interspersed with a few dull cavatinas here and there and a large *claque* thrown in.

Although captivated by the spectacle in *Robert le diable* and rendered as giddy as those around him ('No one will ever stage anything like it! Meyerbeer has made himself immortal!'), Chopin's taste was actually for Rubini in *Il barbiere di Siviglia*, Pasta in Rossini's *Otello* and Lablache in *L'italiana in Algeri*. This music, which he heard repeatedly, with wonder and admiration, coloured his palette in a way that the showmanship of Meyerbeer never would.

With these sounds and spectacles in the air, Chopin stepped gingerly through the diplomatic and musical minefields of his adopted city, through the claims and counterclaims, flattery and jealousy, advancement, disingenuousness and sabotage. He planned his Paris debut in a programme including Véron's singers (postponed), Kalkbrenner's assistance (postponed), and finally the contrivance of both. On 26 February 1832, at Les Salons de MM. Pleyel et Cie. at 9, rue Cadet, he played his Concerto in E minor and his courteous Variations on 'Là ci darem la mano' – the tender-tense duet from Mozart's *Don Giovanni* in which Giovanni attempts to seduce the peasant girl Zerlina on the eve of her wedding to the oafish Masetto. Colleagues performed Beethoven's String Quintet, Op. 29, and a few arias, before Chopin joined Kalkbrenner and others in Kalkbrenner's new Polonaise for six pianos, its scale no doubt inspired by recent goings-on at the Opéra. François Fétis in *Revue Musicale* wrote perceptively of the evening: 'There is a difference between music for the piano, which Beethoven wrote, and music for pianists, a field in which M. Chopin's inspiration has created a revitalization of forms which could carry in their wake a great impact on this type of art.'

Thus were many of the patterns and expectations of the decade established. This largely self-taught pianist deflected the vain, mercenary Kalkbrenner's attempts to bind him into a long, expensive apprenticeship. He shook off the remnants of his upbringing in conservative Warsaw: obeisance to Beethoven and the Viennese school; the extrovert concert pieces he had written in late adolescence; the expectation that he would earn his living as a public performer; the assumption that he would become Poland's national composer, producing one patriotic opera after another. He discarded his homeland's parochial habits too, which inspired other Polish musicians in the 1820s and 1830s to seek either tuition or validation in Vienna or Paris. Almost by chance Chopin had discovered a city and a culture in which he could become himself.

6

Paris, 1839

In the early months of 1839 Fontana had assiduously followed each of Chopin's detailed, almost obsessive instructions from Majorca. Consequently, in the middle of the year, with Chopin not yet back in Paris, editions of the Preludes appeared more or less simultaneously in Germany, France and England. Breitkopf & Härtel was first, publishing a single volume in July (costing 2 *reichstaler* in German Confederation states); Ad. Catelin et Cie. (two volumes costing 7 francs 50 centimes each) and Wessel & Co. of Frith Street, Soho (also two volumes, 6 shillings each) followed a month later. Only the Germans managed to include an opus number, and only the French and English the correct dedicatee.

Later in the year Schumann wrote in *Neue Zeitschrift für Musik* a perplexed though ultimately admiring review of this startling publication. He maintained a complicated friendship with Chopin, a puzzled admiration guarding their every encounter; it was in this vein that he responded to the new collection:

> The Preludes are strange pieces. I confess I imagined them differently, and designed in the grandest style, like his Etudes. But almost the opposite is true: they are sketches, beginnings of Etudes, or, so to speak, ruins, eagle wings, a wild motley of pieces. But each piece, written in a fine, pearly hand, shows: 'Frederick Chopin wrote it.' One recognises him in the pauses by the passionate breathing. He is and remains the boldest and proudest poetic mind of the time. The collection also contains the morbid, the feverish, the repellent. May each search what suits him; may only the philistine stay away!

Aside from Schumann, no one in England or France wrote publicly about the new volume. It is not that it sank without trace, but this delicate raft of miniatures certainly attracted little attention. Partly this was because the culture of criticism we know today – a largely German invention – was only finding its feet in the 1820s and 1830s; partly it was the fault of the elusive Preludes themselves.

There were private encounters with them, of course, and personal responses too. Friederike Müller knew at least a handful of them, for they turned up on her study list when she became Chopin's pupil in October 1839. Ignaz Moscheles (whose playing Chopin greatly admired) heard Chopin perform a few or all of them at around the same time – probably in the apartment on the rue Tronchet, or in Sand's on the rue Pigalle – finally understanding Chopin's rhetorical gestures, grateful that Chopin had sidestepped the weighty orchestral effects that German composers, performers and pedagogues were replicating in piano music this decade, himself included.

A week or so after this informal performance Moscheles attended a salon hosted by a relative of his wife, the Hamburg banker Auguste Léo, and once again heard some Preludes. Léo was resident in Paris from 1817 to 1848 and a good friend to Chopin, not least with his finances. With his wife Sophie he hosted a salon popular with Chopin and other artistic émigrés, both those settled in Paris and those passing through: Mendelssohn, Moscheles, Meyerbeer, the pianists Ferdinand Hiller and Stephan Heller, and Clara Wieck, still denied her father's permission to marry Schumann. Moscheles and Meyerbeer each wrote about Chopin's performance on this occasion, and about Prelude No. 17 in particular: Meyerbeer recorded in his diary his love of this *himmlisch* (heavenly) work, while Moscheles scribbled in a letter how his wife and eldest daughter were captivated by it, not least the eleven A-flat pedal notes punctuating the last page or so. Mendelssohn had a similar response on another occasion: 'I love it, I cannot tell you how much or why; except, perhaps, that it is something which I could never have written at all.' Mostly, though, the Preludes escaped notice.

This crowd, this banker, brought out in Chopin the anti-Semitism that hummed away in the cultural background of many European cities in these decades. Léo was the subject of an anti-Semitic tirade to Fontana over dealings with foreign publishers for the Preludes. (It seems Chopin owed Léo money at the time of his Majorca trip and the banker was merely trying to make good the debt.) So Léo was a Jew, a scoundrel, hysterical. In negotiations over the Preludes, others were similarly painted: 'I did not expect such Jewish behaviour from Pleyel . . .' When it looked as though Breitkopf & Härtel was faltering: 'Schlesinger has swindled me all along . . . go carefully with him, for this Jew would like to cut a figure in the world.' And to Wojciech Grzymała, 'Jews will be Jews and Huns will be Huns – that's the truth, but what can one do? I am forced to deal with them.'

This last rhetorical flourish shows up Chopin's anti-Semitism for what it was: the paranoia of those short of money when convinced they are being bilked by the wealthy – nourished from the deep seam of anti-Semitism then found in many gentile Poles. Later in the century Édouard Drumont would turn this socially accepted prejudice into a sturdy platform, which would find its apogee in the Dreyfus affair. In *La France juive* (1886) Drumont, arguing with all the sophistication of a doomsday street preacher clutching a crayoned sign, wrote, 'Jews, vomited from all the ghettos of Europe, are now installed as the masters in historic houses that evoke the most glorious memories of ancient France . . .' He maintained a fanatical hatred of the Rothschilds, though it was never quite apparent whether it was more due to their difference or their assimilation – their proud, Jewish, familial business empire housed in the grandest mansions in all Europe's capitals, or the arriviste nonsense of commissioning a coat of arms and learning to hunt. So there were definitely legacies of the sort of talk and stereotypes in which Chopin engaged – the 'sordid Jew' Sand watched him impersonate in her salon once the music had stopped and the charades begun – but they did not play out in his lifetime, or not quite. His friendships with the Rothschilds, with Léo and his associates, with Heine too, were genuine and admiring.

Chopin enjoyed Léo's salon and those like it because they were hosted in the grand houses of the *nouveaux riches*, a class largely uninterested in the customs of the *ancien régime* (aristocratic rivalries between one ancient family and another could not have interested them less), or only so far as they overlapped with their own desire for social currency. Heine encountered these *ancien* crowds at the salons he visited in the year he and Chopin each arrived in Paris, where attendees looked like relics from a curiosity shop on the Quai

Voltaire, he thought: Egyptian idols with dogs' heads standing next to bold musketeers with happy memories of Marie Antoinette; *Montagnards* alongside Jesuits of the Restoration; grand empire dignitaries, faded diplomats, the decayed, deposed gods of old times, all faith in them lost.

Chopin dipped into such streams, especially when first in Paris, but was almost as dismissive of them as Heine. He liked the forums in which music was a prized part of everyday conversation and culture; if occasionally those who patronized musicians did so because they were attracted to more than their work – as with the Marquis de Custine – that did not bother him. Custine's salon was a complete intersection of old and new France in the Paris of Louis-Philippe, the type Berlioz had in mind when he wrote of how, around midnight, 'when the big butterflies of the salon had left, when the political questions of the day had been discussed at length, when all the gossips had exhausted their supply of stories, when all the snares were set, all the perfidies consummated, when one was thoroughly tired of prose', Chopin finally sat at the piano. There he would play for Hugo and Lamartine, the Countess Merlin and the Duchess of Abrantès, Sophie Gay and Sand.

At his own gatherings, or those in Sand's house, Chopin was a generous, graceful, occasionally reluctant host. Liszt wrote of the apartment in the rue de la Chaussée-d'Antin, with its thicket of candles round the Pleyel (which sounded like a German glass harmonica, he decided), leaving the rest of the room in shadows, its large mirror offering an extra perspective of the slight man at the piano, the single portrait on the wall seeming to listen to the 'ebb and flow of the music, which moaned and roared, murmured and died upon the instrument near which it hung'. Caught in the candlelight were Heine, Meyerbeer, Nourrit (the tenor at whose funeral Chopin played on his way home from Majorca), the great poet and advocate of Polish independence Adam Mickiewicz, Hiller, Delacroix, and Sand, deep in an armchair and in shadow, listening intently.

Because of his experiences performing as an adolescent in grand Polish houses, there was nothing unusual or difficult for Chopin in these salons. (Public recitals were another matter.) Moreover, as artistic gatherings and harbingers, they were more important than they seemed: the dismissive soubriquet 'salon composer', which attached itself to Chopin with grim persistence in the following decades, is twice a misnomer, for it misreads both the quality of his music and the artistic and intellectual significance of the forums in which it was performed. It was in these salons that other pianists saw how Chopin played: if so minded they adapted (as best they could) his unusual technique, reconditioning fingers and minds trained on the brilliant style then so fashionable, with its fast double octaves, sequences of repeated notes, and sheer physicality. Or they merely watched and listened in the flickering candlelight, admiring Chopin's singularity, but not at all sure whether his music would ever catch on.

Prelude No. 17, which Meyerbeer, Moscheles and Mendelssohn so admired, is full of chromaticism and cheek, of cyclic modulations that take it far from the home key, the eleven pedal notes in the last half minute or so emphasizing just how permanently it has returned. Chopin's pupil Madame Dubois (Camille O'Meara) told the young Paderewski in a lesson not to make these pedal notes softer as each bar passed since Chopin struck them all with the same strength and accentuation. 'The idea of that Prelude is based on the sound of an old clock in the castle which strikes the *eleventh* hour,' Chopin told Dubois. Each chime must be the same 'because the clock knows no *diminuendo*'.

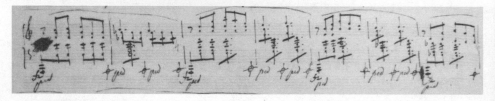

There is something folkloric about a clock striking none but the eleventh hour, as unsettling as the thirteen chimes mentioned in the opening sentence of Orwell's *1984*. It could be completely benign, of course, a precursor of Baudelaire's 'L'invitation au voyage', his essay on nostalgia for countries never known, 'where clocks strike happiness with a deeper, a more significant solemnity'. Or comic: perhaps the castle clock is meant to mark midday and midnight, but the gears clog on the last few chimes, or the snail-shaped cam, worn down from endless markings of the *meridiem*, can never quite trigger a twelfth. (Each of the first eight rings lasts for two bars – regular clockwork – but between the ninth and tenth tolls there are three bars, between the tenth and eleventh four: it is as though the whole mechanism is seizing up.) Whatever Chopin's exact intention, this Prelude is one of the few instances in which he incorporated a specific programme or image and admitted it to a pupil or peer.

He certainly enjoyed such mimicry outside his composing. In summer 1846 he entertained friends at the piano with a pitch-perfect imitation of a music box, which rippled and vibrated and, at one point (in a performance of a Tyrolienne), muscled its way ahead of whatever other tune was being played. Chopin even managed to give the impression that the delicate cylinder driving the box was missing a tooth or pin, which caused the note to snag each time. He admired the intricate technology of these boxes, and could write to his family enthusiastically about the more recent inventions and events he read about in the French press: Morse's telegraph line running between Washington D.C. and Baltimore; Leverrier's discovery of Neptune; Faber's singing automaton.

Similar artefacts were on display in these decades in the arcade windows of the *deuxième*, and in the parlours of wealthy Parisians too: exquisite *boîtes à oiseau chanteur* (singing bird boxes) made by the four Rochat brothers in their atelier in Geneva. They were decorated with fingernail slices of mother-of-pearl and delicate carvings of turquoise, with gold detailing and tiny *champlevé* enamel leaves and flowers. Yet their interiors far outshone their gilded exteriors, interiors jammed with pistons and fusees, rotating cams and fly-controlled wheel trains, pin barrels activating tuned teeth the shape of grasshopper wings, and small circular bellows blowing air through sliding whistles to re-create the birdsong that piped away with the dexterity of Malibran's coloratura.

Each splendidly feathered bird was no bigger than a thimble, and was perched on a leaf or branch wrapped with gilt tendrils. There it sat, wings flapping, head turning, tail wagging, beak opening as birdsong rang out (the duration of which was directly proportionate to the complexity of the cogs and combs tucked beneath it). Without warning it would stop flapping, look straight ahead, and then disappear through

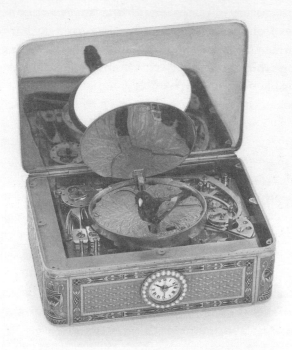

a trapdoor or medallion, a scallop shell or bunch of peonies – like Malibran or soprano Pauline Viardot retreating from the stage at the Théâtre Italien into the cool, silent darkness, applause in their ears, until an audience once more assembled and the show began again.

Such precious items offered Chopin a more interesting metaphysical template in the Preludes than an old castle clock, as No. 13 (the most perfect of them) suggests. Although it begins as a droopy barcarolle, for a mere eight bars in the middle the texture, key and mood suddenly change: above a harmonically static though rich bed of chords Chopin introduces a beautiful *cantilena*, which he spices with the gentle embellishments his friend Viardot – not yet twenty but already a sensation throughout Europe – often improvised in her lyrical repertory in the same tessitura. The *cantilena* is over as abruptly as it begins, replaced by the texture and tonality of the opening page; listeners are left unsure whether they heard it or simply imagined it.

But then the final two bars recapitulate the shadowy aria, sending a delicate haze of reminiscence over the whole piece, suggesting that the mind was not playing tricks after all, that there really was something exquisite in the middle of the surrounding fabric. It is a wholly unexpected shift of scene and character, which mesmerizes those listening: the art of the great improviser who knows not to make the next step predictable, yet also knows how to remain comprehensible.

Long after Chopin composed the Preludes, Walter Benjamin wrote, 'The interior was the place of refuge of Art.' The middle eight bars of Prelude No. 13 – even more spellbinding than the sections encasing them – were Chopin's place of refuge, away from the exterior displays of Romantic music that Liszt and his confrères were promulgating, ones he found too literal, too extravagant, entirely lacking in magic.

Such interior worlds did one more thing: they suggested a way of shaping the structure of a work – from inside out. Midway through the previous century Jean-François de Bastide achieved this with perfect clarity in his novella *La petite maison*, the story of a nobleman who uses the refinement of his impeccable summer house – the wall paints (by Dandrillon) infused with the fragrance of either violet, jasmine or rose, the dining room serving a luscious banquet on a *table machinée*, course following course – to help him seduce a beautiful woman. The proportions, symmetry, furnishings, colour and decorations of each room play a role – so much so that in the intimate chamber at the top of the house (bathed in subtle light and containing the finest artworks from the nobleman's collection) the woman almost loses her moral resolve. Bastide's innovation lay in structuring his episodic narrative around the proportions of the house: the size, shape and design of each room find a direct correlation in the size, shape and design of each chapter.

While some critics late in the nineteenth century regretted that the interior section of the thirteenth Prelude is so small, Chopin knew it could be no bigger; the Prelude's proportions are as superbly balanced as the rooms and chapters in *La Petite maison*. A lesser composer would have squeezed more from the transitions, and would certainly have allowed more time inside the small inner chamber. But Chopin chose instead to present a concentrated burst of intense beauty. And then, in the penultimate bar, he allows some notes of nostalgia for a world that is gone.

7

Paris, 1841

In fewer than twenty years the pianoforte had become an integral part of the French cultural imagination, and in December 1839, for the second time that decade, Camille Pleyel inaugurated a new concert hall, atelier and showroom, all at 22–24, rue Rochechouart, only a street away from the firm's original and smaller premises in the rue Cadet, and a short walk from Sand's apartment in the *deuxième*. Édouard Renard's etching of the new venture in *L'Illustration* depicts grand neoclassical facades fronting large rooms over three floors – the ceilings higher at no. 22 than at no. 24, the window cornices and modillions more ornate – behind which spacious inner courtyards can just be made out, all on a broad street inhabited by Parisians in their smart spring dress.

A plan from later in the century for Salle Pleyel, inside the more handsome building at no. 22, specifies four hundred seats in the Grand Salon, including those on the large stage itself, which stood only a foot or so from the floor. Drawings made during Chopin's lifetime illustrate a smooth barrel-vaulted ceiling with an attractive frieze at the wall join; a cupola above the stage not unlike that today in London's Wigmore Hall; French crystal chandeliers dropping from decorated ceiling roses; gaslight wall sconces on either side of mirrors the size of the largest paintings in the Louvre; three hundred chairs grouped with much space around them – a little like the way poetry was then published, buffered by wide margins and vast gutters – patrons sitting upright, or perched in the Salon's three window seats, or standing in the two large entrances close to the stage on which a pianist is acknowledging the applause. It was an altogether better dressed, more richly adorned sibling than the *salle* on the rue Cadet, though the filial bond between the two was underlined by yet another showy piece from Kalkbrenner in the opening concert, this time for eight pianos, thirty-two hands – a grotesque display by Chopin's standards.

Sand had Pleyel's new concert hall in mind when, in April 1841, she wrote to Viardot. 'A great, astounding piece of news is that little Chip-Chip is going to give a Grrrrand Concert. His friends have plagued him so much that he has given way ... This Chopin-esque nightmare will take place at Pleyel's rooms on the 26th. He will have nothing to do with posters or programmes and does not want a large audience. He wants to have the affair kept quiet.' Unknown to Sand, Chopin had originally asked Viardot to share the platform with him, but when her absence from Paris prevented her from doing so, he turned to the soprano Laure Cinti-Damoreau, a favourite of

Rossini and star of both the Opéra and Opéra-Comique, and to his friend Heinrich Ernst, a worthy successor to Paganini.

Sand's remedy for the stage fright that crippled Chopin in large auditoriums ('So many things alarm him that I suggest that he should play without candles or audience and on a dumb keyboard') indicates a relationship of solicitous regard and teasing humour, fully two years after their return from Majorca. Not everyone shared her excitement. 'A little spiteful clique is trying to resuscitate Chopin who is going to play at Pleyel's,' Marie d'Agoult told a friend five days before the concert. 'Madame Sand hates me and we no longer meet.' Ill will had been brewing for a while. Liszt wrote to d'Agoult in January 1841 about how ridiculous he found Chopin and Sand, and of the subtle blow he had in mind for them, whatever this might have been. He was playing to a very small gallery.

D'Agoult's letters repeated the mean-spiritedness she had been trotting from one salon to the next: that the only thing permanent about Chopin was his cough; that he resembled an oyster sprinkled with sugar; that Chopin did not visit Liszt when he was ill, so jealous was he of his friend's brilliance; and so on. It was one more indication of her foolish desire for a duel between two wary friends, one complicit, the other with no intention of even choosing a weapon. Sand refused to counter the gossip with either excuses or explanations on Chopin's behalf lest he feel he ought to do the same, a wasting, wearying process. All she wanted for him was the space to think and write.

What with sickness and travel, with summers and salons at Nohant, Chopin seemed to have been absent from Parisian life for such a long time. Tickets for his 'Majorcan programme' – twenty francs each, double the price of a seat in the *premières loges* of the Théâtre Italien, ten times a worker's daily wage – sold quickly to 'the most elegant ladies, the most fashionable young men, the most celebrated artists, the richest financiers, the most illustrious peers, indeed all the elite of society, all the aristocracy of birth, fortune, talent, and beauty', as Liszt described them in the *Revue et Gazette Musicale*. 'And as for the brilliant audience which flocked around the poet, who for too long has remained silent, there was no reticence, no reserve, only praise on every tongue.'

In addition to the social padding – the sketch of the atmosphere and audience, the clothes and high spirits – and the list of works performed (a selection of Preludes, Études, Nocturnes and Mazurkas, with another two Études and a Ballade as encores), Liszt attempted to say why Chopin was both unusual and important. A year younger than Chopin, Liszt was only in his twenties when, in the environment of catastrophe and opportunity created by the artistic, social, industrial and political upheavals of the 1830s, his astounding career took off. He could only admire that Chopin refused to play the game he himself was so clearly winning: the travelling virtuoso soloist filling large auditoriums without recourse to associate artists, the modern-day recitalist (a term coined in England in 1840 for a Liszt performance) able to earn 10,000 francs in an evening. Perhaps the admiration was grudging or disingenuous, yet here was the most celebrated pianist of the day tipping his hat to another, someone uninterested in dominance among the hordes of their fellows in the capital, who ran his career on his own terms, valued scarcity over ubiquity, and somehow remained buffered from the storms of competitiveness and jealousy that defined the industry. 'Is not the noblest and most justifiable satisfaction an artist can experience that sense of being above and beyond his fame,' Liszt concluded, 'superior even to his success, greater still than his glory?'

Afterwards, when Chopin and Sand had read and absorbed the long review, there was a feeling that Liszt's reluctance to discuss the new works was intentionally glancing, that his wholehearted tribute to Chopin the pianist was a slight on Chopin the composer, a field in which Liszt was seeking pre-eminence. Did he really mention the Ballade in F only in passing? 'To new ideas he has given new forms,' Liszt writes, which is true yet foggy. 'Oh yes,' Chopin would say to friends about the review, 'Liszt has thought fit to find me a place in his kingdom.'

Yet this was a graceless response, for Liszt was part of a culture in which leading pianist-composers regularly incorporated new works into their programmes without fanfare and which critics absorbed without fuss. In any case, he admired the Preludes. 'They are not simply, as their title would suggest, pieces intended as an introduction to something further; they are poetic preludes similar to those of a great contemporary poet [Lamartine], which gently ease the soul into a golden dream world and then whisk it away to the highest realms of the ideal.' He needed to examine them further before he could write on them properly, Liszt said, yet even so 'they still retain the appearance of spontaneous improvisations produced without the slightest effort. They possess that freedom and charm which characterize works of genius.'

It was not Liszt's first introduction to the Preludes. He had called on Chopin after his return from Majorca – probably in April 1840 when visiting Paris, their friendship still intact – finding him with face and fingers smudged with ink, hair dishevelled, yet in a hospitable mood, happy to play through eight or ten of his recent works. Long after Chopin's death, Liszt could recall this play-through in perfect detail and with the greatest tenderness, especially Chopin's performance of Prelude No. 8, 'a work replete with enormous difficulties, which he wove intricately under his fingers, [so] that at times a wailing melody was unravelled, and then again completely absorbed

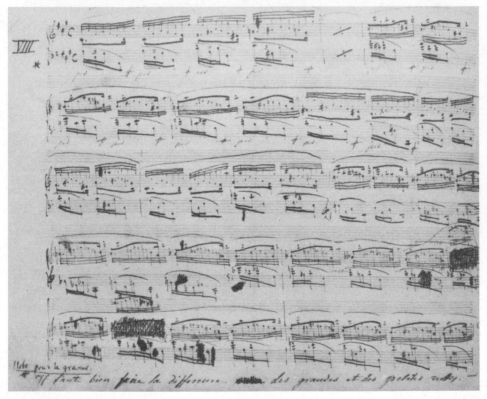

by wonderful arabesques and chromatic progressions. It was so enchanting that he complied with my earnest entreaty, and repeated it *twice*. Each time it seemed more beautiful, and each time he played it more ravishingly.'

These early encounters with the Preludes clearly cast a spell, for whenever Liszt returned to them in print he grappled with greater specificity, though still often found himself stranded behind poetic generalities. In his biography of Chopin he draws a comparison between the Preludes and the works of the seventeenth-century writer Jean de La Fontaine, whose original and marvellous fables carry great moral weight within a compact frame. The comparison is a good one, for though the characters in the Fables are as familiar today as they were to Liszt – doves and frogs, thieves and acorns, oysters and astrologers – their behaviour and fate can still catch out readers. 'It is likewise with Chopin's études and préludes,' Liszt writes, 'pieces of no lesser perfection in genres he himself created, which sprang, like all his works, from his distinctive poetic genius.'

In genres he himself created: this is what Benjamin would later say of Proust – that a great work of art either invents a new genre or dissolves an existing one (Frank Kermode, later still: 'Literature which achieves permanence is likely to be "transgressive"'). But critics and performers – Liszt and Schumann among them – were stumped as to which of the two applied here, invention or dissolution. Over time, however – even as Bach haunted the landscape and Kalkbrenner's protégés continued to thump away immediately offstage – a consensus emerged that in the Preludes Chopin really did invent a new genre. He created something wholly his own, as unsettling as anything in La Fontaine's curious yet muddily familiar world, a wild and motley assortment of ideas assembled under a singular banner, their ideas fleeting, their endings too sudden, their overriding character momentary. To their credit, Liszt and Schumann recognized that they did not quite have the language for the task in hand. Perhaps they even knew why: no matter what they heard, taught, played themselves or studied in French, German or English editions, Chopin's most personal vision was too alien for them to write about with any confidence. Poetic similes and comparisons with great artists in other fields were safer.

*

When words failed, Lamartine and La Fontaine were reliable compass points for cultured Parisians. Yet the better literary parallel with the Chopin of the Preludes is Georg Christoph Lichtenberg, the eighteenth-century German scientist and satirist who, over a long and distinguished life, wrote hundreds of silly-profound aphorisms: on tiny scraps of paper or on envelopes and menus, which he assembled only once the pile was big enough, sticking the fragments together like clothes on a paper doll. 'A book is a mirror: if an ape looks into it an apostle is hardly likely to look out.' Or, 'Nothing can contribute more to peace of soul than the lack of any opinion whatever.'

It is not solely the brevity of his aphorisms that makes for a good comparison with the Preludes: Lichtenberg also conjured up a sly description of how composers before Chopin thought about musical form. 'He marvelled at the fact that cats had two holes cut in their fur at precisely the spot where their eyes were.' However luxurious the coat or splendid its colours, the holes still had to line up with the eyes. It wasn't just composers who thought this way: audiences raised on Classical sonata form also needed surface and structure to align; when Parisians in the 1820s were left bemused or stupefied by late Beethoven sonatas, they were responding in accordance with their experiences and expectations.

This conflict between sound and form was the dominant battle in nineteenth-century music. (The corollary in painting – in this century as in others before – was between *colore* and *disegno*: colour and drawing.) Beethoven was primarily a composer of sonatas, string quartets and symphonies, and regardless of how much he stretched the formal conventions of each genre, his oeuvre is recognizably a legacy of Classical thinking, a legacy of his teacher Haydn. Yet after Beethoven, composers in thrall to the colours and potential of powerful pianos and the large Romantic orchestra increasingly took their cue from the new sounds and scale at their disposal, rather than from the formal models of their upbringing. This distinction seeded the divergent philosophical stances taken by Brahms and Wagner later in the century: Brahms wrote symphonies and sonatas, their formal shape apparent to anyone conversant with Mozart's sonatas, whereas Wagner wrote huge, self-mythologizing dramatic works, basking in the original sounds he was able to draw from the stage and the pit.

Chopin could certainly do form when he needed to. His Piano Sonata No. 2, which menaced him in Majorca and Marseilles before he finished it at Nohant in the summer of 1839, demonstrates a thorough understanding of Classical principles, notwithstanding the many deviations and innovations: a Grave introduction and Scherzo followed by a March funèbre and then a Presto Finale. The architecture of individual movements – with their evident debt to middle-period Beethoven sonatas (he was particularly fond of Op. 26 in A flat, whose opening movement is a theme and variations) – is perfectly clear, as it is in the preceding sonata and the one to follow. So Chopin knew the rules; it's just that he didn't muster very much enthusiasm for them. He was more taken with the brilliant outer layers than the skeleton beneath.

When in the following century André Gide grappled with the meaning and function of Prelude No. 2, Édouard Ganche told him to look no further than the discordant church bells of Chopin's childhood,

which were identical to those Ganche remembered from his own; on windy days they produced the off-key, funereal tolling Chopin replicated in the piece. Yet the second Prelude is too offbeat, too radical, for Ganche's conventional explanation. In just twenty-three bars Chopin weighted aesthetics over function, sensuousness over structure, sound over form. It is certainly more complex, more abstract, than anything from Ganche's belfry.

Chopin's scores are so often like patchworks constructed from the most brilliant but unexpected juxtapositions – like separate weather phenomena (tree-rattling winds on a clear day) that do not seem to belong together – scores he compulsively revised and polished, even after publication, until he could be certain they represented precisely his musical intentions. His intention was not always that clear, however: when Wilhelm von Lenz criticized him for not highlighting the variation theme enough on each transformed appearance in a domestic performance of Beethoven Op. 26, he responded offhandedly, 'I indicate . . . it's up to the listener to complete the picture.'

This is a better way of thinking about Chopin's music than Lamartine's sentimentality or La Fontaine's naughtiness. It also points to why Chopin was so taken with the wild *bel canto* arias he had heard as a youth onstage at the (Italianized) Warsaw National Theatre – Elsner in charge of opera – and in his twenties at the Théâtre Italien: these were nothing if not fantastic collections of virtuosic leaps and dives, of rich, embossed sounds and gestures and improvisations and tricksy embellishments almost (but not quite) puncturing the confines of the form binding them, a stunning embroidery in which the individual needle threads are as captivating as the picture they complete.

Rossini, the great exemplar of this style, had already stopped composing operas by the time Chopin met him. (Bellini, by contrast, whom Chopin also admired and befriended in Paris, remained active.) In the 1830s Rossini continued to live handsomely in Paris on the commission and staging fees he had accumulated, and, from the middle of the decade, on the generous annuity first granted him by Charles X. In many ways the style of opera he represented was already an anachronism, kept alive by the bourgeois pretensions of the July Monarchy, but now shown up by what was going on at Véron's Opéra. Yet to Chopin this old-fashioned style remained attractive. No less a

musician than Paganini embraced it, after all – notably in the concertos he wrote through the 1820s, which bend and twist with every
phrase, each gesture as gravity-defying as the best *cantilenas* on the
Italian opera stage – as Chopin experienced at first hand in 1829 when
the show-off violinist visited Warsaw for a series of ten concerts.

A year later in Warsaw, Chopin met the refined German coloratura
soprano Henriette Sontag, navigating a path through the admiring
senators and generals, adjutants and chamberlains who filled her
ante-room like extras in the first act of *Der Rosenkavalier*, and he
was completely smitten. It was the effect of her kindness, of course,
her warm personality and charming manners; but it was also her
outstanding musicianship: the scales and *portamenti* she dispatched
without effort in the cavatina 'Una voce poco fa' from *Il barbiere di
Siviglia*, or the florid passagework in *La gazza ladra*. 'You wouldn't
believe how different it is from what you have hitherto heard,' he told
Tytus Woyciechowski, captivated, half in love, before drawing comparisons with the last great musician whose concert tour took in
Warsaw. Her ornamentation was completely original, he wrote, so
distinct from Paganini's travels on similar terrain, more understated,
her genre more contained. In place of the violinist's ostentation, 'she
breathes over the stalls of the theatre a scent of the freshest flowers'.
    All such descriptions must be viewed with Sand's note of caution
in mind: her lover's genius was his ability to transform the sounds

he encountered, to change them into something sublime, something dislocated from reality. Even so, the image of Chopin in Sontag's chamber – devouring every crumb of Rossini she was prepared to flick his way, later transfiguring them inimitably in his own scores – is difficult to resist.

This is the quality that Liszt couldn't quite come to grips with in Chopin's music: its lack of flashiness and its simultaneous refusal to line up the slits with the eyes. Chopin appeared unwilling to tack to either one course or the other, which left his friend grappling for the meaning of what he heard. It did not seem to matter that Liszt himself had, by the late 1830s, set off on a path away from the formal arguments of his youth and training, inspired (like Jean-Joseph Laurens) by the journeyman in *Wilhelm Meisters Lehrjahre*. Liszt's footing was not yet firm, which made his friend's strides along an altogether more precarious trail all the more bewildering. In his preface to *Années de pèlerinage* (the title lifted from Goethe's novel) he acknowledged that the two men's goals were distinct. His intention in these pieces was to re-create the impressions, sensations, sights and emotions he experienced in the countries he criss-crossed on concert tours. It was music as travelogue – not a new concept, but one with a particular Romantic twist as the Continent opened up and interest in cultural similarities and differences became widespread.

Implicit in Liszt's aim was the understanding that some of this musical portraiture could unfold in real time, since the crutch of Classical form was being replaced or modified by something altogether more nebulous: a narrative arc plotted over a defined span – the duration of a piece in performance. For comprehension it helped that, in the three *Années de pèlerinage* volumes and in other programmatic works from these decades, Liszt signalled his pictorial intentions in large letters: 'William Tell's Chapel', say, or 'St Francis of Assisi preaching to the Birds'. This was Liszt as creator of musical *feuilletons*, taking his lead from Alexandre Dumas, Eugène Sue and George Sand herself, and from the literary genre's strident declamations, plot twists, cliff-hangers and neat resolutions. (In England at this time Dickens was doing much the same thing, injecting a single word with great narrative and structural power: 'Suddenly'.) None of this diminishes what were undoubtedly innovative scores, which shifted dramatically from the Classical ideal of time and structure. Liszt and his followers were moving out of Beethoven's dense shadow in the direction of instrumental storytelling; Chopin, of course, had never seen himself in it to begin with, and instrumental storytelling could not have interested him less.

All of this, then – the uncertainty, the innovation, the febrile cultural atmosphere and the bourgeois taste of Parisian audiences, Liszt's showmanship and programmatic ideas spurring on other pianist-composers, the tension between those who pursued sound over form and those who remained loyal to the ingrained structural arguments of the Classical period, Chopin's own lack of engagement with his contemporaries and the latest trends: all of this was played out in Liszt's review of the first public performance of the Preludes.

Establishing exactly what the blue-blooded, rouged and powdered crowd heard that evening in Salle Pleyel is paradoxically easier now than it would have been a hundred years ago. Some surviving Pleyel pianos from the 1840s have been fully and authentically restored, whereas in the early decades of the twentieth century they would have been neglected or junked, or pushed to the corner and replaced by a modern instrument – much like the unfortunate Bauza. They have been given new soundboards of pine veneered with mahogany across the grain, as Pleyel started doing in 1830 to enhance individual registers – silvery in the treble, penetrating in the middle, vigorous in the bass. They have new dampers and hard wooden hammers with outer layers of deer leather, the angle at which the head strikes the string changing as the notes get higher. Or the hammers have a coating of soft, expensive and quick-wearing felt made from rabbit or hare down, bound together with cashmere fibres (as Pape's patents in the 1830s specify) to produce a particular *moelleux* quality. There is new buckskin on the butts and catchers, new pin blocks glued and bolted into place, and replacement ivory: from old instruments, or from auction houses or repositories, sanded down slightly to fit the thinner keys. The stencil work has been touched up and new lacquer applied, often from an historical recipe incorporating seedlac or gum mastic. And the light action of the Pleyel pianos has been carefully regulated to facilitate the flighty finger work of the music written for them.

They look magnificent, yet it is their sound that captivates, a sound so fundamentally different from that of a modern concert grand that it is sometimes difficult to believe both instruments belong to the same genus. Block out the clackety action in fast or thick passages (as loud as a telegraph machine); listen instead to the slightly hollow yet distinct tone in the straight-strung bass, to the intimate, silvery colour in the treble, which floats in the air, refusing to decay. Their over-dampers operate by weight and gravity alone, no springs, and the soft-edged hammers hit the strings with less vehemence than hammers today – less even than the hard-felt ones used by some of Pleyel's French and Viennese contemporaries, and by Pleyel himself later in the decade – which varnishes the whole texture with a radiant film of upper partials.

These are the characteristics Chopin admired and exploited in his preferred Pleyel instruments: the soft attack, the hazy harmonics, the fine gradations between dynamics, the woody, burnished sound in one register, the bright, glistening tone in another, the way the hammers' hard inner layers pushed through and changed the tonal colour in louder passages. Chopin preferred these qualities to those of the more even, powerful pianos of Pleyel's great competitor Erard, which he thought too forceful, too insistent, the double-escapement action inhibiting his technique. (Liszt's advocacy of these pianos comes as no surprise.) 'When I am indisposed, I play on one of Erard's pianos and there I easily find a ready-made tone,' Chopin told a pupil. 'But when I feel in the right mood and strong enough to find my own tone for myself, I must have one of Pleyel's pianos.'

Listening to an 1841 Pleyel today is a bit like smelling a classic vintage perfume: its lineage is apparent, even if its individual character and quality make it difficult to correlate with its modern equivalent. Or perhaps a better analogy is listening intimately to a soft-spoken conversationalist: you lean in, certain the precious sounds are intended for you alone, that the wind will carry them away at any moment. To modern ears there is something so delicate about the soft-grained voice of these pianos, their sound blurred by an otherworldly sheen that clings to distinct pitches, a transient quality that casts over each of the fifty-odd public concerts Chopin gave in his lifetime a sense of even greater impermanence.

It is easy enough to hear these pianos today – in museums, small halls, private homes and recordings. Yet the difficulty in conjuring up the impact of the Preludes in their first public outing has less to do with the sound of the piano than the style of the playing. Besides Liszt and Solange, so much has been written about the way Chopin played the piano: Chopin's pupils on his rubato ('The hand responsible for the accompaniment would keep strict time, while the other hand, singing the melody, would free the essence of the musical thought from all rhythmic fetters'); others on his ability to make every performance sound improvised, as though each thought had only that second occurred to him; Moscheles on his love of soft colours and rich swatches of harmonics; Chopin's veneration of Bach and clear contrapuntal lines in recital; his disdain for Liszt-style thumping ('Why, she plays like a German,' Chopin said discouragingly of a prospective pupil brought to him by her mother). Elise Peruzzi heard him play numerous times in Paris in 1838 and said that his fingers seemed so elastic that they could not have bones. Émile Gaillard admired the beautiful song he unfolded in the left hand of one of his Nocturnes, while the right produced a magnificent, affecting lacework. Custine told Chopin after the April concert in Salle Pleyel that he played on the human soul, no mere piano, never content to serve up meaningless notes. Mendelssohn compared his originality to Paganini's. Balzac called him an angel, Liszt a demon. Berlioz wrote that he injected his performances with a sense of the unexpected. Nonetheless our picture of Chopin as pianist remains – appropriately perhaps – unfinished.

Chopin's most famous pupil, Karol Mikuli, who studied with him between 1844 and 1849 and thereafter established himself as a teacher and chronicler of Chopin's music and intentions (his lessons and editions based 'for the most part on the composer's own indications', he would later write), died when the gramophone was in its infancy. This would be another unfortunate dead-end were it not for the fact that in his seventies Mikuli began teaching an eight-year-old boy of phenomenal talent and prospects.

Over four consecutive summers Raoul Koczalski, born in Warsaw, was Mikuli's pupil in the city today called Lviv. Daily lessons lasted for two hours and were arduous, for Mikuli's sense of discipleship was as strong as his determination to leave a worthy heir to the

Chopin tradition. Even at this young age Koczalski was aware of his own new-found responsibilities, later writing about Mikuli's revolutionary teaching, his marriage of technique and thought, his emphasis on posture and pedalling, finger work and phrasing, the use of legato and staccato, rhythm and rubato, and his many *fiorituras* – those florid embellishments of melodic lines. Chopin's authentic voice had to be heard, Mikuli stressed: no camouflage, no cheap rubato, no useless contortions were to disguise his originality.

Given this charmed apprenticeship, Koczalski's recorded Chopin performances are unsurprisingly revelatory. In the sad-spirited Nocturne in D flat, Op. 27, No. 2, recorded in the last year of his life in Warsaw's Belweder Palace (where Chopin as a youth performed for Russia's Viceroy of Poland) and on Chopin's own Pleyel of a hundred years earlier, Koczalski is so intimate and personal that the audience seems barely in his thoughts, his freedom as evident as Chopin's structure. In his discs of the Preludes, made in 1938–9 on a modern instrument (one of the great achievements of early electrical recording), he tosses off the impossible *fiorituras* in Liszt's favourite with mocking ease, his thumb smoothing out the 'wailing melody', his own boneless fingers effortlessly filling in the arabesques. His performance of No. 2 is a full forty seconds shorter than Alfred Cortot's from a few years later (Cortot's is only two minutes long) and has none of its doom-laden air, though even at this brisk pace Koczalski manages to magick up a melancholic dance for a solitary figure, the music briefly stopping twice as if from a scratch on a gramophone record.

Throughout the recording there are plenty of instances of Chopin's *tempo di rubato* (Peruzzi's reference to his great elasticity), along

with glistening cascades of sound and colour and wild oratorical declamations, though not a scrap of narrative. There are the softest
dynamics, as distinct as they were said to be in Chopin's playing, and
beautiful *legatissimos*, for which Mikuli was renowned. And there is
subtle pedalling throughout, smudging the textures at one moment,
bringing out a dislocated melody the next – which is exactly what the
French pianist Antoine-François Marmontel said Chopin achieved in
his own performances, how he created ravishing harmonies and
melodic whispers through careful fingering and pedalling, which left
his audience astonished and charmed.

There are numerous flaws in the idea that a teacher passes on wholesale a performance tradition from one generation to the next: teachers
change their minds or lose their touch, students hear things differently, outside influences infiltrate. Certainly as the nineteenth century
progressed – as railways bound together different countries, as annotated critical editions of composers' works appeared, as pianos changed
in shape and power and concerts changed in function – the idea of
a single performance lineage was impossible to sustain. Yet Mikuli
was serious about his responsibilities as flame-keeper, and Koczalski
was an outstanding artist aware of his privileged musical education.
His recordings, together with contemporary re-creations of instruments from Chopin's time, establish a way of thinking about what
those three hundred people heard that night in Salle Pleyel: an otherworldly, sensuous, shivery sound, full of bold tricks and gestures and
references barely understood yet somehow still recognized, startling
improvisations rather than stoic interpretations, as unsettling now as
Liszt and others clearly found it then.

8

Paris, 1842–8

After his performance in April 1841, Chopin gave only two more public concerts in Paris, each in Salle Pleyel, and both incorporating a number of Preludes. In February 1842 he finally persuaded Viardot to appear alongside him, teaming up also with Franchomme as he had when first in Paris – a lifetime ago, really – for his Grand Duo for cello and piano, which they had knitted together from themes from *Robert le diable*. (At his valediction to Parisian audiences in February 1848, he would couple this early piece with his late Cello Sonata, Op. 65.)

The concert in February 1842 was as momentous as that in April the year before, the crowd as distinguished, the coffers as full. Sand made her entrance alongside her cousin Augustine Brault and daughter Solange, the three women very much at home in this parade of ribbons and veils, roses and jewels, clouds of perfume and extravagantly coiffed hair – though Sand, through her fame, association and temperament, stood just that bit apart. 'What must it feel like to be such a literary celebrity?' one reviewer asked.

Aside from four Preludes, Chopin played an Andante (probably Op. 22, which he often used as a curtain-raiser), three Mazurkas, three Études, four Nocturnes (including the one in D flat that Koczalski played so beautifully a hundred years later), the Impromptu in G flat and the Ballade, Op. 47. Léon Escudier, reviewing the concert in *La France Musicale*, did not mention the Preludes individually or by number, though he did describe Chopin's playing and the qualities of Pleyel's instrument: 'one cannot help but think he is hearing the faint voices of fairies sighing under silver bells or showers of pearls falling on crystal tables'. The poetic exaggeration of Chopin's music had begun.

More insightful are Escudier's thoughts on how the many sounds and nuances in Chopin's hand 'pour forth one after the other, weaving about each other only to disengage and then reunite once more as they give shape to the melody', which is a good description of Chopin's kaleidoscopic vision of colour and structure. The unnamed critic of the *Revue et Gazette Musicale* was similarly acute, writing that Chopin wove 'a certain connecting thread through the most brilliant digressions so that the diverse portions of his work remain skilfully bound together in a unified whole'. He continued: 'Liszt and Thalberg, as we know, can transport us by the thundering violence of their styles. Chopin can also do the same but in a more subdued, less fiery manner, precisely because he is able to strike the most intimate strings of the heart and arouse its deepest emotions.' Here were two critics managing to keep up with Chopin's aural magic, able to complete the picture he had provided in light-sketched outline, and doing so earlier than most contemporary musicians.

Chopin did give private performances between his Salle Pleyel concerts in 1842 and 1848. In January 1843 he played in the stately Paris residence and offices of James de Rothschild at 19, rue Laffitte, with its seven salons and many bedrooms, grand staircases and furnishings, richly deserving Heine's sobriquet that it was the Versailles of a financial potentate. 'Just look! Look at those glass portals,' wrote Escudier, 'those regal tapestries, those magnificent paintings, those furnishings swathed in gold! On all sides there's a magical brilliance that overpowers you. It's like an incredible dream. Such fairy-tale luxury is within the realms of kings and princes alone!' Joseph Filtsch estimated five hundred people attended, which, if accurate, was Chopin's largest Paris audience to date. He was in distinguished company that night: Viardot, Lablache, Giulia Grisi and Giovanni Matteo Mario also performed, as did Joseph's brother Karl, whom Chopin, on a second piano, accompanied in his own Concerto in E minor – a reminder of his debut concert in Paris eleven years earlier.

A few weeks before this performance Joseph wrote about a dinner with Sand in Paris, observing her intelligence and efforts to preserve her former beauty, despite what he characterized as her advancing age. (She was then all of thirty-eight.) Having dispatched his double-edged gallantry, Filtsch wrote of her touchy, capricious, jealous disposition, speculating that she could not be easy to live with. 'But since I have been playing chess fairly often with Chopin I have been close to this genius too often not to become aware of the other side of the coin.' This young-man censure aside, Filtsch had the grace to acknowledge how devoted Sand was to Chopin. If he did not appear as planned or was customary – at dinner, or for guests, or to play at her salon ('his playing is stupefying and unbelievably moving – in the almost complete darkness his varied inspirations now lull us, now electrify us, or throw us into the darkest recesses of our own thoughts,' Filtsch told his parents) – Sand quickly asked his servant whether he was in or out, working or sleeping, his mood good or bad.

Letters in 1842 and later reinforce Filtsch's impression of mutual rapport and respect. From Paris in November 1843 Chopin wrote encouragingly to Sand at Nohant about her work (and slipped into the envelope a note from Maurice): 'Everything you do must be *great* and *beautiful*, and if we don't write and inquire what you are doing it is not because we are not interested.' Or he wrote when the weather or her health was poor, when her travel plans were upset, when the winter in Paris was too cold for her to visit (Chopin dining by the fireside in his frock coat, three layers of flannel underwear beneath his trousers), when her garden in Paris was frosted with a swan's-down layer of snow ('as white as Solange's hands or Maurice's teeth'), or when he was undertaking tasks on her behalf – having the chimneys swept, say. Or he sent letters, daily, merely because he missed her. 'I imagine it is morning and that you are in your dressing gown with your darlings around you. Please give them kisses from me, and accept for yourself my devoted regards. As for my spelling-mistakes, well, I'm too lazy to look in Boiste's dictionary. Your old-as-a-mummy Ch.'

Such solicitations were not one-sided. In November 1843 Sand implored Carlotta Marliani and Marie de Rozières to look after Chopin once she had sent him away from Nohant, with its cold rooms and absence of things to do. 'Go and look in on some pretext or other to see what the aforesaid Chopin is doing – whether he gets any lunch, whether he forgets about himself – and you should *denounce* him to me if he behaves like a silly fool with regard to his health.' When Chopin's father died in May 1844, Sand begged Franchomme to visit him and raise his spirits, and then wrote a moving letter to Chopin's mother, who responded with grace and gratitude. 'After the first shock,' Chopin's mother wrote, 'my thoughts flew to the dear boy who, alone in a distant land, with his frail health and highly sensitive nature, could not fail to be struck down by such shattering news.'

Sand was not the only one supporting him. Chopin had lost Julian Fontana to America in 1841 and thus leant on other friends for practical help – with the production and sale of his scores, of course, but also simply with the increasingly gruelling task of living. These friends included Grzymała (Chopin asking him casually in October 1843 to post some manuscripts to Leipzig); Franchomme (in September 1844 regarding payment from Schlesinger); and Léo (in July 1845 urging him to negotiate a fee of 600 francs for the German edition of the Three Mazurkas, Op. 59, and Two Nocturnes, Op. 62). But otherwise life continued as before: a steady stream of pupils new and old, good and bad, alongside a gradually ebbing tide of new works. And dinners, an endless succession of dinners – with the Marlianis and Franchomme, Delacroix and Grzymała – which formed a colourful backdrop to the ongoing vagaries of his health.

Since September 1842 Chopin and Sand had been living almost side by side in the Place d'Orléans, just off the rue Saint-Lazare, their apartments separated by the Marlianis' home. To his parents Joseph Filtsch described Sand's suite at no. 5 (for which she paid 3,000 francs a year): the handsome drawing room with the billiard table she rented for another twenty francs a month; the cigars and ashtrays on her mantelpiece; the small salon with piano.

A watercolour of Chopin's drawing room at no. 9 (a mere 600 francs a year) suggests a much more modest though congenial living space. His Pleyel 'Petit Patron' is by the window; a slightly gaudy clock sits on the mantelpiece (more Louis XV than Louis-Philippe) next to ornate candlesticks; while rugs, chairs, cushions, sofa, muslin curtains, fire screen and a single painting (by Théodore Frère, according to a pupil, of a caravan in the desert) fill and soften the space. The entrance to the bedroom is not in the frame. Nor is Chopin's Pleyel *pianino*, the instrument on which he demonstrated phrasing or fingering to the pupils who filled his days, the same model he had enjoyed in Majorca during those few weeks at the beginning of 1839.

Although the original painting no longer exists, the piano in it is probably the 'Petit Patron' (Pleyel no. 13819) delivered to Chopin

immediately after its completion in January 1848, which does still exist: it is in the keyboard collection at Hatchlands Park, a gorgeous Georgian mansion in Surrey, England. Pleyel's accounts show he was billed 2,200 francs for it. It is a handsome instrument, with wooden beading all the way round like a trail of marzipan from a piping bag; an elaborate scroll either side of the fallboard; and lyre pedals, a commonplace if kitsch addition to grand pianos and square pianos from early in the century onwards, borrowed from Biedermeier furniture makers. Chopin almost certainly performed some of the Preludes on it: less than a week before his final Paris concert he told his family, 'I already have got the piano I am going to play on at home.' At this concert he performed, in addition to a smattering of Preludes, a Mozart Trio (with Delphin Alard and Franchomme), some of his own Études, Mazurkas and Waltzes, and the final three movements of the cello sonata. Tickets at twenty francs each soon disappeared, and those who missed out put their names on a waiting list, forlornly hoping Chopin might repeat the programme another evening. Patrons who successfully acquired tickets were not merely aristocratic ladies in elegant dresses (the *Revue et Gazette Musicale* reported), but the aristocracy of artists and music lovers too, all of them pleased with themselves for catching a glimpse of this elusive musical sylph. No one knew quite how sick he was.

'The papers say Chopin is giving a concert *"before he leaves"*,' Sand wrote to Maurice from Nohant nine days before the performance. 'Do you know where he is going? To Warsaw, or merely to Nérac? You will find out at the Square . . .' Sand would not be joining the artistic aristocracy there that night: she and Chopin were now estranged.

The separation happened so quickly, and so pointlessly. In March 1847 Delacroix could write about wading through a blizzard and slush to visit Sand in her apartment off the rue Saint-Lazare, where that 'enchanting talent' Chopin played for them all, and where Auguste Clésinger talked a little too intensely and self-importantly about his own work for Delacroix's liking. Two months later Sand wrote despairingly to Grzymała the most passionate, exasperated and honest letter of her life. She was sad at the slow hollowing out of the great artist Chopin, his affection and jealousy the source of his illness, she was sure, which left him immune to the confidence, creativity and peace she should by rights be able to inspire in him. She was aware that onlookers thought her passion or distance was killing him, aware also that he was too weak for either, and that, as a consequence, she lived like a virgin in his company, growing old too soon. 'You see how I am placed in this fatal friendship, in which I have consented to be his slave, whenever I could do so without showing him an impossible and wicked preference over my children, and when it has been such a delicate and serious matter to preserve the respect it was my duty to inspire in my children and my friends.'

She had come to resent aspects of their relationship, a relationship in which she was almost as much a mother to Chopin as she was to her own children, a highly sexual woman in a physically unfulfilled partnership. She was peacemaker when Maurice came to resent Chopin's tacit authority in the household and started claiming some for himself. She was nurse when Chopin's health failed, which happened more and more often as the decade progressed. She watched helplessly as he fought with the lingering religious dogma of his upbringing – not least its terrified anticipation of death – which he applied to his own life and fate with 'every superstitious fancy of

Slavic poetry'. ('Pole that he was, he lived in the nightmare world of legend.') And she was forever putting out the fires sparked by Chopin's jealousy: of the men with whom she conversed all too easily, of her own public profile in the 1840s, of not very much at all.

So it took only a tiny spark to set the whole thing off. Having stage-managed Solange's courtship with Clésinger – four years Chopin's junior and yet another competing masculine voice in the Sand household – Sand then withdrew her favourable opinion, unable perhaps to contemplate the impending marriage. Maurice also grew to despise Clésinger: the two came to blows at Nohant in July 1847, Sand intervening, Solange stirring the dispute with icy ferocity, lies and filthy stories (Sand's words), before the newlyweds fled into the night. Pregnant and stranded in La Châtre, Solange wrote to Chopin, begging to borrow his carriage since the journey to Paris by stage-coach was an unbearable prospect. Despite his now intense dislike of Clésinger, despite thinking Sand had done her family and daughter a great disservice by allowing the marriage to go forward, Chopin sent his carriage and then wrote Sand a gentle letter of admonishment, full of affection, and with a clear explanation for his actions. 'This misfortune must be very powerful today,' he told her, 'if it can forbid your heart to listen to any mention of your daughter, at the beginning of her real life as a woman, at the very moment when her physical condition calls more than ever for a mother's care.' He signed off, expressing his devotion to her and his regard for Maurice.

> If you are ever caught, no matter how well you've concealed it,
> Though it is clear as the day, swear up and down it's a lie.

It is a couplet from one of Ovid's love poems. It was also Sand in this moment, swearing up and down that the fault was not hers. Chopin's letter was a challenge to her authority, and to the viability of their relationship as well. She responded equally rationally, but hurt, affronted, furious with Solange, her sign-off far more devastating. 'Adieu, my friend. May you soon recover from all your ills: I hope you will *now* (I have my reasons for thinking so); and I shall thank God for this queer end to nine years of exclusive friendship. Let me hear now and then how you are.' And that, more or less, was that.

Leaving the Marlianis in March 1848, Chopin bumped into her. He played the impassive courtier, informing her of the birth of her granddaughter, before tipping his hat and walking down the stairs, as wooden as poor Armand's father in Dumas's *La Dame aux camélias*. Feeling the encounter inadequate, Chopin sent back his companion to tell Sand that Solange and her daughter were both fine. Sand came down to talk, but read in Chopin's face only anger and hatred, she told a friend. She was fairer in *Histoire de ma vie*, though equally sad. 'I shook his trembling, icy hand. I wanted to talk; he escaped. I suppose it was my turn to say he no longer loved me, but I spared him this suffering, and left all in the hands of Providence. I was never to see him again.'

Sand was mistaken about his travels, for Chopin had in mind neither Warsaw nor Nérac (where Solange and her father were staying): he was bound for Great Britain. In one sense it did not really matter where he was going: he found the ghosts and chance encounters at the Place d'Orléans unsettling, though Sand remained mostly at Nohant, avoiding these same ghosts. Yet it was not solely the damaged emotional terrain – represented daily by the expanse between his rooms at no. 9 and her suite at no. 5 – that drove him away: he was also escaping the political unrest that percolated through Paris and rippled throughout Europe.

The immediate source of discontent was the crippling winter of 1846–7. The public mood turned with the lingering cold, with the ruined crops, food shortages, unemployment, and further migration to the slums of Paris in search of work. 'I do not like these symptoms,' Heine wrote in August 1847. 'When there's poison in the blood even a small pimple can set off the malady. A mere graze can lead to an amputated limb.' So it proved. The Citizen King was the first major casualty: only eight days after Chopin's farewell recital at Salle Pleyel, Louis-Philippe abdicated in favour of his nine-year-old grandson and fled to Britain, settling into a Palladian mansion in Surrey (only ten miles from Hatchlands) where he spent the remaining two years of his life. But his departure was deemed too small a price: a day later the people rose once more, and on 26 February 1848 the grandson was dispatched and the Second Republic declared.

The uprising is the subject of Félix Philippoteaux's *Lamartine refusant le drapeau rouge devant l'Hôtel de Ville* (*Lamartine Refusing the Red Flag*), a flag that to supporters of a Second Republic symbolized only further repression, terror and bloodshed. Around Lamartine white-sashed student militants cheer and wave their *Tricolores* (the flag he would help retain), while soldiers attempt to control the crowd. Cobblestones have been pulled from the streets as weapons or barricades, looted goods are everywhere, cannons point aimlessly, and an overloaded donkey is dead on the ground, wounded citizens close by. Philippoteaux's canvas is the perfect bookend to Delacroix's *La Liberté guidant le peuple*, the same sides slogging it out, exactly the same flag, cobbles and chaos. How fitting that Chopin's Parisian life was framed so neatly by these two seismic events, represented in these two epic paintings.

Hugo thought Louis-Philippe a better leader than his fate suggested, devoting a full chapter to him in *Les Misérables*. 'What is there against him? That very throne. Take the king out of Louis-Philippe, there remains the man. And the man is good. He is sometimes good to the point of being admirable.' But that was the Louis-Philippe of 1832, a leader in an age of social unrest doing his best to modernize France. Hugo lists the terrible problems diminishing French society and needing Louis-Philippe's attention: 'poverty, the proletariat, wages, education, sentencing laws, prostitution, the fate of women, wealth, misery, production, consumption, distribution, exchange, money, credit, the right of capital, the right of labour.' No amount of early-bloom enthusiasm for Louis-Philippe's ascendancy could ameliorate these difficulties.

There was one final eruption. Dismayed by the conservative turn that the fledgling government quickly took, socialists and workers once more rose in protest. In June 1848 Alexis de Tocqueville observed the barricades between the Palais Bourbon and the rue Notre-Dame-des-Champs, some abandoned, some captured; he heard the drums and trumpets, the gunfire, the sound of an impoverished populace rallying; he saw National Guards searching houses, and workmen in blouses clumped together reading the ominous signs of the rally and the cannon. Blood slicked the cobbled streets, a revival of the scenes of 1832; corpses were stacked up on the pavements or in the public gardens and later thrown into the Seine or tossed into common graves, some 4,000 in total, as bad as Sand's wall of human masonry during the previous insurgence; manhunts ended in summary executions of those whose lips or hands were blackened by gunpowder. The uprising was viciously put down, though doing so irreparably damaged the government: in December a large majority of the population elected Louis-Napoleon Bonaparte – Napoleon I's nephew and heir – President of the French Second Republic.

Chopin missed the events of June, for on 20 April 1848 he followed Louis-Philippe to Britain, taking the train to the coast and then the slow boat to Folkestone, his luggage filled with letters of introduction, drug prescriptions, scores, concert dress, gloves, hats, and so forth. His Pleyel 'Petit Patron' followed soon after. He was escaping revolutionary Paris, his dislike of politics, his own dwindling finances and health, and the pain of his ruined relationship with Sand. To his old friend Fontana he wrote that Poland might yet rise again in opposition to Russian rule – within a month, perhaps, or a year, as France's contagion quickly spread – but his heart was not really in the fight.

9

London, Scotland, Paris, 1848–9

In London (the abyss, as he called it) Chopin had to struggle with the unfamiliar language and the solicitations and expectations of fashionable society, which was aware of his prestige if not necessarily how or why he had acquired it. He thought English musical taste too crass, too conservative – Mozart, Beethoven, Mendelssohn, but no further – and England's principal orchestra, the Philharmonic, like its turtle soup: strong and efficient, but nothing more. It was a country of huge posters and monstrously long concerts, he told a friend. 'Whatever is NOT boring here is NOT English,' he railed. He hated the smoggy air – he coughed incessantly and spat blood, sipping ices and lemonade as palliatives – the bleakness of the city, the dull, heavy people (so different from the French, 'whom I have become attached to just as if they were my own people'), whose love of art was built entirely on their love of luxury.

He was conscious too of the expense of the place, of how few pupils there were who would pay him a guinea a lesson, and how many of these might go off to the country without warning, leaving their accounts unsettled. He caught cabs rather than take carriages to the endless sequence of social occasions he thought would launch his London career, which earned the derision of his Italian valet. 'He refuses to accompany me in the evening if I take a cab rather than a privately hired carriage,' Chopin told a friend. And the news from Paris and Poland was bad: he feared for his friends in homes around the rue Rochechouart: Pleyel and Valentin Alkan, Grzymała and Delacroix. He was miserable, Chopin wrote to Grzymała in July, yet he deadened his thoughts, avoided his own company, lest depression and illness capture him. 'If only I were younger I might let myself become a machine: I would give concerts all over the place and play the most tasteless trash (anything to make money!).' And in other letters he picked at the scab left by Sand, mentioning her almost in passing, inviting news or derision, showing genuine concern for Solange, scared that she might be caught up in the upheavals in Paris, either political ones or those of her mother's making.

There were compensations. He had three pianos at his disposal – the Pleyel now at Hatchlands, an Erard, and an unexpected Broadwood – which scarcely made an impact on the large drawing room of his light-filled lodgings in Dover Street, just off Piccadilly, for which he paid twenty-six guineas (650 francs) a month, an astronomical sum (almost exactly his rent in Paris for a whole year) that soon increased to forty. And friends and colleagues from Paris were in town – for the concert season, of course, but also to escape the political unrest; Lablache and Grisi, Mario and Viardot, and the baritone Antonio Tamburini and the contralto Marietta Alboni were among them. Viardot sang her own arrangements of a handful of Chopin's Mazurkas at Covent Garden one evening, generating acclaim and her friend's gratitude. At the Theatre Royal in Haymarket – in a stalls seat costing two and a half guineas, Queen Victoria in the royal box, the Duke of Wellington sitting beneath it like a guard dog, Chopin thought – he heard Jenny Lind sing in Bellini's *La sonnambula*, bathing the audience in a brilliant light, her soft singing 'as smooth and even as a thread of hair'. And then, at a dinner a week later, Lind performed Swedish songs just for him.

Slowly he began to make an impact, in the salons of Lord Falmouth and Mrs Sartoris, at parties hosted by Lady Combermere and attended by the Duke and Duchess of Cambridge. He met a remarkable array of aristocrats – lords and ladies of great houses, including Lady Byron ('I can well believe she bored Byron,' Chopin wrote to his family) – as well as ambassadors and émigrés, instrument makers and deposed royalty, Carlyle and Dickens. 'Old Mme Rothschild asked me how much I *cost*,' he wrote to Grzymała, bemused, as though she were hiring a farrier. At the Falmouths' house in St James's Square, with tickets a guinea each and net earnings close to 200 guineas (5,000 francs), Chopin performed some of the Preludes. Here too he was perceptively reviewed, George Hogarth writing in the *Daily News* of the unpremeditated quality of the music. 'The

MONSIEUR CHOPIN'S
Second Matinée Musicale,
FRIDAY, JULY 7th, 1848,
AT THE RESIDENCE OF
THE EARL OF FALMOUTH,
No. 2, St. JAMES'S SQUARE;
TO COMMENCE AT FOUR O'CLOCK.

Programme.

ANDANTE SOSTENUTO ET SCHERZO (Op. 31)........Chopin
MAZOURKAS DE CHOPIN, arrangées par *Madame Viardot Garcia*
Madame VIARDOT GARCIA et Mlle. DE MENDI.
ÉTUDES (19, 13, et 14)..............................Chopin
AIR, "Ich danke dein"........................Beethoven
Madame VIARDOT GARCIA.
NOCTURNE ET BERCEUSE.......................Chopin.
RONDO, "Non più mesta"......(Cenerentola)......Rossini.
Madame VIARDOT GARCIA.
PRELUDES, MAZOURKAS, BALLADE, VALSES.........Chopin
AIRS ESPAGNOLES, Madame VIARDOT GARCIA
et Mlle. DE MENDI

performer seems to abandon himself to the impulses of his fancy and feeling, to indulge in a reverie and to pour out unconsciously, as it were, the thoughts and emotions that pass through the mind . . .' It is a good description of Chopin's studied improvisation, especially as little of his music was then known in Britain.

He had arrived late in the season: summer loomed, and after that the winter temperatures so detrimental to his health; such thoughts preoccupied him even as the heat made the city uncomfortable. On 5 August he took an express train from Euston to Edinburgh. The journey lasted twelve hours, so Broadwood bought a second ticket for him in the seat opposite to give him some privacy. In Scotland, under the generous if suffocating ministrations of his pupil in Paris, Miss Jane Stirling – long-fingered, her face framed by loose cork-screw curls – and her sister Mrs Erskine (who had invited him to Britain in the first place), he performed a series of concerts, for £60 here, £90 there.

His wit frequently outstripped his health: at Calder House near Edinburgh, the seat of Mrs Erskine's brother-in-law Lord Torphichen – a huge pile in beautiful parklands, with maze-like corridors that were haunted at midnight, and eight-foot-thick walls lined with gloomy ancestral portraits, the subjects kitted out in kilts and armour and farthingales – he described himself in a letter to Franchomme as a donkey at a fancy-dress ball, a violin E string on a double bass. The people were nice but ugly, he decided, the cattle fierce looking though productive, the countryside populated with out-of-towners here for the hunting season and the balls and fêtes that accompanied it. He could skewer them without difficulty: the proper Scottish lady who played terrible tunes on a concertina, a fug of serious faces surrounding her; the pupils who 'look at their hands and play wrong notes most soulfully'; the noblewoman who stood at the piano while singing French songs with an execrable accent; another *grande dame* who whistled tunes to a guitar accompaniment. 'There are fine dresses, diamonds, pimply noses, lovely heads of hair, marvellous figures, the beauty of the devil himself and the devil minus the beauty!'

Their breeding gave them all perfectly good French, yet the general conversation took place in English, a language Chopin had neither time nor inclination to learn, he said. In any case, the topics discussed were mostly chosen on genealogical lines, since those participating were all related one way or another, just like in the Gospel, Chopin decided, in which 'such a one begat so-and-so, and he begat another, who begat still another – and so on for two pages, up to Jesus Christ'. Yet even with Scotland's open skies, with magnificent trees far older than Bonaparte, with expansive mountains and lakes, he could not breathe, he wrote to Grzymała, and daydreamed about Warsaw or Paris or Rome or just about anywhere else.

He was glad of his reception – playing to his largest audience ever in late September, 1,200 people in Manchester's Merchant Hall – but nevertheless felt as though his time was passing, especially now he was surrounded by people who thought of music as a profession, not an art. 'No one plays now to my taste,' he wrote to Fontana, sensing the aesthetic shift that would take place in the decades following his death. On 4 October he performed some Preludes once more in Edinburgh, at the Hopetoun Rooms, earning the admiration of his audience (five encores) and the critic of the *Edinburgh Advertiser*. But, as he wrote to Grzymała, he was mostly whirring and clunking like his old castle clock, unable to compose, scarcely good for anything before lunch at 2 p.m., stuck at the dinner table at night watching the menfolk talk, listening to them drink, then carried by his manservant to his bedroom where he was left to gasp and dream, before the whole dreary, wearying process began once more. 'We are a couple of old cembalos on which time and circumstances have played out their miserable trills,' he wrote to Fontana. 'The sound-board is perfect, only the strings have snapped and a few pegs have jumped out.'

Back in London in November he gave his last ever public performance, playing for an hour at a Guildhall ball in aid of a Polish charity. 'Mr. Chopin, the celebrated pianiste, was also present, and performed some of his beautiful compositions with much applause,' the *Illustrated London News* reported. 'The dancing commenced soon after 9 o'clock . . .' No doubt he included some Preludes. His health was terrible, the winter putting down early roots, which prompted one of his Scottish ladies to talk a little too insistently about how the next world was in any case so much better than the present one. 'This world seems to slip from me,' he wrote to Grzymała, 'I forget things, I have no strength. I no sooner recover a little than I sink back lower still.'

He plotted his escape, asking Grzymała to find him a new apartment in Paris, one warmer than his rooms in the Place d'Orléans, and with space for his servant, on the boulevards perhaps, or the rue de la Paix, south-facing and on the first floor – not too far to climb, with every chance of getting above the shadows, catching whatever sunlight there was – and certainly nothing on the city's dark, narrow streets. He needed a new instrument from Pleyel, and wanted Grzymała to make sure it was waiting for him in his rooms, along with firewood and fir cones for kindling. And in this despondent mood he wrote bitterly of Sand. 'I have never cursed anyone, but everything is so unbearable that I should feel easier if I could curse Lucrezia. But they too must be suffering down there [Nohant], suffering all the more since they are growing old in their fury. I shall never cease to be sorry for Solange.' He left London on 23 November in a resigned fury of his own, dining in a Folkestone inn on one side of the Channel, stopping the night in Boulogne on the other, and arriving in Paris at noon the following day.

He sat for a photographer soon after his return, perhaps Daguerre or the gifted Louis Bisson, whose fashionable studio, close to the apartment that Chopin had taken behind the Madeleine on his return from Majorca, was a salon for the Parisian intelligentsia: in the 1840s one could encounter Baudelaire and Delacroix, Gautier and Nanteuil, Rothschild and Saint-Victor, all passing round prints, marvelling at the new art form, gossiping as they went.

In the photograph Chopin's face is swollen – perhaps from the neuralgia he wrote about to Solange before leaving London – and he seems easily in his fifties, though he was actually not yet forty. Exposure times were speeding up but were still slow, so Chopin glowers for the full length of time the lens is open to the silver plate. His hair is long and limp, which hinders him in his letter writing, he tells Grzymała, draping his eyes, requiring him at regular intervals to sweep it behind his ears with an inky hand, his concentration broken for the second that each gesture takes. He looks like an emaciated, ageing traveller shunted into a photographer's studio at some dismal point on a Grand Tour.

Some scholars have dated the picture to 1846 or 1847. But in those years Chopin still walked the boulevards, travelled to Nohant, played the piano in Sand's salon, took carriage rides with Delacroix, attended the opera, bought trousers from his tailor Dautrement, composed a few Nocturnes, completed his cello sonata, ate with the Marlianis, walked to the Tuileries, played charades, looked out for Solange's best interests, worried about the type of young man Maurice was becoming, wrote letters full of wit and humour and puns, sat attentively as Sand read to him long passages from *Lucrezia*, failing to see the connection that Delacroix thought so obvious. None of this Chopin comes across in the photograph: he is a sick man, near the end of his life. It is a world away from the double portrait that Delacroix made of Chopin and Sand in his studio in the rue Notre-Dame de Lorette, just before their winter in Majorca.

In his diary Delacroix charts his friend's final year. There were still salons and occasional carriage rides – along the Champs-Élysées and through the Arc de Triomphe de l'Étoile, the two men held at the city walls while their possessions were checked – but most vital was the conversation, Delacroix playing the eager student, writing down every-thing he remembered. Chopin responded warmly when asked by Delacroix whence music derived its logic. He explained harmonic rhet-oric and that fugue was an encapsulation of pure reason, that Berlioz did not really know the difference between the two (you could tell by the way he plonked down harmonies in manuscript and then did his best to fill in the gaps), and how shallow Meyerbeer was in *Le Prophète*. He was unfolding a grand Romantic panoply, characters coming from nowhere, ostensibly unrelated, sharing ideas or butting heads.

Without prompting, Chopin tackled the difference between Mozart and Beethoven. 'Where Beethoven is obscure and appears to be lacking in unity, it is not, as people allege, from a rather wild originality – the quality which they admire in him – it is because he turns his back on eternal principles.' It was Chopin's shrewd assessment of Beethoven's attempts to innovate yet remain comprehensible, which were not always successful. In his journal Delacroix added his own interpretation:

> The fact of the matter is, that true science is not what we usually mean by that word – not, that is to say, a part of knowledge quite separate from art. No, science, as regarded and demonstrated by a man like Chopin, is art itself, but on the other hand, art is not what the vulgar believe it to be, a vague inspiration coming from nowhere, moving at random, and portraying merely the picturesque, external side of things. It is pure reason, embellished by genius, but following a set course and bound by higher laws.

Also without prompting they spoke of Sand, 'of her strange life and extraordinary mixture of virtues and vices'. Chopin was sure she would never write her memoirs; she had forgotten the past, he told Delacroix. All her great outbursts of emotion in any case soon blew over. 'For instance, she wept for her old friend Pierret, and then never thought of him again.' Delacroix predicted an unhappy old age for her, but Chopin disagreed. 'She never appears to feel guilty about the things for which her friends reproach her,' he said simply in response. 'Her health is extremely good, and may well continue to be so. Only one thing would affect her deeply, the death of Maurice, or his going wholly to the bad.' It was an exchange of perfect equanimity – or at least of graceful resignation.

There were good, lucid days when Chopin looked from his sitting room over much of Paris, to the Tuileries, the Tour Saint-Jacques, Notre-Dame, the Panthéon, the church of the Invalides, the Chamber of Deputies, to Saint-Étienne-du-Mont. But the bad days were now more frequent, when he could scarcely breathe, when boredom seemed his greatest malady, when not even Delacroix's sensitivity and erudition could buoy him. When Delacroix asked him whether he too occasionally felt 'the unbearable sense of emptiness', Chopin replied that before his illness he could lose himself in one occupation or another, which kept depression at bay. But illness, time to think, brought its own grief, something quite distinct.

In *A Song to Remember*, Charles Vidor's clunky film of 1945, Chopin's boyhood teacher Elsner (transplanted to Paris for the whole of the composer's time in the capital, and played by Paul Muni in a strange Harpo Marx routine) visits Delacroix's studio and asks Sand (Merle Oberon), sitting for her portrait, to go to Chopin (Cornel Wilde), his time left so sadly limited. 'Frédéric is mistaken to want me,' she replies in a clipped English accent, haughtily brushing Elsner off. 'I was always a mistake.' Elsner returns to Chopin's deathbed – Liszt (Stephen Bekassy), with very odd teeth, is playing in the adjoining room – and makes Sand's excuses. 'She was too ill to come.'

There actually were attempts to reunite the former lovers. A mutual acquaintance wrote to Sand telling her how much Chopin missed her, to which Sand responded thoughtfully, regretting they had not been able to transfer their great affection and admiration for each other into an ongoing friendship, but certain that it was Chopin who did not desire it. In September, Sand wrote to Chopin's sister Ludwika, now in Paris, asking for word of his condition, and stating her love for him. The letter remained unanswered.

Chopin died at two o'clock in the morning of 17 October 1849 in his apartment at 12, Place Vendôme, surrounded by a small number of friends, Solange and Grzymała among them. Tuberculosis was the most likely cause. Delfina Potocka sang for him in his last hours – arias by Bellini and Rossini, as Grzymała attested, or a Marcello psalm or some Pergolesi, as others said – and after his death her place was taken by Clésinger, who made a cast of Chopin's left hand and a death mask of smooth-skinned, youthful beauty, the sculptor tidying up the diseased and puffy features, making the lines cleaner, the face nobler, so different from the scowling, sick old man in the photograph of only a year earlier.

Grieved and angered, Grzymała lashed out against Sand in a letter to Léo, obsessed with the thought that if Chopin had not had the misfortune to meet the poisonous woman he might have lived as long as Cherubini. It was a boorish assessment of Sand's character and her relationship with Chopin, but would prove remarkably tenacious in the years to come – for musicians and biographers, and even, in time, for Hollywood film directors.

Acting on Chopin's superstitions and instructions, Ludwika insisted her brother's heart be removed and placed in a glass jar filled with preserving liquid, which was deposited inside a mahogany and oak reliquary and, in the following months, smuggled out of France. (It is now in the Holy Cross Church in Warsaw, the columbarium inscribed HERE RESTS THE HEART OF FREDERICK CHOPIN.) The funeral, at noon on 30 October, was a grand ceremony at the Madeleine, paid for by Jane Stirling and attended by up to four thousand mourners, Delacroix, Franchomme, Gutman and Meyerbeer among them. An orchestra and chorus from the Conservatoire performed Mozart's Requiem, with Viardot and Lablache two of the soloists, before Chopin's coffin was carried by hearse the three miles to Père Lachaise cemetery, some mourners on foot, others following in carriages, curious onlookers at every turn. Mozart was not the only music performed during the service: at the offertory the Madeleine's organist Louis Lefébure-Wély played two Chopin Preludes, No. 4 in E minor and No. 6 in B minor. The posthumous life of this miraculous collection had begun.

10
Paris, New York City, London, 1851–88

Between the Great Exhibition in London's Crystal Palace in 1851 (six million visitors) and the Exposition Universelle in Paris's Champ de Mars in 1900 (thirty-nine million), railways, revolutions and recreation shrank the Continent. In his memoirs Berlioz writes about visiting Russia a year before Chopin's death for performances of parts of *La damnation de Faust*, travelling first from Paris to Brussels and then Berlin by rail, thereafter by stagecoach, and then, for the final four days, through icy landscapes on a covered sledge. Returning there twenty years later he caught trains direct from Paris to Berlin and then Saint Petersburg, journeying all the way in heated carriages with leather seats. A few years hence he would have been served hot meals on bone china in a dining car. These were not new frontiers, but they were certainly now more comfortably traversed.

France's Revolution of 1848 lit fires throughout Europe and brought forth a shared liberal ideology that in certain ways transcended the circumstances fuelling individual uprisings. There were no coalitions between countries, no gatherings under a single banner (Marx's *Das Kapital* was still many years away, though *The Communist Manifesto*, written with Engels, was published at the beginning of the revolutionary year), yet the radicals and reformers in one place were not so different from those in another, and their common political purpose brought their respective countries closer.

These years affected musicians in other ways. It was not simply that in the railway age soloists travelled easily and on arrival spoke a common language. It was also because in the aftermath of 1848 audiences across Europe gradually migrated from private salons to public concert halls, surprised to find themselves rubbing shoulders with an expanding, moneyed middle class hungry for art music – or, at the very least, eager for access to a culture that had hitherto been the domain of their social superiors. Music had different currency in different countries: the effect of social and political shifts on concert-going varied according to patronage, public halls, states and municipalities, education and aspiration. In France the salon had been the incubator of Chopin's music, but the concert hall would be its guardian.

The revolutionary fissures in France's social fabric were greatest in Paris, which experienced political and cultural upheavals greater even than those Chopin witnessed. Denied by Parliament (and the Constitution) the chance of running for a second term as President of the French Second Republic, in 1851 Louis-Napoleon Bonaparte staged a *coup d'état*, appointed himself Emperor, and a year later ascended the throne as Napoleon III. It is impossible not to admire the social and urban reforms he undertook during his reign, notwithstanding its shoddy origins and many repressive characteristics. Sanitation, water, transportation, architecture, public monuments, parks, gardens, hospitals, boulevards, gas street lighting, schools, Garnier's exquisite opera house, the redesign of Paris, an ambitious foreign policy: these were all implemented or transformed by him.

In the wake of the traumatic events of 1848, Louis-Napoleon's modernizing zeal was not without a healthy element of political self-preservation. He wanted to clear out the workers' suburbs in the capital, the *faubourgs* that Balzac described as 'seminaries of revolution, which contain heroes, inventors, practical servants, rascals, rogues, virtues and vices, all compressed together by poverty, stifled by necessity, drowned in drink, worn out by strong liquor'. But the Emperor's vision was driven simultaneously by his belief in the need for social reform, his desire to open up major arteries in the city, to build new and more housing with lower rents, and to give greater self-sufficiency and self-respect to Paris's *classes laborieuses*. So he set about building a great capital city from (under) the ground up, demolishing the light-starved, plague-ridden slums, accumulating huge public debt as he went.

Louis-Napoleon's Prefect of the Seine, Georges-Eugène Haussmann, was either his Svengali or his Speer, and the controversy that the two men ignited was immediate and lasting. 'Alas, Old Paris is

disappearing at terrifying speed,' Balzac wrote in 1855, not yet knowing the half of it. Twenty years later, with Louis-Napoleon dead and
most of Haussmann's vision realized, Henry James echoed Balzac's
despondency, decrying the smell of newly lain asphalt, the imperial
scale of the buildings and boulevards ('it must make the late Napoleon
III smile with beatific satisfaction as he looks down upon it from the
Bonapartist corner of Paradise'), the bland facades (he thought), the
vanity and anonymity of it all. 'The deadly monotony of the Paris that
M. Haussmann called into being – its huge, blank, pompous, feature-
less sameness – sometimes comes over the wandering stranger with a
force that leads him to devote the author of these miles of architectural
commonplace to execration.'

Balzac and James were nostalgic for lost alleyways and chance
encounters, for the inconvenience and unscriptedness of the old city.
Haussmann had no such nostalgia: in his memoirs he gleefully records
razing one part of the capital, building up another, as though doing
nothing more than idly stoking a fire. In commissioning the illustrator-
turned-photographer Charles Marville to take his camera to areas of
Balzac's fast-disappearing city, Haussmann was not mourning lost
Paris: he was instead making the comparison between the old and the
new, to the advantage of the latter.

The majority of Marville's photos look strangely impersonal: a city
abandoned as though due to catastrophe, or a filmset once the cam-
eras have stopped rolling, the actors back in their trailers. But he was
obviously entranced by this eerie element of absence, even if he
remained neutral on the value of the loss. His work evinces this quality both because the streets and buildings in his photographs no longer
exist, and because of the exposure time needed for an image to be
fixed on collodion-coated plates, which would be sabotaged if people
moved within the frame.

Marville's photo of a deserted rue Sauval shows how parts of central Paris became ghost towns after Haussmann reclaimed whole
streets and evicted long-standing tenants with ruthless application.
Twenty years earlier the *premier* had been Chopin's *arrondissement,*
an area teeming with vendors and shoppers, *flâneurs* and grain merchants, the rue Sauval a mere kilometre and a half from his apartment
in Place Vendôme.

Perhaps the change was too great, too fast, too unsettling: a certain cultural insularity kicked in as Parisians tried to hold on to what they once had, what they could remember. France's increasing binary divisions exacerbated the tension: aristocrats versus peasants; Catholics versus secularists; monarchists versus republicans; a (small) forward-looking industrialist culture versus the proud traditions of craftsmen. Rising through the middle of it all was a new middle class. These were the entrenched conflicts in French society and culture, conflicts that simmered then boiled over, first in 1789, then in 1815, 1830, 1848, and, finally, in the radical Paris Commune of 1871.

France's disastrous showing in the Franco-Prussian War (which prompted this last eruption) only exacerbated the ingrained national uncertainty. Bismarck's armies constantly outmanoeuvred those of Louis-Napoleon, with France's north-eastern border falling first, then the eastern one. When in September 1870 the Emperor was forced to capitulate after the calamitous Battle of Sedan, the Second Empire fell with him, only to be replaced by a new French Republic that refused to accept the terms of surrender. Prussian troops marched on Paris and encircled the city. It was May 1871 before the Commune, which ruled Paris for two months in the spring – at war with its own army – could be put down in the bloodiest episode in French revolutionary history. A final peace treaty with a newly united Germany was signed at the Palace of Versailles, which would host another such ceremony – much more punitive to the defeated – almost fifty years later.

France licked her wounds and hunkered down. She kept to herself as best she could and slowly rejuvenated, looking on with undisguised horror as Germany strengthened her national infrastructure with ever more railways and factories, trade treaties and mining licences, all cheered on by a populace in thrall to Bismarck's sure political instincts and tactical successes. The French Third Republic, which began life as a transitional government, lasted until France's next capitulation to Germany, in the terrible summer of 1940, when German troops once more marched into Paris, a merciless, mechanized reprise of a blurry, monochrome memory.

Romanticism in all the arts, including of course pianism, evolved against this giddying backdrop of conservatism, nationalism, industrialization, radicalism and war. This evolution was intrinsically linked to shifts in musical taste as the century progressed: as Gare Saint-Lazare replaced the train station a few streets along from Chopin's apartment, connecting bankers with their summer houses, workers with the seaside, and musicians with ever more concert venues; as Haussmann cut through the capital's slums and distinctive *quartiers*; as the concept and sound of the mid-century Parisian salon came to seem quaint to most (foreign) people; and as the works of the salon's greatest musician moved on to fill large concert halls across the world, the works utterly transformed in the process.

These cultural changes also affected the pianoforte itself. On 20 December 1859 the U.S. Patent Office – soon to move into Robert Mills's splendid neoclassical temple on the strip running between the White House and the Capitol (now home to the National Portrait Gallery) – awarded Henry Steinway, Jr., a patent for a new type of grand piano, its internal footprint and construction startlingly original. By tilting the bass strings only ten degrees or so on the keyboard axis, crossing them over the lower-middle range of the instrument, Stein-way was able to place the bass bridge near the resonant centre of the soundboard, which granted the low octaves unparalleled power and definition. No piano maker had attempted this before: the physical tension was too great for a wooden frame, notwithstanding any but-tressing. Steinway solved this problem by binding the whole lot into a single cast-iron frame the size of a concert harp laid flat. It was such a simple idea, as good design so often is.

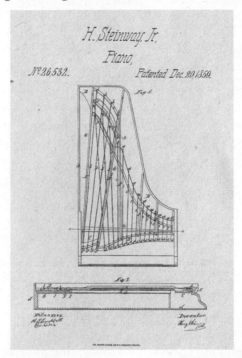

Pleyel had used wrought iron in its piano frames since the 1820s, soon after Bostonian Alpheus Babcock made the first full cast-iron frame for a square piano, smelting pig iron along with scrap metal, carbon and limestone, pouring it into a specially constructed mould of his own design. Yet most makers – Pleyel included – were initially blind to the full implications of Babcock's invention: they carried on reinforcing their wooden frames with iron braces and brackets – as though trussing a bridge once the first cracks had appeared – running bolts through the soundboard to keep them in place, compromis-ing its spring along the way. Other makers experimented with cross-stringing, though they missed Steinway's trick of placing the bridge near the most resonant part of the soundboard.

The next great innovation was outlined in a patent by Henry's brother Theodore: a device that shaped the piano rim into a single piece of hardwood, rather than multiple bits of wood and joist thrust together, Viking style.

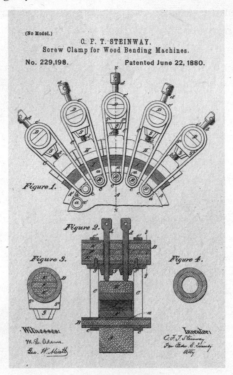

This inspired bit of peacock-tail engineering allowed the casing for those big iron frames to be made from thin sheets of wood glued together like plywood and held firmly in place by the curved vice. Once set, the rim retained the shape of the concert grands we know today, ready to be varnished with a mixture of French polish and vegetable black, applied with a large camel-hair mop, each coat left to dry hard before being sanded with very fine glass-paper, primed for the next application. The iron frame could then be slipped inside, on top of an inner rim incorporated into the outer one, all fitting together into a continuous piece of carpentry. Theodore's aim in each of the patents of these years was to simplify all aspects of production, to have as few separate parts as possible so that nothing subtracted from the instrument's governing principle: a resonant, dynamic soundboard transmitting the vibrations of a hammer-struck string.

Camille Pleyel's new partner August Wolff recognized the challenge posed by Steinway's instrument, even before the American company established a factory in Hamburg in 1880 in order to circumvent crippling European import taxes, transforming the Continental market in the process. In the 1860s Wolff resolved to increase the volume and tone of Pleyel pianos while retaining their inherent sweetness. Steinway's powerful new instruments were not the sole motivating factor here. Wolff was thinking too of the large concert halls springing up throughout Europe and the United Kingdom: Budapest's Vigadó (1859); Vienna's Musikverein (1870); London's Royal Albert Hall (1871) and the string of grand town halls built throughout Britain during Victoria's long reign; Dresden's Semperoper (1878); the original Leipzig Gewandhaus (1884); Prague's Rudolfinum (1885); and Amsterdam's Concertgebouw (1888). These were secular cathedrals, built in response to advances in engineering and taste and cultural reach. Audiences no longer lived exclusively on or near the Wiener Ringstraße or the rue de la Chaussée-d'Antin, and they travelled, on increasingly good public transport, from suburbs further afield than Kensington. Art music was now middle class.

Yet Wolff was not wholly successful, for Pleyel continued more or less on its own path, tweaking and refining, borrowing and adapting, a company run by craftsmen, not inventors or entrepreneurs. Most French piano makers were similarly minded. They resisted cross-stringing and full iron frames, scornful of the very idea (according to the editor of *Musical Courier* when he visited Europe from America at the end of the century). They retained softer hammers and lighter actions; they kept their imprecise dampers, which on Pleyel instruments produced those bursts of sonic perfume; and they seemed not to care that their market was almost entirely domestic. They built pianos that were beautiful and subtle and possessed a character all of their own, as in Chopin's lifetime; yet in the age of Steinway they seemed a throwback to a gentler time.

French makers and consumers told themselves that these distinctive qualities were a mark of cultural superiority, which conveniently allowed manufacturers to stick to their old ways. (This same think-ing led to France's rejection in 1884 of the Greenwich Meridian as the international standard; it continued with the rival Paris Meridian for another thirty years.) The foreign competition came with its own ready-made tone, they sniffed (much as Chopin had done about Erard pianos), and required little artistry to produce its bland singing sound, lacking character and colour. And nationality: Steinway was peddling a homogenized tone counter to the Romantic spirit of indi-viduality. The ground was fast shifting, though. In these same years French firms lost their virtuoso champions: in 1876 Saint-Saëns and Gounod, Berlioz and Auber, appeared on Steinway's list of exclusive 'eminent artists'. Pleyel's spacious atelier in the rue Rochechouart and its factory in Saint-Denis were simply no match for Steinway's new premises on New York's Fourth Avenue (now Park Avenue). Stein-way's factory was driven by the same Corliss steam engines then powering breweries, sawmills and industrial plants throughout North America, German being the common language of its floor workers.

The industry's growth in the second half of the nineteenth century and first decade of the twentieth was astonishing. The Great Exhibition displayed pianos from France, Germany, Belgium, America, Austria, Switzerland, Canada, Russia, Denmark and England – thirty-eight from England alone, showcasing sixty-six different instruments and garnering twelve medals or citations. Even latecomer Spain was rep-resented by ten different makers (Juan Bauza not among them). England produced 23,000 pianos in the year before the Exhibition, France 10,000, America the same. By 1870 annual production was more or less stagnant in England, yet had doubled in both France and the United States. (Germany, not yet unified, was then managing fewer then 15,000 instruments each year.) In 1890 production in England was double what it had been twenty years earlier, in Amer-ica triple, in France the same, while Germany – in factories in Prussia, Saxony, Hamburg and Bavaria – was now manufacturing no fewer than 70,000 instruments annually. In 1910 the figures were 25,000 in France, 75,000 in England, 120,000 in Germany and a massive 370,000 in America. Domestic music-making was driving the indus-try's expansion – a cultural shift every bit as significant as the move from the salon to the concert hall. At the end of the century the

English piano maker Collard was praised for his 'little Quaker-like pianos of white wood, fine tone and most moderate price . . . Offered to the public of small means – the needy clerk, the poor teacher, the upper-class mechanic'. (It could be Auden writing.)

Hippolyte Taine was haughty about such industrial fairs, writing in 1855 of the Exposition Universelle, 'All Europe has set off to view goods.' George Bernard Shaw was more genial, later poking fun at the piano merchants present, the foreign gentlemen with their fur collars and long moustaches (straight out of Dostoevsky), hammering their instruments recklessly, fistfuls of wrong notes, carnival barkers attempting to lure in customers. But there was a serious point of comparison to be made at these expos, one that could not be achieved anywhere else: which countries and makers were winning what became the piano wars?

Heine thought pianists were hostage to their instrument long before the Steinway revolution – more or less what Marcellin Desboutin would say of Edgar Degas and his monotype press later in the century. 'This predominance of piano playing,' Heine wrote in 1843, his friend Chopin still very much alive, 'not to speak of the triumphal processions of the piano virtuosos, are characteristic of our time and bear witness to the victory of mechanism over spirit. Technically proficient, the precision of an automaton, self-identification with wired wood, the resounding instrumentalization of the human being, all this is now praised and celebrated as the highest of things.' He was foreshadowing the great battles of the century's second half, when the Germans and Americans – convinced of the ascendency and authority of science, of social progress made possible only through industrial advancement – were pitted against the Romantic French, resistant to change, blinkered to international trade and progressive ideas, still caught up in the distinctive identity and purpose of their regions and districts, their *arrondissements* and *quartiers*, their squares and streets, their salons decorated with paintings and bibelots, clocks and candelabras, French pianos, and all the other iconography of the *ancien régime*. Progressives versus reactionaries, Haussmann versus Balzac.

Two-thirds of the way into Günter Grass's *The Tin Drum* the protagonist Oskar – who at the age of three vowed never to grow and thereafter watched others from within his tiny frame – feels his joints swelling and his upper and lower legs stretching (three and a half to four inches, he tells a nurse), his body somehow, at last, becoming a good fit for his adult mind. This was the fate of the pianoforte in the second half of the nineteenth century. Steinway put the instrument into a bigger frame, releasing potential that had hitherto been locked into a body wrongly shaped and too small for the big concert halls it now had to fill. Through design, materials, a refined understanding of acoustics and physics, and by harnessing the best aspects of industrialization, the company made the instrument sing. The music historian Malcolm Gillies has a neat line: Chopin grew into the piano only after his death. He means that Chopin's music was quietly waiting for the changes Steinway initiated in performance style in the second half of the century, and only then filled out to fit its proper frame. Yet it is just as true to say that the piano grew away from Chopin.

In fact it wasn't quite Haussmann versus Balzac. There were French and English piano makers who were analysts, not mere nostalgists, craftsmen at Pleyel and elsewhere who believed something fundamental had been lost in Steinway's bold march to the future. Some musicians still wonder about this. Only a few years ago Daniel Barenboim launched a straight-strung concert grand built by the Belgian piano maker Chris Maene, inspired by a restored piano once owned by Liszt, which Barenboim had encountered in Siena four years

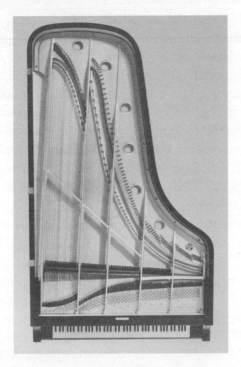

earlier. It is a beautiful instrument, with frame bracings running more or less perpendicular to the keys, not angled across the soundboard as in a big Steinway. The soundboard's veins and grain run parallel to the strings, not (again as in Steinway pianos) with the bridge, and not perpendicular, the preference of a few nineteenth-century makers. Its main feature, though, is its emulation of the distinctive register colours of Liszt's piano – indeed of most pianos before Steinway: a curious yet hypnotic sequence of different characters across the instrument's compass – what Bartók called the autonomous 'register life' of the pianos of his boyhood. Maene's undertaking is the most radical change to the concert grand in 130 years.

Barenboim's reaction to Liszt's instrument was like that of European pianists late in the nineteenth century and early in the twentieth who occasionally found Steinway pianos too rich, too powerful, the action too heavy. 'Chopin would not have been able to play more than a few bars on a modern Steinway,' mused the pianist Stephen Hough in an appreciation of Josef Hofmann, whom he considers the first great modern pianist because he was raised wholly on the American Steinway.

Uli Gerhartz, Steinway's chief technician in London, thinks Chopin would have found his sound on one of these pianos just fine, adapted his touch, and exploited all its soft colours, leaving its bruising dynamic power to others. This is precisely what the pianist Aleksander Michałowski thought: 'Are we to believe that Chopin, had he known the modern pianoforte, would not have explored all its sonorous effects?' Gerhartz thinks Barenboim simply fell in love with Liszt's old instrument in Siena after a lifetime of playing on these same Steinways, deciding there and then to do all he could to re-create its essence in a potent, contemporary keyboard. 'Here is a very old idea transplanted back into a modern instrument.'

The old idea continues to have a certain appeal. Johann Baptist Streicher, for quite some years the finest piano maker in Vienna (at different times his instruments were owned and appreciated by Brahms and Liszt), skilfully made a virtue of necessity in this regard, as illustrated by a surviving instrument from 1843. Streicher No. 3705 is nearly eight feet long, with a mahogany case, ivory keys, English action (more powerful but also more sluggish than a French one), five iron struts supporting a wooden frame and six and a half octaves of parallel strings. The keys are shallower than on a modern piano, but not substantially so. The fallboard proudly displays the firm's medals: *Goldene Medaille* in 1835 and again in 1839 (laurel wreaths in dull gold leaf or enamel), their provenance most likely the expos in Vienna in those years. (Streicher would go on to win handsomely at the Great Exhibition, and once more, four years later, in Paris.) It is similar to the Streicher that Chopin played and admired in Warsaw in October 1830 – three weeks before setting off on the travels that would conclude in Paris the following year – in the first performance of his Piano Concerto in E minor. (He had only just finished the piece and thought it too original to be a success with the public, though afterwards he wrote to Tytus Woyciechowski that the premiere, to a full hall, was a great success, his nerves nowhere to be seen.)

The music historian Edward Swenson found No. 3705 in Stockholm, imported it to America, and then set about restoring it. Peter Roennfeldt bought the fully restored piano for the Queensland Conservatorium of Music and remains its champion, gracefully deflecting the scepticism of students whose preference is for red-meat Steinways, performing on it as much Beethoven and Brahms and Schumann as he can, revelling in the markedly different colours of each register. 'You never feel like you're fighting with the piano,' he says. 'You don't force: because it has that natural warmth, you don't feel as though you have to help it. It has its full size, length and resonance. You don't have to worry about the voicing because the instrument does it for you.' And because of the parallel strings, 'nothing competes for overtones. Each register has its own resonating space.' This could be Bartók talking.

There is indeed something mesmerizing about this piano's register life. In Beethoven's 'Waldstein' Sonata the Streicher growls away low in the keyboard, but without any burring of its remarkably pure tone – not at all the complex mix of ingredients that makes up a modern Steinway. It is good Viennese fare: a little starchy, perhaps, but not at all heavy. In Schumann's *Fantasiestücke* the sound is completely clear in the loudest passages – neither muddy nor overly resonant – and tremolos produce a great effect: no individual hammer attacks, just a wash of sound, whose start and finish are indistinct. In the final movement of Schubert's Piano Trio, D. 929, scales whirr up and down the keyboard with thrilling virtuosity, adopting a different character every octave and a half as registers are passed like milestones: sonorous, glassy, brilliant, shivery. It is the quality and clarity Barenboim sought in his new piano – Liszt's sound, Brahms's sound: Chopin's sound.

The possibilities and limitations of parallel stringing were central to the way composers thought about their own piano music before Steinway. Schumann was completely alive to the quirks and character of the pianos he played and composed on: pieces inhabit specific areas of the instrument's compass and toy with their idiosyncrasies. Brahms also exploited the distinct register colours of his favoured Streicher instruments. Chopin too, as the Preludes show.

Yet Steinway's catalogue of technical innovation in the last decades of the nineteenth century was ultimately only partly about sound and power, only partly about the creation of a more homogeneous colour across the entire compass of the instrument. This was the single quality that other makers emulated over time (even, reluctantly, Pleyel), which Gerhartz admires, Roennfeldt dislikes, and which Barenboim and Maene have now rejected. It was only in part that other piano makers followed Steinway's technical lead in so many ways once mettle, metal, industry, politics or taste permitted: they grew their instruments to a length that allowed strings to vibrate sympathetically – not too big that they could not be moved with relative ease, not too small that the sound would not fill a concert hall. They positioned the hardwood bridge at the reverberant centre of the soundboard. And they ran the strings a little beyond their metal pins (or started them before the tuning pins) to create duplexes – small areas that zing with harmonics in sympathy with the fundamental tone – and produce a richer, more complex sound.

For Steinway's innovations spread far beyond the instrument itself. In building a large, cross-strung, iron-framed piano the company both allowed and stimulated the creation of the modern concert, modern touring, virtuosity as never before, specialists in particular repertory or composers, and the arrival of the producer and agent and a new performing style. These instruments accelerated the acceptance of standardized pitch throughout Europe (before then something of a musical smorgasbord), since they were so much harder to jack up or loosen out depending on the players with whom they were coupled. All of this was unleashed by that inventive and determined family from their factory on Fourth Avenue. Barenboim and Maene's new piano takes us back in time, quite thrillingly, but cannot now uninvent any of what Steinway did.

11

New York City, 1889

In 1889 Mary Elizabeth Adams Brown added 270 'obsolete' instruments to Joseph Drexel's seedling donation to New York's Metropolitan Museum of four years earlier, her generosity admirably explained in an accompanying letter. 'The collection is of value as a whole, as illustrating the habits and tastes of different peoples. It will become more valuable every year, as many of the instruments ... in the collection are rapidly disappearing and even now some of them cannot be replaced.' By the time of her death in 1918 the collection numbered some 3,600 items, much of it her doing. It would come to include a Graf made only seven years after Chopin was daily at his shop in Vienna, practising hard, misspelling Graf's name, its frame entirely wooden, its case a swirly walnut veneer; a harpsichord–organ hybrid in cherry wood, its natural keys black-stained wood, its accidentals light bone, and with a cumbersome eighteen-note pedal board at its feet; a beautiful rotary-valve cornet – a fiddly thing, whose valves operate like sluices or penstocks on a dam, engraved with an ornate patch of lichen that spreads along the bell; and violins and a cello by Stradivari. And there are instruments that, as Brown predicted, have disappeared from human cultures. In some instances the cultures disappeared right alongside them – particular Native American tribes, say, the instruments of which fascinated Brown.

One of Brown's proudest and most stubborn acquisitions was the world's oldest surviving pianoforte, a scrappy Cristofori of 1720 made of cypress, boxwood, fir and leather, which looks a little rough-and-ready, though, up close, it boasts a glistening patina. In recordings it sounds closer to a harpsichord than a piano, though its ingenious escapement action – the first keyboard ever to incorporate a hammer that strikes rather than plucks the string, the hammer then falling

away without dampening it – allowed dynamics through touch, a crucial step towards the modern piano. This Cristofori is the piano-forte's Burgess Shale: a repository of the earliest evolutionary form of the modern instrument, miraculously captured in a single artefact, frozen in time, its internal workings to be marvelled at, though no longer replicated. Sadly, Cristofori had no idea of the wonderful things his invention would initiate.

The Metropolitan Museum's keyboard collection illustrates what a Wild West the 1830s and 1840s were in terms of what was tonally acceptable in a piano: experimentation and innovation were rife, and consolidation among divergent local and national makers and trad-itions was consequently almost impossible. Yet there was another reason for this tonal wildness. Before the widespread acceptance and adoption of equal temperament at the beginning of the twentieth century, there was no consensus on the best method to tune a Western instrument. It is a problem of physics. Pile three pure major thirds on top of each other and you should, in theory, reach an octave: C–E; E–G sharp; G sharp (A flat)–C. In practice, the top note is less than a pure octave above the starting pitch, so you widen the thirds just a little to compensate. Voices, strings, and wind and brass instruments can make this adjustment aurally depending on context, key and tempo. Fixed-pitch instruments – harps, pianos, harpsichords, organs – have no such facility.

Competing systems each presented a different way of carving up the Pythagorean cake into more or less even slices; distinctions between them are found in the details. Just intonation uses an untempered scale: on a keyboard, certain fifths need to be sacrificed in order that the vast majority of thirds and fifths, in the most popular keys, remain pure. In meantone temperament a tone is exactly half a major third, which results in some more obscure keys – dense, black-note ones – sounding uglier than others, tuners having cut their losses to favour more popular keys. As late as 1913 Alphonse Blondel, head of Erard for forty years, wrote in the *Encyclopédie de la Musique et Dictionnaire du Conservatoire* that the system he recommended for his keyboards (as 'harmonious and possessed of a charm which makes plain the natural qualities of the instrument') was one that alternated pure fifths with ever so slightly narrower ones; this leaves seven of the twelve fifths of a chromatic scale pure, the remaining five slightly smaller.

Equal temperament put paid to all this: to the different character of each key, to the sighs and moans preserved in older methods of tuning. Although advocated by certain theorists and performers from the end of the sixteenth century onwards, it was fundamentally a child of positivism. This philosophy originated in France and swept through Europe in the 1830s and 1840s, preaching rationalism and scientific explanations for natural phenomena – including the physics of sound – and Steinway was its legitimate offspring. In equal temperament major thirds are wider than acoustically pure thirds, a compromise brokered to keep the tonal ship afloat, but it means that every note and interval, bar the octave, is artificially tuned. Equal temperament eventually made redundant the commonplace practice of string players treating A flat and G sharp as different notes, though Joseph Joachim held out, tuning the open fifths of his violin to slightly different spans, earning Shaw's disapproval for his poor intonation. The arguments rumbled on and on. As late as 1972, Pablo Casals could tell his pupils not to be afraid of being out of tune with the piano for it was the tempered instrument at fault, its tonal scale an unfortunate compromise.

Mostly, though, musicians fell in with equal temperament, which slowly crept into their vocabularies in the decades after Chopin's death.

Berlioz, no pianist, loved the noble sonority of the new Steinway because it solved what he considered a long-standing problem in earlier pianos, the 'terrible resonance of the minor seventh', which buzzed away at the bottom of the instrument, ruining the lowest eight or so notes, he thought, turning even straightforward chords *cacophonique*.

Advocates of older systems of temperament propose that in pre-twentieth-century music string players make the intervals of their open strings slightly smaller, and play major thirds narrower, minor thirds wider, since this is how composers conceived and heard their own music. Yet this would leave pianists dangling, as Casals thought they should be. It is alluring yet strangely illicit to hear a piano tuned in such temperaments. In certain keys and instances – as sharps and flats pile up – it is slightly rank, like meat on the turn. In others, where a piece sets out specifically to exploit a wilder key's quirks of temperament, it can be mesmerizing. It is as if these works we know so well leave a hazy shadow from across the centuries.

Chopin was alive to the characteristics of temperament, never more so than in his Prelude No. 15 in D flat, which explores the difference between A flat and G sharp. The ostinato (Sand's raindrops) starts lightly, evenly, on the first of these pitches, yet a third of the way in – as the drops become heavier, stormier, and a growling chromatic line beneath takes the piece to its climax – it is played on the second pitch, G sharp. It works so well because the repeated note in the new key (C sharp minor) sounds uglier in meantone temperament, the chromatic underpinning more threatening, more fantastic. In equal temperament a player must create these storm clouds through other means, since A flat and G sharp sound exactly the same in either key.

On his British tour Chopin met and liked the tuner Alfred Hipkins, himself a talented pianist. Hipkins was then technical adviser to Broadwood, where he had recently introduced equal temperament on all the firm's instruments, far ahead of any consensus on its universal applicability. Soon after meeting him Chopin – ill and homesick and frustrated with the British – wrote a forlorn letter to Fontana about his favourite tuner at Pleyel, who had recently died. 'All those with whom I was in most intimate harmony have died and left me. Even Ennike our best tuner has gone and drowned himself; and so I have not in the whole world a piano tuned to suit me.' It is impossible to

say from this whether Chopin, now faced with Hipkins's equal temperament, was nostalgic for the distinctive tuning Ennike employed on his pianos in France or whether time spent with Hipkins reminded him of his favourite technician in Paris, so similar were they in approach. Was Chopin inviting an invidious comparison or a sympathetic one?

Neither shines light on the temperament of Bauza's piano, though it is safe to assume it was not equal temperament. To Chopin, the middle section of Prelude No. 15 probably sounded menacing on the Bauza, less stable than the key it had left and to which it would return, Sand's storm far more ominous than on well-maintained pianos today. (A conceptual flaw in Maene's 'Barenboim' piano is that, for all the care lavished on re-creating the sound of a mid-nineteenth-century instrument, it is nonetheless tuned using equal temperament, which was a possibility in Liszt's piano, though an unlikely one.) These characteristics of temperament – together with Chopin's letter to Fontana – are a reminder of how intimately his music is bound up with whichever instrument he composed it on. Bauza's limitations as a piano maker, as much as his apparent skill, are in the DNA of the Majorcan Preludes. In these pieces Chopin was forced to overcome the peculiarities of the piano at hand, though he was just as likely, through temperament – his own, but the instrument's as well – to take advantage of them. The temperament of Bauza's piano left Chopin in No. 15 scratching away at two itches: the sound of a repeated note in one key, the interval of the fifth in the next. And in such fashion, in the distinct tonal world of this Prelude, a flaw became a feature.

12

Paris, Saint Petersburg, Berlin, 1849–1900

Four days after Chopin's death the *Revue et Gazette Musicale* – his greatest cheerleader during his lifetime – published an obituary, little anticipating the way in which the great advances in trade and technology would take its subject hostage in the years to follow. Although hugely admiring, the obituarist wrote of Chopin's physical weakness, of the solitary dreamscape he occupied, of how contact with the outside world was to him wounding, a torment, a clap of thunder, a dose of poison. 'He was as frail in body as his music was delicate in style, almost merging into the impalpable and imperceptible.'

Henri Blanchard, writing in the same paper a few days after attending Chopin's funeral, nudged closer to his subject, identifying a singular characteristic of the fast-forming Chopin historiography. 'This talent was especially understood, profoundly felt by women,' Blanchard began, 'by ladies, if not of high, then at least of good society, where one always recognized an aristocracy, that of talent.' Then came his key point. 'Mmes de Belgiojoso, de Peruzzi, etc. were the disciples, the admirers, the friends of the poor melancholic artist, of vaporous, fine, delicate inspiration. They loved to follow him when he lulled his intimate audience with his capricious melodic arabesques over an unforeseen harmony, strange, but distinguished, classic, pure, and nevertheless sickly, which seemed a swan song, a hymn of death.'

Thus the underlining trope of sickliness in the man and his music was given a specifically feminine identity. Liszt took the same line a few years later in his biography, writing that Chopin's frailty instilled in him a uniquely feminine sensibility. The writings of the composer and critic Hippolyte Barbedette show how entrenched this view had become by the early 1860s. Although enthusiastic about the Preludes ('a jewel-box of precious stones'), Barbedette damned Chopin's wider influence on modern pianists and pianism, singling him out as a sick man who enjoyed his suffering and who wrote weak music to express his sadness, casting a spell of imperfection and melancholia on listeners and players alike.

Danger, sickness, suffering, adorable accents, melancholic thoughts: these words and phrases were attached to Chopin indiscriminately in the decades after his death and remained in place at the end of the century. When Charles Willeby published his biographical study in 1892 he nominated six Preludes he felt sure were composed entirely in Valldemossa – nos. 4, 6, 9, 13, 20, 21 – since to him their character was morbid, azotic, infected with a faint strain of disease, each displaying 'something which is over-ripe in its lusciousness and febrile in its passion'.

Cortot in the following century was more perceptive about what feminine championship meant for Chopin's music after his death. He was careful to unpick the thread that had been sewn between women, disease and Chopin's music, keen to give credit to the discerning female students who perpetuated the composer's name and authentic performance traditions. In her occasional charity performances – the single forum in which it was possible for a woman of her class to play in public – Marcelina Czartoryska, the most talented of Chopin's (amateur) pupils, was able to reproduce with great skill Chopin's nuanced instructions in her lessons. The Princess de Chimay, the Countesses Potocka and Esterhazy, Mlle de Noailles and the Baroness de Rothschild also received from Chopin tuition, the dedication of various works, and patient loyalty, which they repaid after his death. But they were nonetheless amateurs: professional advocacy was some years away.

Clara Schumann facilitated the transition. In the 1840s and 1850s, following Liszt's lead, she performed solo recitals, from memory, without recourse to streams of associate artists or potboiler repertory; from her and Liszt's initiative emerged a more serious tradition of concert programming. Chopin agreed to this model only once, at the recital in Edinburgh's Hopetoun Rooms in October 1848. Hipkins no doubt serviced the fine Broadwood piano that Chopin played in most of his British concerts, and a number of Preludes were almost certainly on the programme. 'Any pianist,' wrote the *Scotsman* a few days later, 'who undertakes to play alone to an audience for two hours, must, now-a-days, be a very remarkable one to succeed in sustaining attention and satisfying expectation.' Thirty years later this performance model would be commonplace.

The most influential pianist to take up Chopin in the second half of the century was the Russian Anton Rubinstein. As a boy he had charmed Vienna but left Paris cold, audiences there largely unmoved by his talent, or perhaps by the phenomenon he represented: the precocious young musician as circus performer. 'The Parisian public,' Chopin told Joseph Filtsch in 1842, attempting to explain the capital's initial indifference to Rubinstein, 'is overwhelmed to an incredible degree by a crowd of virtuosi of all kinds and all ages, and people are no longer satisfied by *relative* perfection, since we have too much of that. What is needed for success is something *perfect* – and then one is extremely sought after and appreciated.' Rubinstein was only eleven when, soon after the concert in Salle Pleyel in which some of the Preludes were given their first public outing, he visited Chopin in his apartment on the rue Tronchet. Late in life he could remember every detail – from the furnishings to the plaque on the Pleyel piano in the middle of the room: 'The gift of Louis-Philippe to Frédéric Chopin' – a surprising detail. (Chopin had performed before Louis-Philippe and his court in October 1839, which perhaps prompted the gift.)

There were scratchy sympathies between the two. Rubinstein also revered Bach's *Das Wohltemperierte Klavier*, as he wrote later: 'If, unfortunately, all of Bach's cantatas, motets, masses, yes, even the Passion-music, were to be lost, and this alone remained, we would not need despair – music were not entirely destroyed!' And Chopin and Rubinstein appreciated the same opera singers – Rubini, Lablache, Sontag, Grisi, Lind – Rubinstein shadowing them on his initial European tour, not so many years after Chopin first encountered them. But in substance they were very different musicians: one an instinctive creator, the other, predominantly, an intellectual and interpreter.

Rubinstein possessed a supple and sophisticated intelligence rare in someone whose schooling had been simultaneously curtailed and narrowly focused from such a young age. He had a carefully measured and mannered way of speaking beautiful sentences, skipping from one language to the next as the need arose, with a highly developed curiosity and perceptiveness about history and politics, revolution and rebellion, high culture, class, who wrote what and when and why. His open-minded intelligence was perhaps partly a consequence of launching his career properly not as a child prodigy, but at the age of twenty-four, on an enormously successful European tour. Before then, after a boyhood full of concerts and promise, he had eked out an existence in Vienna teaching students, living on his wits and fingers, as Chopin had done before him. It was easier for Rubinstein to establish a career in his twenties than in his childhood: his performing style and approach borrowed more than a little from Liszt, by then a Europe-wide currency. And now that Liszt was preoccupied composing the sprawling works that came to define the second stage of his creative life, a dauphin was needed.

It is not fanciful to imagine Rubinstein meeting Heine in Paris at the same time he met Chopin – perhaps at Salle Erard on the rue du Mail in late 1840, with Chopin and Liszt in the audience for one of the boy's first concerts in the capital. Or a year later at the apartment on the rue Tronchet when Chopin played Rubinstein his Impromptu in F sharp, Op. 36, composed at Nohant immediately after the Majorca trip, his health and optimism slowly returning. As an adult (and composer) Rubinstein often returned to Heine's poetry as though visiting an old friend, not least a year before his death in 1894 when he set Heine's valedictory poem 'Wo wird einst des Wandermüden letzte Ruhestätte sein?' ('Where will be the final resting place of the weary hiker?')

The adult Rubinstein thought like Heine too. Just before the poet moved to Paris in 1831, he predicted that the age of art and culture that had begun in Goethe's cradle (1749) would end in his coffin (1832): the new age would beget a new art, isolated from the dead touch of the past. Rubinstein had a similar idea in the early 1890s when discussing the history of music with Madame von —, the two of them cosy in Rubinstein's richly furnished villa outside Saint Petersburg. Palestrina, he said, represented the beginning of music as a proper art form, with Bach and Handel being the culmination of the organ and vocal epoch. (Bach died a year after Goethe's birth, Handel nine years later.) Then followed the instrumental age, built around the emergence of the orchestra and the piano, which ran from Carl Philipp Emanuel Bach to Beethoven. The third and final epoch – the lyric-romantic, in Rubinstein's phrase – was the age of Schubert, Weber, Mendelssohn and Schumann; Chopin was 'its last representative', and his death, along with Schumann's seven years later, represented nothing less than *finis musicae* – the end of music. When a startled Madame von — asked him to explain his pessimism, Rubinstein responded very simply: 'With the excess of colouring at the expense of drawing; of technique at the expense of thought; of frame at the expense of picture.'

Rubinstein was inserting himself into the century's great cultural argument – art's dispute between colour and line, music's between sound and form. In his grand scheme he could make no room for Wagner or Verdi, Brahms or Bruckner (notwithstanding these last two composers' deference to Classical form), though he did find a chair for Chopin, who was actually uninterested in sitting down. *Après nous le déluge*: after us, the deluge. Rubinstein was hopelessly wrong, of course, to a startling degree; Romanticism continued to evolve in his lifetime, in brilliant and fascinating ways. But he did not place any value on the innovations he witnessed, and was determined to direct young musicians away from 'a false road in art' (as he told a friend), to guide them towards the great works of the past, which he thought far surpassed anything else on offer.

Chopin could never have talked like this about his own music or that around him; he was too modest, and his contemporaries left him cold. In any case, he did not think this way about history, nor really about posterity. He did not position himself in a linear narrative: his musical taste was too particular, his empathies too unfashionable. And he would have disdained the way Rubinstein was so sympathetic to attempts to identify programmes in his music, which the younger musician came to hear as a collective hymn to Poland's greatness, a sob of despair at its downfall, a battle cry for its survival. Perhaps a sensitive, politically astute Russian in the nationalistic second half of the nineteenth century was bound to see the music in this light, though such thinking meant nothing to Chopin himself.

Despite his reactionary viewpoint, Rubinstein was perceptive about Chopin's contribution to the evolution of modern pianism:

> Whether the spirit of this instrument breathed upon him or he upon it – how he wrote for it, I do not know, but only an entire blending one with the other could call such compositions to life. Tragic, romantic, lyric, heroic, dramatic, fantastic, soulful, sweet, dreamy, brilliant, grand, simple – all possible expressions are found in his compositions, and are all sung by him upon this instrument in perfect beauty.

When Madame von — accused him of extravagance, of unduly deifying Chopin when he deserved no such thing, Rubinstein listed the pieces he thought justified his assessment: the Nocturnes and Ballades; the scherzos in B flat minor and B minor; the sonatas in the same keys, 'the first of which is a whole drama, with its last movement (after the very typical Funeral March), which I would name, "*Night winds sweeping over churchyard graves*"'; the greater portion of his Études; the Mazurkas; and a large number of the Polonaises. Above all, the Preludes, 'to me the pearls of his works'.

It is the career of this prodigy, who was still alive when the teenage Stravinsky was composing his first notes – devouring everything on offer at the nearby Mariinsky Theatre where his father was a soloist – that best charts the transition from the style of Chopin playing that Rubinstein heard as a boy to the one he perpetuated as an adult. This shift to a more gargantuan approach to Chopin's scores was starkly evident in the series of seven 'historical concerts' that he curated and presented in 1885–6 in different European and Russian cities, beginning with Byrd and ending with contemporary Russian composers, an exhaustive and exhausting affair. He dedicated one enormous concert in each city to Chopin: the F minor Fantasy, the B minor Scherzo, Sonata No. 2, the Barcarolle and Berceuse, all four Ballades, four Mazurkas, three Waltzes, three Nocturnes and three Polonaises, two Impromptus and six Preludes. The critic Oscar Bie was scarcely alone in describing Rubinstein in such concerts as a musician who 'rushed and raved, and a slight want of polish was the natural result of his impressionist temperament'. Or perhaps he meant a slight want of Polish, for in the final years of Rubinstein's life, as Poland's circumstances seemed irredeemably grim, and as musicians started talking about a disappearing school of Chopin playing that had little to do with Rubinstein's ego and flashiness – national ownership of Chopin's music became a matter of some importance.

It was a Polish-Jewish pianist – with aristocratic looks and a friendship with his teacher Liszt (with Brahms and Wagner too) – who first programmed a Chopin retrospective in Europe. In Berlin in 1867, a

few years before his early death from typhoid, Carl Tausig performed a series of four Chopin recitals, which no doubt included the Preludes, though probably not yet all of them.

Tausig was in many ways ahead of his time, for Chopin in the 1860s was still no competition for Beethoven. He was even in danger of being overshadowed by the young Brahms, who, by 1867, had composed his three piano sonatas and first concerto. Yet Tausig believed Chopin was a (Polish) composer of substance, not a peripheral figure of Parisian salon life, and was intrigued by his pianism, grilling Wilhelm von Lenz on the subject when the two met in Berlin in 1868. The composer and critic Caesar Cui recognized what Tausig was doing. 'In his hands Chopin was transformed and emerged in a very unusual form for us: the composer's ultra sensitivity, sentimentality, eternal sorrowfulness and whining had disappeared, and playfulness, flirtatiousness and vivacity came to the foreground. I have to admit, such a new and piquant way of interpreting Chopin affected me refreshingly and nicely.'

The American writer and critic James Gibbons Huneker, who in Paris in the late 1870s observed the classes of Chopin's pupil Georges Mathias, thought distinct national approaches to Chopin's music began to become apparent in the final three decades of the century. 'If the Germans treat him in a dull, clumsy and bruited manner, the Frenchman irritates you by his flippancy, his nimble, colourless fingers and the utter absence of poetic divination.' By the time he wrote this (1900) it was possible to identify four distinct national schools of Chopin playing. Poland and Russia each claimed him for his Slavic blood, which allowed them in their different ways to distinguish themselves from Austro-Germanic culture and traditions (seemingly an especially important distinction following the Austro-German Alliance of 1879). Germany countered that she was the acknowledged gatekeeper to the Western musical canon, and that it was only because of the various Breitkopf & Härtel collected editions of his music (particularly that of 1878–80) – along with various major biographies and works of analysis – that Chopin had been given his ticket of admission. France declared Chopin her own since the vast majority of his scores were composed on her soil, and the poetry and intimacy of the music were in any case quintessentially French. England for the most part just liked the pretty tunes and simpler melodies, fodder for the domestic market.

The conductor and pianist Hans von Bülow, Tausig's senior by almost twelve years, should rightly have been expected to fulfil Huneker's stereotype of the brutish, autocratic German musician. Bie suggested as much when he wrote that von Bülow was a skilled draughtsman who 'drew carefully the threads from the keys . . . while every tone and every tempo stood in ironbound firmness, and every line was there before it was drawn'. He was describing von Bülow's playing, but it works just as well as an assessment of his character. There was something alluring about this pike-faced law-school dropout with abrasive manner, liable to insult his audience as readily as perform for it, often demanding that two pianos be set onstage, head to tail, so he had the choice of presenting his listeners with his back or his face, depending on his mood.

Von Bülow thought nothing of playing the last five Beethoven piano sonatas in a single recital, recognizing that in them the composer was hewing his own monument from craggy stone. Performing them in sequence was not about thematic connections or tonal relationships, but instead about scale, power and endurance, the pianist as mountain climber – *Ein Heldenleben* (*A Hero's Life*) decades before Strauss got there. Von Bülow was the teacher who instructed his pupils that, now and then in concert, they should claw a wrong note to underline the difficulty of a leap or figuration. And he was the first truly modern opera conductor, scheduling rehearsal upon rehearsal for any new production: coachings, ensemble calls, sectionals, orchestra calls, stage rehearsals, piano dresses, orchestral dresses, *Sitzproben*, *Halbproben* and *Hauptproben*; the rehearsals and premieres (*Tristan und Isolde* and *Die Meistersinger von Nürnberg* among them) conducted from memory; his loyalty to Wagner enduring even after he had lost to him his wife, Liszt's daughter, the redoubtable Cosima. It was, after all, the Age of Wagner, the age of monuments and monsters.

Yet von Bülow behaved in an entirely un-German way regarding Chopin. It was he who came up with the tortuous list of titles for the Preludes – 'Uncertainty', 'Tolling bells', 'The Polish dancer', and so forth – his attempt to identify each fleeting vision, to pin down each delicate butterfly in a specimen case and put a label on it. He tagged No. 8 'Desperation', which was hardly an advance on Delacroix's characterization of it ('This music,' Delacroix told Baudelaire, 'swift and passionate, resembles a brilliant bird flying over the horrors of an abyss'), and for No. 10 – which Koczalski dispatches in a little over twenty seconds – von Bülow concocted a programme more baroque than anything Sand ever attempted:

> A night moth is flying around the room – there! it has suddenly hidden itself (the sustained G sharp); only its wings twitch a little. In a moment it takes flight anew and again settles down in darkness – its wings flutter (trill in the left hand). This happens several times, but at the last, just as the wings begin to quiver again, the busybody who lives in the room aims a stroke at the poor insect. It twitches once . . . and dies.

The formidable American critic Harold Schonberg later observed, 'It takes about as long to read this programme as to play the piece itself.'

Despite von Bülow's best efforts, pianists born in the second half of the century drove the great change in attitude and pianism from the programmatic narratives Liszt initiated in Chopin's day. It was not simply that to play in the age of the modern Steinway was to play in a different way from those who came before. It was also that pianists had to choose between exploiting the potential of these new pianos or honouring the very different instruments for which their repertory had been conceived. This was not yet a common way of thinking, though it would become so in the following century. But in the late nineteenth century few pianists could resist the power of these new pianos, nor the heightened Romantic narrative – the pianist as storyteller and superstar – accompanying them. Audiences too were beguiled by the heft of a Steinway grand, which seemed to contain a whole world of drama and inner revelation. The thoughtful, intimate communications between composer, performer and listener initiated by Chopin and perpetuated by Tausig were shouted down by a more boisterous crowd.

Inevitably this same crowd came to think the smallness of the Preludes was something of an inconvenience. To them structure and grand musical architecture were Romanticism's underpinnings and the century's most important legacy. This was the basis of Brahms's fight with Wagner, after all, Strauss's response to Liszt, Mahler's to Beethoven – in Mahler's own ten symphonies, of course, but also in his edition of Beethoven's ninth, with its woodwind doublings and extreme dynamics, so shepherding the work into an age of larger orchestras and more powerful string bodies. And insatiable audiences too.

This gargantuan mindset was a better fit for a newly united and expansionist Germany than for a recently bloodied France: in Germany the Preludes seemed a foreign language, one full of small words and characterized by gnomic utterances. So, in compensation, pianists at the end of the century began to think of them as a cycle: it was a way of sidestepping the criticism that had dogged Chopin since the 1830s, that his music was too slight to add anything of substance to Romanticism's cause. Chopin's admirers were attempting to save him from his perceived flaws by presenting the Preludes as a sequence of intricately jewelled, individual parts that constituted a far more imposing and valuable whole.

It is possible that Chopin performed them as a complete set in private. In October 1839 Moscheles wrote that 'Chopin played me his Etudes and his most recent work, the Preludes', though this is too ambiguous to determine whether Moscheles heard them all. Chopin certainly identified particular connections between individual pieces. On the back of a published copy of his Nocturne in B flat minor, Op. 9, he scribbled programming suggestions for Jane Stirling: two groupings of four Preludes each, which highlighted and juxtaposed specific tonal characteristics, notably the binding interval of the fifth. It was almost modern programming: Chopin creating a garment from scraps, a faggot out of sticks, at a time when audiences did not really look for such cohesion. But it was nothing more sophisticated than this.

Yet the notion of the Preludes as a cycle was already gaining traction at the beginning of the twentieth century: in his biography of Chopin (1900) Huneker writes of the Russian-German pianist Arthur Friedheim performing all twenty-four as a set 'with excellent effect'. (His teacher Liszt, however, was aghast to learn of Friedheim programming all six *Paganini Études* in a single concert; Liszt only ever performed two of them together at a time.) Such thinking would soon influence Schirmer's complete edition of Chopin's music (1915–18) – a new-century replacement of Mikuli's volumes for Schirmer from the 1890s (first published by Kistner). Both Huneker and Friedheim were intimately involved in the new edition, each determined to exert some control over the 'real' Chopin performance tradition in the twentieth century. 'All-Chopin programs fill concert halls,' Huneker begins his introduction to the Preludes. 'Thanks to this the old Chopin is gone for most of us. It is not that he is played too often, but that he is badly, sadly played.' Friedheim thought he knew why. Open any page of Mikuli's edition (he suggests in his preface to the Études) and you will be confronted 'by a hedge of stubborn, thorny fingerings and shapelessly twisted, truncated expression and tempo markings, behind which a naughty rogue seems to be calling out mockingly at the trustful beginner: "Come along, keep on trying! You'll never get through."' Empty expanses dominate; liberty reigns untrammelled; pedal marks are scattered like seed; metronome markings are mostly twenty notches higher or lower than they should be. 'Only one who feels impelled to follow up this "legitimate" apostle of Chopin bar by bar, is in a position thoroughly to appreciate all that has been achieved here on the basis of a most intimate misunderstanding of the instrument.'

There is actually very little difference between Mikuli's edition of the Preludes and the much later Urtext editions based on various original manuscripts and the fine copies made by Fontana, who was acting on the detailed instructions Chopin sent from Majorca and Marseilles. Yet to Friedheim, Mikuli (and by extension Hiller, Hallé, Tausig and Koczalski) stood outside the performance style and tradition created by Rubinstein and Friedheim's great idol Liszt. This made Mikuli both unfathomable and unfashionable among many pianists for the simple reason, to Friedheim's way of thinking, that Rubinstein's pedagogical influence long and rightly outlasted him, and continued to shape the 'authentic' Chopin performance tradition well into the twentieth century.

Huneker was not so sure. He flinchingly remembered Rubinstein's brawny performances of Chopin's music, remembered too how 'a few of the old guard' – those who had studied with Chopin or heard him play – 'still hobbling about in Paris declined to accept the Russian lion, with the velvet paws, as an authentic interpreter ... The unearthly element in the music was absent in the noble, full-blooded treatment of the glorious Anton.' This did not delay Friedheim. Having dispatched Mikuli, he outlined his editorial purpose and presented his bona fides. 'To a certain extent, therefore, a tradition actually exists – is alive; but as no one has hitherto thought to set it down on paper in a form as uncorrupt as possible, it was time that this should be done by one who is justified, by his own past experience, in giving his opinion in the matter.' And so, drawing on memories of Liszt's Chopin recitals three or four decades previously – in Saint Petersburg, Weimar and Rome – and on the playing and lessons of his teacher Rubinstein (who, from Liszt, 'greedily absorbed everything that suited his temperament', in particular how to play Chopin), Friedheim produced an edition that in its interventionist fingering, phrasing, pedalling, articulation, metronome marks, dynamics and other expressive directions contradicted earlier Chopin scores – but respected the more accurate performance tradition that he thought these two giants of the keyboard, Liszt and Rubinstein, had created between them.

The two spirits hovering over all these shifts in taste and technology were Chopin and Liszt themselves. The argument about how to play

Chopin's music had really not progressed much since the 1840s. All these pianists – Mikuli, Friedheim, Rubinstein, Tausig, von Bülow, Koczalski, and the hundreds more who, in the last decades of the nineteenth century, performed Chopin's music on new concert platforms throughout the world – all these critics and scholars working away at new Chopin editions, all these publishers making claims on the large domestic market growing alongside the burgeoning piano industry: all of them swore allegiance to either one performance tradition or the other.

Paradoxically, Liszt had the advantage over Chopin: he lived a long time, taught streams of eminent and influential pianists – not solely Rubinstein, but Tausig, Moriz Rosenthal and Lamond as well – traded on his early friendship with Chopin, and wrote and revised his intimate biography. 'The Chopin best known in our time is without question, that of Liszt, which the Prince Karol [in *Lucrezia*] of George Sand resembles sufficiently to serve for a confirmation,' the critic Joseph Bennett wrote at the end of the century.

Sand would not have agreed on either point. Liszt, she wrote, 'in his *Life of Chopin* (which, though somewhat rank in style, is yet full of good things and good pages), went far astray with the best will in the world'. Apart from this throwaway line and some guarded reminiscences spread over ten more pages in *Histoire de ma vie*, Sand in later years never sought to tend Chopin's grave or legacy. So Liszt, Rubinstein and Friedheim filled the vacuum. And as the century ended and living memory of Chopin the performer faded, musicians held on to whatever they could in the sheer ephemerality of his playing and scores.

'Dans les arts il faut faire grand': the arts must be large. It was a common expression of Liszt's, Rubinstein attested and emulated. It suited the exponents and instruments of high Romanticism, yet it turned out to be a terrible match for the nineteenth century's great musical miniaturist. Fresh troops were arriving, however, to relieve Paris's hobbling old guard. Chief among them was an astounding young Polish pianist and scholar, who would soon challenge the way the twentieth century viewed a whole swathe of composers and scores from earlier centuries.

BOOK TWO

An Old Jewess, Crazy About Music

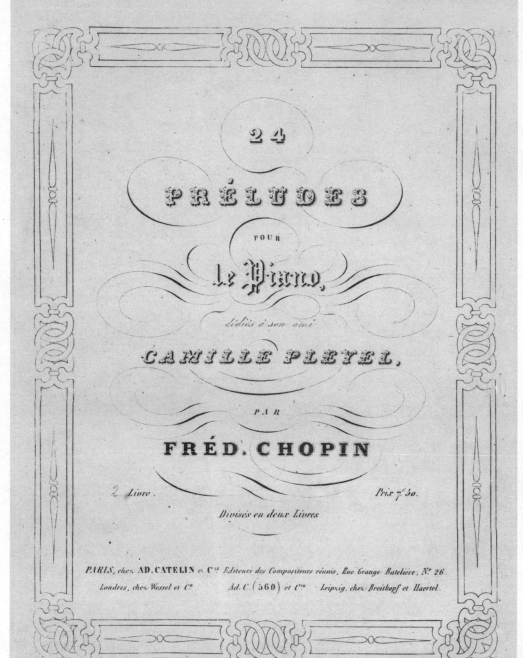

24

PRÉLUDES

POUR

Le Piano,

dédiés à son ami

CAMILLE PLEYEL,

PAR

FRÉD. CHOPIN

2.ᵉ Livre.   Prix 7.ᶠ 50.

Divisés en deux Livres

PARIS, chez AD. CATELIN et C.ⁱᵉ Editeurs des Compositeurs réunis, Rue Grange Batelière, N.º 26.

Londres, chez Wessel et C.º   Ad. C. (560) et C.ⁱᵉ   Leipzig, chez Breitkopf et Haertel.

Gravé par A. Viaton.

13

Valldemossa, Warsaw, Paris, Berlin, 1879–1913

Her party disembarked in Palma early morning, her date book listing its arrival in her trademark purple ink and handsome *écriture cursive*.

Wanda Landowska and her retinue had left Barcelona at 10 p.m. on 27 January 1911, sailing the 160 miles south in eight hours. In the seventy-odd years since Chopin and Sand traversed this exact route the journey time had been shaved of ten hours, and pigs no longer accompanied passengers on the return leg; everything else, essentially, was the same. In the days immediately prior to travelling to Palma, Landowska gave two recitals in Barcelona, and before then concerts in Vitoria, Malaga and Valencia. It was a long tour, over two months in total, which would include in its latter weeks German cities hugging the border of her homeland, the Kingdom of Poland, and its neighbour, the future Czechoslovakia.

Her date book reduces the hard graft of touring to a series of gnomic entries: travel times, towns or cities visited, number of concerts performed: two in most, often a day between them, a separate programme in each. Landowska in these years was still recognized as a pianist, performing repertory by Haydn and Mozart, Schubert and Schumann, Weber and Wagner, Chopin and Liszt. As part of the Grand Festival Chopin in June 1909, held in Paris's Palais du Trocadéro, she played Mazurkas and Waltzes, and a sole Prelude, No. 15. Yet six years earlier she had given her first public performance on the harpsichord – pieces by Byrd and Praetorius, Morley and Chambonnières, Rameau and Couperin, names then seemingly from folklore – and she was now most renowned on this instrument. She lugged it from town to town, tuning it herself before and during each recital, proselytizing these obscure works with the zeal of a travelling preacher.

Many artists fell under her spell. Four years before her Spanish tour she accepted Tolstoy's invitation to spend Christmas with him at Yasnaya Polyana, his grand house and estate near Tula, where he wrote *War and Peace* and *Anna Karenina*. Countess Tolstoy photographed Landowska at her two-manual harpsichord, Tolstoy a few steps behind her, transfixed by the music on offer.

Two years later she was photographed in Auguste Rodin's studio in Paris. She is sitting at the same instrument, her half smile the same as at Yasnaya Polyana, the bearded Rodin standing a few steps behind, concentrating on her, much as Tolstoy did.

They were captivated by the allure of the unknown, these artists and their friends and families, of scores excavated from past centuries. Those who thought the instrument belonged, at best, in Brown's collection at the Metropolitan Museum in New York, a gallery or two away from Rodin's *L'Âge d'airain*, were quickly put in their place. 'The harpsichord is an instrument with a brilliant past and a promising future,' Landowska would write in 1949. Yet in 1907 in Russia, in 1909 in France, its future was by no means assured. Britain aside, where at the end of the nineteenth century and beginning of the next century Arnold Dolmetsch and Chopin's tuner Alfred Hipkins gave harpsichord concerts and lecture-recitals, and in a few centres on the Continent (Salle Pleyel the most important of them), there was no widespread revival under way, no cultivated public interest in the instrument and its shadowy sounds. It fostered mostly condescension or ignorance.

There was thus something almost wilful in Landowska's dedication to the harpsichord and its repertory. On the day before she visited Majorca, Ernst von Schuch had conducted the first performance of Richard Strauss's *Der Rosenkavalier* – only a few months before the premieres of Ravel's *L'heure espagnol* and Stravinsky's *Petrushka*. It was the year of Mahler's death and the posthumous first outing of his

astonishing *Das Lied von der Erde*, the repeated final word 'Ewig . . .'
('For ever . . .') of the last movement, 'Der Abschied' ('The Farewell'),
left floating in the air, a fitting epitaph. In the background Schoenberg was beginning to dismantle tonality – in *Erwartung* (1909) and
in other equally startling works. Playing the harpsichord in the first
decade of the twentieth century was a curiosity, an eccentricity, a
neat reminder of music's great progress since the instrument's zenith.
Tolstoy and his wife, Rodin and his guests, believed they were hearing performances that were not simply rare, but ephemeral as well:
there was no reason to expect that this music would be around in
another twenty years. Turn away for a moment and they might miss
it for ever.

Auguste Wolff, Camille Pleyel's successor, had sowed the seeds of
the instrument's revival in the late 1880s, assisted by his son-in-law
Gustave Lyon. Under Lyon's direction the company built its first ever
harpsichord, exhibiting it at the Exposition Universelle of 1889 in
an act of almost deliberate provocation: the Exposition was a celebration of the hundredth anniversary of the storming of the Bastille,
the beginning of the end of the *ancien régime* with which the harpsichord was historically associated. Pleyel based its design on
antiquated plans in treatises and manuals made by long-dead instrument makers for their apprentices or assistants, and on surviving
seventeenth- and eighteenth-century harpsichords in private hands.
Lyon matched its sound and projection to the bigger spaces it now
had to fill by giving the five octaves on each keyboard a number of
registers and stops, controlled by six pedals that could change couplings and registration mid-flow; he weighted the keys and regulated
the tuning via a complex mechanism adapted from the modern piano;
and over time he traded the original rococo-style case for one of
hardy rosewood to help ameliorate the damaging effects of climate
and transportation.

In 1906 Lyon's invention gave rise to one of the most spectacular
group photographs in the history of music, a gathering at either Salle
Pleyel or the Paris home of Lyon ('the restorer of the harpsichord', as
one newspaper called him) featuring friends and colleagues of
Francis and Henri Casadesus. At the beginning of the century these
brothers had founded La Société des Instruments Anciens, which in

concerts at Salle Pleyel showcased little-known instruments – a viola da gamba, or gittern, or hurdy-gurdy. Koussevitzky, Rachmaninoff, Saint-Säens, Rimsky-Korsakov, Chaliapin and Landowska (standing in the middle row, second from the right) were just some of the crowd.

Five years later Lyon would accept Landowska's commission for a harpsichord built to her specifications, a husky instrument with a sixteen-foot register; leather plectra (which had to be replaced too often); couplers linking two keyboards; lead-weighted keys; seven pedals to satisfy the need for tonal contrast in the age of the modern piano; and a complex system of coarse- and fine-tuning, which looked like the wirings of a telephone exchange. Later still the company would incorporate a full-iron frame, which rendered it almost indestructible, as the 1940s would underscore. This powerful new keyboard was only beginning to formulate in Landowska's mind when she travelled to Majorca, taking with her the robust Pleyel instrument, which thereafter musicians only learned to negotiate ever so slowly, intrigued as they were by the lost sounds it recovered.

This was never meant to be Landowska's path. She was born in Warsaw in 1879 to middle-class parents, her father a lawyer, her mother similarly educated, both Jewish, though they had converted to Catholicism before Wanda's birth. They belonged to that well-to-do cultured set in Warsaw in the trailing decades of the nineteenth century, conversant in Wagner and Liszt, the Romantic poets, and even, improbably, the works of Mark Twain, which Landowska's mother translated into Polish.

She began piano lessons at the age of four with Jan Kleczyński before studying with Aleksander Michałowski at the Warsaw Conservatory – both specialists in Chopin's music, as most Polish pianists then styled themselves. In the year Landowska became his pupil, Kleczyński delivered a series of lectures later translated and published as *Chopin's Greater Works (Preludes, Ballads, Nocturnes, Polonaises, Mazurkas): How They Should Be Understood*. It is a frustratingly superficial book, not least on the Preludes, about which strange pronouncements pile up. 'The Prelude in C must be played twice, the first time with less, the second with greater haste in the middle part, the speed becoming slower towards the end.' (This is quite close to how Ferruccio Busoni plays it in a 1920 piano roll.) And, 'Prelude 2 ought not to be played, as it is bizarre.' Passionate and committed, Kleczyński nonetheless gives the impression that comprehension of the Preludes had not progressed much since the 1840s.

Michałowski was a more significant figure and influence. Although his principal teachers had been Moscheles and Tausig, his friendship with Mikuli – who generously shared his knowledge and experiences as Chopin's pupil – lent authority to his playing and nudged his teaching in the direction of that performance tradition. And it was as Michałowski's pupil that Landowska blossomed into the most captivating, musical and intelligent adolescent, passionate about music, religion, talent, family, ambition, personality, politics, love and literature.

As a glint-eyed fourteen-year-old she described her own character, listing in her journal twelve vices ('besides these, surely, 12 others of which I have not the slightest conception'): her conceitedness and ignorance; her ego and envy; her sudden enthusiasms ('when I hear a beautiful work, I dream day and night about how I might play it'); her evasiveness and capricious personality; her lies and lazy disposition; her disorderly conduct and false convictions. 'My extreme fault is that I am very, very stupid.' It is an unforgiving analysis (though a year later Landowska's mother was happy to corroborate it, citing her daughter's conceited nature, fogginess, sulks, discourtesy and general unbearableness).

Landowska was particularly critical of her own appearance. 'Why are you thinking about all these things, you ugly girl, you!':

> Leave those thoughts to beautiful and . . . rich girls; rather work hard, do not let your head be turned by the flippant. I am ugly, in fact, very ugly; my only exterior quality is in my teeth and my hair; otherwise, I rarely look good in any kind of dress. Perhaps I am best off at the pianoforte at which I am queen on a throne . . . Perhaps, though, I look best when I crawl in bed and cover my face; but I cannot stay in bed all my life!

The reverse side of such adolescent conceitedness and self-loathing is the way she writes about her development as a musician. She tells how she transposed the chromatic jumble of a fugue in E minor from the first book of Bach's *Das Wohltemperierte Klavier* into six different keys – most of them belonging to a black note – as a surprise for Michałowski, and performed them at an examination, earning the highest mark. ('Bach is a genius so great, so powerful, that it is difficult to believe that he was a human being; does he not seem more a kind of divinity?') She giddily records the night at her house when Michałowski dropped in for a glass of wine ('my good fortune . . . was equal to insanity') and stayed to play on the family's box of nails (Landowska's description) some Gluck, and two Études and a nocturne by Chopin, of course, which left her beaming. She writes about the recital of her own compositions she undertakes at Michałowski's urging – the whole thing topped off with a Chopin Mazurka – which generates idiotic reviews, she thinks, the first critic enthralled by the richness of melody in her music, the second despairing at its lack of form, the third appreciating the influence of her composition teacher, the fourth despondent about it. 'Why does Wanda Landowska seek strange gods, alien protectors?' one asks presciently. And in early 1895 she writes:

> How could I live without Chopin, whose nostalgic, capricious melodies shake one's soul; his *obereki* [Polish folk dances], his *mazurki* which remind me of the village girls, of familiar hamlets, of the fields and the meadows . . . How, oh how, could I ever separate myself from my beloved masters. I can stand in awe of these masters in the

execution of the works of others, but I wish to give them myself, to give to them and their works my soul, my thoughts!

Late the same year she played for the Polish-German virtuoso and teacher Moritz Moszkowski, who asked whether she was Jewish. 'Making a funny face, I replied, "Oh, no!" He replied: "What: you are not a sweet little Jewess, and I was so enchanted at the thought of it." ' It caught her by surprise, shame somewhere in the mix. When the following year she pondered the character and prospects of Bogumil Zepler, a young composer courting her ('A woman sees a husband in every single man,' she writes, Jane Austen at her shoulder), she concluded that 'Jews have a totally different way of thinking than do Christians. With them everything tends toward marriage or toward money.' It was hardly an unusual observation for the time: the following year evidence exonerating Captain Alfred Dreyfus from a charge of treason was suppressed by high-ranking military officers, which left his incarceration unchallenged. When she disclosed to her father Zepler's interest, he told her he would never allow her to marry a Jew. She laughed him off, a little too heartily, suddenly wary, yet cocky too. 'And am I not a Jewess, except that I have been baptized?' she asked. 'No, now you belong to the "true-believers".'

She was unflinching in recording these experiences and transgressions: she wrote down everything that happened to her, everything that came to mind. Inevitably this included the moment she discovered the harpsichord. In Berlin in 1895 she went with Zepler to an exhibition of ancient instruments. There she saw and played a two-manual cembalo purportedly once owned by or associated with Bach (a provenance later disputed), made some time after 1700 in Harrass's workshop in Gross-Breitenbach, and sold in 1890 to

Berlin's new Sammlung Alter Musikinstrumente, precursor to the Musikinstrumenten-Museum. It was much modified in the eighteenth century, its registrations and couplings changed. Yet this did not prevent various German makers treating it as the Rosetta Stone when, in the early decades of the twentieth century, they began to build their revival harpsichords. 'The tone however is very sharp, almost shattering,' Landowska writes. 'One senses a certain storminess arising as the vibration winds itself about the room. It does not permit for too much differentiation or variation and theme-change. It is, though, a magnificent creation.' It was an unpromising encounter, perhaps, though a fire was lit, and in this single moment the fate of much musical performance in the twentieth century was set.

All these different threads came together on 31 January 1911 when, after two concerts in Majorca, Landowska made a pilgrimage to the monastery in Valldemossa. The village was then much as Chopin had found it, though change was in the air. At the end of this year it would be possible to travel from Palma to Sóller (a short distance north-east of Valldemossa) on board a steam engine pulling beautiful art deco rolling stock with oiled panelling, pretty brass detailing and slatted seats on ornate wrought-iron bases, passing over a graceful five-arch viaduct and a series of rough-hewn bridges, through thirteen tunnels excavated from the Serra de Tramontana, along shallow inclines and steeper gradients, the entire route mapped on English narrow-gauge track, all of it built on the profits of the citrus trade and a burgeoning tourist industry. This is the Valldemossa that Édouard Ganche would discover in 1928, a monastery and village groggily waking to the gift left them almost a century earlier by their most famous residents.

On Landowska's trip passage was still via the maze of dirt roads Chopin described so well, which funnelled into a single track through the near-impenetrable limestone of Coll de Sóller, where tired coach horses were watered and rested before the final push north. The journey was hardly simpler than when Sand and Maurice made their way from the monastery to Palma to beg customs officers for the release of Chopin's Pleyel, before turning around and making the journey back, in that insistent rain.

There is a lovely symmetry to Landowska undertaking her pilgrimage in this manner, for in the cell in which Chopin worked and slept, and in whose overgrown courtyard she was photographed smiling joyfully, she found not the piano that Sand and Maurice finally secured at the docks (which remained for a long time in the possession of Madame Canut's family), but instead the instrument made by Juan Bauza in his workshop in Calle de la Misión. It had sat there, probably barely touched, for over seventy years.

It belonged to Lorenzo Pascual Tortella, a local doctor who had grown up in Buger, a tiny municipality forty kilometres north of Palma. Tortella had bought the piano from the Lapenas, a Majorcan family who traditionally spent the summer months in cell number four and who sold all the fixtures and fittings to him when they gave it up. The piano 'aroused in me an emotion and an interest easy to understand,' Landowska later told Ganche. 'I would have liked to carry away the relic.' But Tortella rebuffed her offer, so the best Landowska could do was instruct a friend in Sóller to buy it if ever Tortella changed his mind.

It was more than a relic to Landowska. Much later – in Paris, following the world war that would unfold three years after her visit to Majorca – she scribbled notes for an article on Chopin and the Preludes, rehearsing Sand's arguments about No. 15. 'One day George Sand went out, Chopin stayed alone at the Carthusian monastery listening to the monotonous drops of the falling rain. ~~The night was falling. GS didn't reappear.~~ In the middle of this groaning storm, in the dark and solitary mystic's cell . . .'

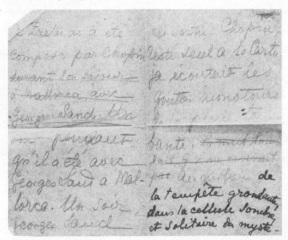

To Landowska, the Preludes and this piano were bound together, each historical object illuminating the other. 'As a matter of fact,' she told Ganche, revealing how the Bauza instrument became part of her collection, 'sometime afterwards, in May 1913, I learned from my friends in Majorca that the piano so much coveted was mine.'

She wasted no time arranging for its transportation to the late-century *Altbau* she shared with her husband Henri Lew. He was the 'zionist and folklorist' (as she later described him in *Who's Who*) whom she had married in May 1900 and lived with successively in Paris's seventeenth, eighth and fifth *arrondissements*, before moving to Berlin for a new position as harpsichord teacher at the Hochschule für Musik. Lew thereafter fulfilled the roles of impresario, collaborator, co-author and travel companion.

A very young Alexander Binder photographed the piano inside their apartment soon after its arrival, in the same year he established his portrait-photography atelier in a cramped room on Motzstraße in Schöneberg. Binder was Jewish and a recent graduate of Munich's Lehr- und Versuchsanstalt für Photographie, Chemie, Lichtdruck und Gravüre (Teaching and Research Institute of Photography, Chemistry, Collotype and Engraving). He quickly established a glittering clientele, capturing with sympathy and technical flair a host of German dancers, singers, artists, musicians, and silent-film actors: they included Lucy Doraine, Lya de Putti, Reinhold Schünzel, Greta Garbo, Leni Riefenstahl, and the English pianist Harriet Cohen. Binder would die suddenly at forty, leaving his widow to run the studio, which in 1938 the Nazis closed without notice.

For his photographs of the apartment Binder used natural light to illuminate the couple's upper-middle-class furnishings and lifestyle: Persian rugs, chandeliers and ornaments, un-flashy artworks on every wall – to the right of the Pleyel harpsichord (which in 1913 had already accompanied her to Moscow and Majorca) a reworking of E. G. Haussmann's famous portrait of Bach, a little further away a sombre icon depicting a saint's coronation in heaven. The dining table is set for six, though could easily seat twelve: there is a forest of silver candlesticks, champagne in the ice bucket, decanters close to hand,

and place settings of heavy silverware, crystal glasses, bone china. There is a grand piano piled with scores, and a glass-fronted cabinet next to it storing others. The whole place displays the certain good taste of a prosperous, artistic couple in the deceptively secure years before the Great War: its furnishings *Jugendstil*, its shadows warm, its ambience calm. A live-in housekeeper, Elsa Schunicke, whom Landowska met in Berlin not long after Binder took his photographs, would soon keep the apartment in order.

Binder's portrait of Landowska at the Bauza piano – taken before Garbo was a client, Riefenstahl a subject, but with all the inspiration of his later work – shows his particular talent. He posed her as though a Greek statue or from a Roman frieze, using a reflector to illuminate her porcelain skin, the sharp texture of her braids, the deep-carved folds of her lustrous dress. Already in 1913, so early in their careers, Binder caught Landowska the commanding artist (as Delacroix had once captured Chopin) as she sat in profile beside her proudest acquisition, Chopin's piano from Majorca, the piano of the Preludes.

Almost everything we know about Bauza's instrument in these years comes from this photograph: its height; its compass; the rippled mahogany or hardwood of its case; the lattice-like inlay above the

keyboard and the exposed strip of whippens or stickers just visible below, looking like a row of teeth; the folding keyboard; the beading around the case; the lathed front legs; the name of its maker and his address in Palma. It is not much. At exactly the time Bauza built his piano Pleyel was recording in his firm's ledgers every step and sequence in the production of each instrument in his factory, ledgers that we can still read today. With Bauza's piano we have only Binder's photograph and Sand's unflattering description to go on.

Landowska was doubly lucky to acquire it: by 1911 Chopin was no longer a peripheral figure in Romantic music. He still resisted easy categorization, still did not fall simply into one of the understood narratives of Romanticism. Yet by the time of Landowska's Majorcan trip he was recognized as a great figure in nineteenth-century music; only Valldemossa's isolation had shielded such an important Chopin relic from public scrutiny.

Sergey Prokofiev, a piano and composition pupil in Saint Peters-burg during the first decade of the twentieth century, illustrated the extent of Chopin's transformation. 'They say you can't give a recital without Chopin?' he remarked. 'I'll prove that we can do quite well without Chopin.' (It is pretty difficult to be a piano major at college today without him.) The Preludes had evolved too, and no longer tot-tered unsteadily on their feet. In 1915 T. S. Eliot wrote 'Portrait of a Lady', a bleak poem about the thwarted friendship between a mean-spirited young man and an upper-class Bostonian woman of a certain age, who invites him back to her house after a lunchtime concert on a foggy December day, her salon lit by four candles (the mood that of Juliet's tomb, the narrator decides), and gently offers her thoughts on the music they had just heard:

> We have been, let us say, to hear the latest Pole
> Transmit the Preludes, through his hair and finger-tips.
> 'So intimate, this Chopin, that I think his soul
> Should be resurrected only among friends –
> Some two or three, who will not touch the bloom
> That is rubbed and questioned in the concert room.'

Proust traces a similar line in *Du côté de chez Swann*, published the year of Binder's photographs (though set in the first decade of the

French Third Republic). He writes of a salon in the fashionable Paris home of Madame de Saint-Euverte, at which a young pianist is playing:

> When he had finished the Liszt Intermezzo and had begun a Prelude by Chopin, Mme de Cambremer turned to Mme de Franquetot with a tender smile, full of intimate reminiscence, as well as of satisfaction (that of a competent judge) with the performance. She had been taught in her girlhood to fondle and cherish those long-necked, sinuous creatures, the phrases of Chopin, so free, so flexible, so tactile, which begin by seeking their ultimate resting-place somewhere beyond and far wide of the direction in which they started, the point which one might have expected them to reach, phrases which divert themselves in those fantastic bypaths only to return more deliberately – with a more premeditated reaction, with more precision, as on a crystal bowl which, if you strike it, will ring and throb until you cry aloud in anguish – to clutch at one's heart.

It is not at all a bad description of Chopin's craft. It does not matter that Madame Cambremer's daughter-in-law, sitting some distance from her, is a passionate Wagnerian, who feels positively ill when she hears Chopin. Nor that Proust held the same low opinion he gave Crambremer's daughter-in-law, describing Chopin in his notebooks as an ailing, self-centred dandy, a great artist who in his music unfolded an intimate aspect of his mind, only to break in on it with another, provoking a spectacular collision of thoughts and images, which to his thinking pointed to a sick heart and solemn introspection. It does not even really matter that Proust was grafting a later response to Chopin – the response he himself formulated in Paris only in the 1890s and 1900s – on to an earlier period: it was all he knew. It does matter that by the time Landowska acquired the Chopin piano, the man and the music he composed on it were ubiquitous.

In 1913, the year in which Binder took his photographs and Proust launched his masterpiece, Landowska directed her thoughts to the musician who had composed astounding music on the old ship's piano she had obtained. Her published articles were never as quick-fire as her journal entries. She began them with the same bursts of energy and thought: scribbling ideas on scraps of paper (like

Lichtenberg), leaving gaps she knew she had to fill and how to fill them, all the sort of shorthand that busy, clever people use every day. Yet as she worked at them for publication, her explicatory prose almost inevitably dammed this attractive stream of consciousness.

celui qui joue
Ch. trop vite
ne comprend rien
à son écriture, si
intense, nourrie
de Bach. Prenons l'é-
tude en fa mineur,
moderato expressif
et juxtaposons à
une intention de
Bach. Ou l'impromp-
tu en Sol bémol –
(autres exemples)

'How Chopin Played Chopin', which the *Musical Standard* published in March 1913, is a good piece on an important topic. Landowska was confidently stepping on to Rubinstein's and Huneker's territory – where she had been a few times before. Five years earlier, as the centenary of Chopin's birth loomed and a year before she performed in the Palais du Trocadéro's festival, she wrote 'The Work of Chopin and its Interpretation' for a French publication, quoting approvingly a line from Niecks's biography of 1890: 'The interpretation of the modern virtuosos does not resemble what was dreamed of by Chopin!' She spells out her reasons. 'If you place before a good musician a work unknown to him,' she begins gently, 'he will play it according to his own ideas.' But place before this same good musician a work by Beethoven or Chopin, then 'he will play just as it was taught to him by his master; and the more competent he is in his profession the more carefully does he follow tradition, the more sensitive his spirit, the more deeply fixed in his soul remain the offerings of the great masters as he heard them from his childhood up.' If Chopin were to rise from his plot in Père Lachaise, Landowska continues, and play his Ballades and Mazurkas, his Nocturnes and Impromptus, the response of audiences brought up on the performing tradition created by Liszt and Rubinstein, then perpetuated by their disciples, would be, ' "How beautiful that is! How beautiful!", we would say; "but it is not the real, not the true Chopin." '

Here and elsewhere she decried the muscularity of contemporary Chopin performances, of pianists crushing the music's fine-spun arabesques, soullessly transforming it into spasms of hysteria, jerky rubato, episodes of bad taste, sudden relapses into sweetness (honey would seem bitter in comparison!), and the heavy flight heavenward of leaden butterflies. It is the tirade of a serious and proud Pole, grateful for the lineage that connects her – through Michałowski and Mikuli – to a Chopin tradition more authentic than anything currently on show. 'The Chopin of the young generation of pianists has no longer any freshness of appearance because they see him through the playing of all his more or less famous interpreters.'

In *Le Monde musical* a Monsieur de Bertha disputed her claim that Chopin was purely a Polish composer, pointing out that his father had been born in Lorraine, no less. In response Landowska traced Chopin's family back to his Polish great-grandfather, the man who established Ferrand et Chopin wine merchants in Nancy in the early eighteenth century, changing his surname from Szop to facilitate local trade. She underlined that in his written French, Chopin stuck to the rhythms and cadences of Polish, and suggested even the least of his works was impregnated with a fierce nostalgia for the landscape of his homeland, then as in 1915 partitioned under Russian rule. 'M. de Bertha says: "Chopin is great enough, and versatile enough to be shared alike by France and Poland." But we are not so magnanimous! Three times our land has been subjected to geographical division, and we could only stand still and suffer. Now we hope to be more fortunate in defending our claim upon the unique genius of a Chopin.' In reply Bertha asked Landowska to concede that Paris at least supplied Chopin with favourable ground for the nourishment of his genius, that

foreign artists in the capital and their supporters ought to show gratitude for the warmth of the city's embrace. Auguste Mangeot, the son
of a piano maker and editor of *Le Monde musical*, swatted away
Bertha's arguments: it was Paris that should be indebted to Chopin for
what he gave it, both during his fragile life and thereafter.

Landowska's pedigree and nationality were not the only things
that made her write this way. Her aim as a musician, she said, was to
immerse herself fully in the life and music of any composer she played,
regardless of nationality; so long as she penetrated his spirit, moved
with fluency in his world and heart, she would locate without effort
Mozart's good humour, Handel's great joy. And Chopin's essence
too. Later she would say something to Pablo Casals about Bach that
would cling to her thenceforth, painting her as haughty, brittle, pig-
headed. Having heard her play and expressed his appreciation, Casals
asked why she executed certain trills from the upper note. Landowska
told him her reasons, showing him passages on eighteenth-century
trills in her original edition of Leopold Mozart's *Violinschule*, though
without moderating Casals's scepticism. 'My dear Pau,' she finally
said to him with a smile, 'continue to play Bach *your* way and I, *his*
way.' At which point they laughed and the conversation changed
tack. The words haunted her, though, the anecdote havered about by
those who intended her ill.

All student musicians (and virtuoso soloists too) must ask these
questions when faced with unfamiliar music and notation, ideas and
rhetoric. Yet in the early 1900s the problems posed were greater than
today. The scores that Landowska played contained a long-lost language, and she was one of the few philologists willing to tackle it. She
translated harmonic gestures and parsed articulation and ornament.
Should this flourish be played on the beat or off it? Before or after?
Or (as harpsichordist Skip Sempé thinks she ultimately decided) what
if there was no beat? And in this moment, this decision, she discovered a sense of scholarly freedom, which shaped her ideas
about improvisation in these early scores and convinced her of the
need for greater fluidity in performance.

From there it was only a short distance to Chopin, whom she har-
nessed to Couperin for their habit of moving the third finger over the
fourth in certain passages, Chopin giving Couperin's trick currency

in a new century, liberating musicians raised on Kalkbrenner's strict methods and disapproving eye. They had an even greater bond, Landowska thought: both used written-out ornamentation in their scores to re-create a sense of improvisation. ('Chopin', she would write on another occasion, 'the great improvisor – can't bear it if one changes the slightest note when playing his works.') She was thinking of chords crossed by lightning flashes of passing notes; rich melismas; lively arabesques – ideas that imbued the music with a suppleness, an element of surprise, a sense of spontaneity. They created melodic lines that stretch on and on, she wrote – 'sustained soliloquies pregnant with thoughts and interrupted by caesuras'. It could be Madame Crambremer writing.

This was Landowska's concern with how pianists played Chopin in the early twentieth century: they appeared to understand neither the soliloquies nor their interruptions. Instead they cleaved to structure over spontaneity, harmonic rhetoric over melodic freedom, power over intimacy. 'It is an actual fact that the present-day interpretation of Chopin's works, because of a distorted romanticism and an acrobatic virtuosity, has absolutely departed from the intentions of the delicate, sensitive composer.'

14

Berlin, Paris,
Saint-Leu-la-Forêt, 1914–27

The calm cloaking Binder's photographs did not last. When war broke out in August 1914 Landowska and Lew, both Polish nationals, were detained as civilians on parole. Their homeland would soon become a slaughterhouse, caught in the middle as German soldiers moved eastward, Russian troops westward. Landowska was allowed to keep her position at the Hochschüle, but travel and other rights were restricted. They were relatively fortunate. Many Poles working in Germany when hostilities began, or caught there on holiday, or finished at university but remaining in the country to enjoy the lakes and sunshine, the cafés and freedom, were interred in detention camps – at Ruhleben, say, on the outskirts of Berlin. A shantytown hastily erected on a former racing track, it was home to over 5,000 prisoners of war, some of them British, most of them for the duration.

In her journal Landowska charted the uncertainty and danger, clutching at the few straws offered her. At the end of November she pasted in a newspaper clipping, underlining a sentence in which an official put forward his proposed resolution of the crisis: *France and Germany reconciled, and as friends work jointly on cultural projects; it seemed to him that this joint effort will surely attain the apex of human culture.* It was a desperate attempt at entente, a characteristic assessment of European national primacy, and a grim rehearsal for the claims of German cultural supremacy in the period 1933–45.

On the same day she and Henri were surprised at dinner by an intelligence officer, who accused them of using their apartment as a meeting place for Russian dissidents. They showed him their papers and answered his questions. He asked Landowska to prove her professional claims – motivated, he told her (in yet another foreshadowing of the war to come), by nothing more than his love of music. She played him some Handel and he left satisfied, though the encounter unsettled both her and her husband.

They were in an impossibly vexing position: the hated Russian Empire was at war with Landowska's adopted country, which had made them civil prisoners. 'The Germans want to liberate us [Poles] from the Russian yoke,' she wrote in December 1914, the war just four months old. 'The Russians are unwilling to permit our falling under the German boot; while Austria wants to give us an Archduke. They growl over us, tearing us apart; we are dismembered, worse, yes, worse than ever before, and the Kingdom itself is no more.'

She captured this confusion so well, squirrelling away on each page the tiny scraps of newspaper clippings she foraged as the weeks and months passed. She writes of more humane weaponry in France; aerial bombardment; explosive devices modelled on the armoury of anarchists; the terrible consequence of gas warfare, then unknown to the German populace. She analyses the make-up of the Russian army, how the Polish, Armenian, Georgian, Finnish and Jewish recruits have no interest in Russia's victory, how they recognized the insanity of laying down their lives without knowing why. She writes how the Busonis were leaving for the States with no enthusiasm for capitalist America, just a desire to escape the depressing atmosphere of Berlin and a war Busoni detested. She relates sceptically information she is told by a man she meets, quite by chance, that German soldiers were surviving on a diet of bread and hay, unsure as she is whether this would be a good thing or a bad thing.

Yet for all the political uncertainties and confusion, Landowska remained clear-sighted about cultural matters. She attended conductor Siegfried Ochs's performance of Emil von Reznicek's Symphony 'Friede' (Peace). 'It sounded poor, empty, fatally noisy and loud. Some music. Everyone about us was horrified by it. If this is "Friede" then we might as well have war.' She thought Ochs's conducting of Bach's Mass in B Minor clumsy, the choirs too loud, the orchestra heavy and churlish. 'It is like attending a showing of calves: noise and from time to time a sound that sounds reasonable, and, again a murmur here and there.' Trying on hats and looking at dresses made by a German acquaintance, she was horrified at the determination to hold on to pre-war notions of elegance and taste. 'After the war, conditions will be altered and, once again, models will be imported from Paris, just as it should be, as, for example, tea from China.' There was in any case something sour in their charade. 'At present only two models seem fitting for a woman in our day: the funereal for those who have lost a loved one; and a very simple type of costume for those who still await their tragic moment to come.' In such ways Landowska and Lew, in the comfort of the apartment Binder had photographed so well, survived the war.

Landowska's own tragic moment came soon after it. European capitals on the eve of the war still looked much like the Paris caught in a photograph of 1909 or 1910 of the Boulevard des Capucines, near the rue de la Paix: a chaotic melange of buses, pedestrians, automobiles, tradesmen with barrows, and horse-drawn carriages, all vying for precedence, lanes and rules nowhere to be seen. Nothing much had changed since Baudelaire wrote in *Paris Spleen* of his 'terror of horses and vehicles' as he had his hero cross 'the boulevard in a great hurry, splashing through the mud in the midst of a seething chaos, and with death galloping at me from every side'. A degree of regulation came with the peace, but it came too late for poor Henri Lew: in April 1919 he was hit and killed by a car, caught out by the fast-evolving rhythms of urban life.

Landowska drafted telegrams in French and German, writing of her grief and nostalgia, which she said she would keep at bay in the company of her old friends Bach, Mozart and Rameau, and her Pleyel harpsichord too. And then she buried herself in work: concerts, teaching, writing. She obtained a passport from the new Republika Polska, a country reconstituted at last at the Versailles Peace Conference, which listed her height as average, her face oval, her hair and eyes black, her profession *musicienne*.

It soon contained a string of stamps and visas: Berne at the end of October 1919; Amsterdam in early November, then Boncourt;

Lugano on the 18th; Basel two days later for a performance of Bach's St Matthew Passion, the first time in the twentieth century that the harpsichord was used as continuo; Lugano once more; Delle at the end of December. Then, with a *Visé à Paris* in her passport, she set up home once more in the French capital, again with her housekeeper Schunicke, this time in the eighteenth *arrondissement*. She taught privately and in Basel, and at the new École Normale de Musique, which Cortot and Landowska's gallant ally, Auguste Mangeot, had founded in 1918.

Landowska was expunging tragedy through travel. She toured Spain, England also, and then, in 1923, leaving from the port of Le Havre on board the three-funnelled *Paris*, America for performances with Leopold Stokowski and the Philadelphia Orchestra, and for her first recordings. On a return trip three years later she was photographed in the Armor Room of the Cleveland Museum of Art, a serene and imperious figure in dark, dowdy 1920s' clothing, light gloves, a fashionable cloche hat, standing incongruously next to an armoured horse and rider. It was a thrilling time for her – the bedding down of her international career as a scholar and performer, the promise of her pre-war talent now recognized on several continents.

ÉCOLE DE MUSIQUE ANCIENNE
DE
WANDA LANDOWSKA
SAINT-LEU-LA-FORÊT
(S. & O. FRANCE)

It was in these years of loss and frenetic touring that she had her most inspired idea. She bought a villa in Saint-Leu-la-Forêt, twenty kilometres north of the centre of Paris, and in 1927 built in the gardens a small concert hall seating eighty, a hundred at a push. The architect Jean-Charles Moreux worked to her exacting brief: in conversations and letters Landowska specified the size, materials, position, acoustic, portico and innovative suspended glass roof, which would bathe the interior in natural light during the long daylight hours of the summer months, and the low stage, which would encourage intimacy between performers and audiences. This hall and the annual summer school she planned to run from it would allow her to work with rare concentration – not solely as a scholar, performer and teacher, but as a gramophone artist too: the age of electrical recording had begun.

Landowska inaugurated the hall on 3 July 1927, playing on harpsichord and piano (her *confrère* Cortot, photographed with her that day in front of the portico, played piano only) works by Chambonnières, Pasquini, Couperin, Rameau, Bach and Mozart. Her harpsichord and Pleyel grand were on the small stage, but she positioned other instruments – a cabinet organ, a clavichord, a table keyboard, the Bauza piano – along the walls of the auditorium. They were in perfect working order, each able to unlock some magical aspect of the music played on it: the weight of the keys, the quality of the sound, the speed of the action all shaped Landowska's thinking.

In the twelve summers that followed, Landowska's *salle* was host to the most exciting developments in early music anywhere in the world. Renowned musicians – Arthur Honegger, Jacques Ibert, Vladimir Horowitz and Francis Poulenc (touchlingly photographed by Schunicke at a session with Landowska on his *Concert champêtre*) – came to perform and listen, pupils to study, audiences to observe. She attracted writers too, and painters and sculptors: Edith Wharton, Paul Valéry and Aristide Maillol became friends. Hart Crane described Paris in 1929 as a city of 'dinners, soirées, poets, erratic millionaires, painters, translations, lobsters, absinthe, music, promenades, oysters, sherry, aspirin, pictures, Sapphic heiresses, editors, books, sailors': many of these also found refuge in Saint-Leu-la-Forêt. The most vibrant voices in French Modernism in the interwar years were drawn not exclusively to the work of their colleagues and competitors, but to the music of the seventeenth and eighteenth centuries, served up by this serious, solicitous artist with mesmerizing talent and ideas.

Inventories of the collection in Saint-Leu-la-Forêt list a sixteenth-century Italian harpsichord (the painting on the inside lid attributed to Verrocchio); another detailed with tooled leather; several table pianos and clavichords, one of them by Ruckers, its keys ivory and boxwood, the interior lid decorated with a pastoral scene of musicians playing seventeenth-century instruments; a zither; a spinet; Bauza's *pianino*, and more besides. Landowska also built up a vast library in these years – nearly every book written on music from the sixteenth to twentieth centuries – which included a complete Bach-Gesellschaft, the first volume published two years after Chopin's death, the last (and forty-sixth) in the year Landowska and Lew moved to Paris, the whole collection a phenomenal achievement of nineteenth-century music scholarship and a key component in the Bach revival.

Yet in no sense was Landowska an antiquarian, a collector of curiosities. She bought books not for their rarity or beauty, instruments not as talking points or objects of sentimental value: this was a living collection, one part of it feeding into the next, the whole lot begetting recordings, concerts, articles, masterclasses, performing traditions, and whole new swathes of repertory. Music collecting had none of the wild currency and speculation of art collecting in these years, spurred on by the genius of art dealers like the Englishman Joseph Duveen, who, having noticed the wide-eyed wonderment of rich Americans in galleries and museums throughout Europe, set to work on an almost limitless market, a vulture in the warm gusts above Paris ready to swoop in at the slightest opportunity. Even great string instruments were not yet nearly as expensive as they would become. Music collecting was dowdy, antiquarian, worthy: it was not beautiful or valuable. There had probably never been as much cultural speculation as there was in Paris in the 1920s, yet it did not bleed into music; it left Landowska entirely untouched as she went about her own collecting, on her very own *voyage dans l'antiquité*.

But it also strained her relationship with the movement that had shaped her, which is why she felt so protective of Chopin. 'To judge Romanticism,' she would later say, improvising her ideas into a dictation machine (perfectly catching her speech patterns and quirks of thought):

we must first silence the sentimental jeremiads and all that stupid crowds misunderstood for true Romanticism. We must let the voice of the most authentic Romanticist, Chopin, pour out in all its purity. In short, there is Romanticism, and there is this foam produced by fatuous agitators who contributed in transforming a movement, very beautiful in itself, into an unintelligible and turbid jargon . . . Let us not forget the contempt of Lully's contemporaries for the polyphonic works of the Renaissance, and let us keep from making the same mistake about authentic Romanticism.

She was arguing, once more, to preserve Chopin's post-Classical lineage, to sever his links with the bloated excesses of what Romanticism had become in the second half of the century: the ecstasies and flights of fancy, the strong emotions and big-boned performances.

Landowska did not engage with these late-Romantic traditions. She chose instead to mount an argument she knew she could win, one in which she would not be shouted down by entrenched traditions, or by the interested parties that maintained a stranglehold on the repertory on which she had been raised and, for the most part, had left behind. 'I had to struggle against the Romantic movement then in full sway,' she would later write of her early decades in the profession, 'a movement which flaunted contempt for the music of the past.' Unlike great virtuoso pianists of the day, she refused to be locked into the nineteenth century, refused to be defined by an instrument that was the embodiment of musical Romanticism (though she remained a dependable ally of the repertory that had ossified along with it). Arguably this quality is what made her seem so modern to those painters and writers who visited her in Saint-Leu-la-Forêt and who, in their respective disciplines, had also moved beyond the thrall and clutches of late-nineteenth-century Romanticism.

15

Saint-Leu-la-Forêt, Paris, 1926–32

From her year-round lessons and summer courses at the École de Musique Ancienne de Wanda Landowska – 'On the Performance of the Masters of the 17th and 18th Centuries' and other such themes – Landowska left a rich paper trail, her adoring assistants transcribing and typing up her teaching notes, each student's file thickening as the summer months passed. Her pupils included Clifford Curzon, who would later include almost no Chopin in his repertory but would have his gentle way with Mozart and Schubert, successfully adapting for piano Landowska's inventive legato fingering; Curzon's wife, Lucille Wallace; Ralph Kirkpatrick, who would take over from Landowska her pioneering love of Scarlatti – not least in his chronological catalogue of the 555 sonatas; and a young French harpsichordist, Denise Restout, only seventeen in 1933 when she first came to Saint-Leu-la-Forêt, who quickly became one of those adoring assistants, thereafter rarely leaving Landowska's side.

Kirkpatrick was in Europe in 1931–2 on a travelling scholarship, studying with Landowska, Paul Brunold and Nadia Boulanger, very much a wolf among the trusting, timid sheep at Saint-Leu-la-Forêt. Landowska liked him as a musician – for a while, at least – this ambitious, young New Englander, with his deep knowledge and love of repertory she had made her own, startling in someone coming so far from where it was composed.

He was not so sure. 'Holy jumping cats, what am I getting into,' he wrote in his journal on first meeting his fellow students in October 1931, alarmed by the 'hocus pocusness of the atmosphere and the general spirit of "Isn't this old music just lovely. And nobody can play it but Landowska!"' And then, 'Some time later came a hush, and Landowska entered. She is a sort of combination of Mrs. Landowsky, the pawnbroker's wife, and Wanda, daughter of Henry VIII, sister of Mary and Elizabeth. I shook her hand, which she withdrew quickly, and said, "Oh, be careful. My harpsichord hand!" However, she was very nice in a sort of come-into-the-parlor-Red-Riding-Hood way.'

It is a Marx Brothers farce, Margaret Dumont as Landowska, and hardly convincing, except that Kirkpatrick never greatly modified his initial impression. He thought the lessons too inconsistent: illuminating one day, a waste of time the next. He hated the Pleyel instruments, which he dismissed as no more in tune than a mousetrap. And he was seeing other teachers behind her back, which made him think of the line by Montaigne about how it is the liar who deserves pity, not the honest man, owing to the list of fabrications and prevarications he must remember.

But there really were illuminating lessons. Working with Kirkpatrick on Bach's Prelude and Fugue in G from the first book of the *Wohltemperierte Klavier*, Landowska quickly dispatched the Prelude ('Don't do an old maid's *ritardando*, but a nice race-horse stop') so as to concentrate on the tangle of a fugue. This was a pastoral coda to the victorious universality of the Prelude, she told him, before gleefully dissecting the inversion of the theme, picking out Bach's scraps and hints of the bucolic melody that would soon emerge. She showed Kirkpatrick how the climax presaged the overture to Wagner's *Meistersinger*, of all things. And she emphasized the inherent problems of musical character, how Bach initially depicts an uncomplicated idyll, yet, as the fugue progresses, transforms the mood into something erotic, then victorious, then human, then superhuman. It was an unabashedly Nietzschean free-fall into one of Bach's great keyboard fugues, a piece that ends like a clock winding down, performer and listener a little uncertain about what has just transpired. And it was thrilling teaching.

There were times too when Kirkpatrick admired her playing. In May 1932, in the 'abominable acoustics' of the new Salle Pleyel, she performed a Haydn piano sonata and harpsichord concerto very well, he thought, though she 'glided on and off the stage for bows as if she were on wheels, walking with arms tight at her sides, reminding me of Mrs. Lowell's saying that on the stage she always looked like a trained seal'. On another occasion he was struck by the way she demonstrated a Haydn sonata in a lesson. 'I have never heard any-thing like it in the world. She is certainly a pure genius when it comes to Haydn and Mozart. One is inclined to forgive her character when with one phrase, she can transport an audience into a perfect para-dise.' But there were other times when he found her mannered, uninspired, her sound resembling not so much a well-tempered clavi-chord as a well-bred typewriter. Nonetheless, she got him to take his technique more seriously – a technique he had more or less invented himself – and she spoke insightfully about how to apply it to the music he brought to each class.

At one point during Madame de Saint-Euverte's soirée in Proust's great novel the Duchesse du Guermantes turns to Charles Swann and says, 'It ends just in time, but it ends badly.' So it was with Kirkpatrick and Landowska. He spoke about her out of school once too often, which got back to her, causing pain and indignation. In the confrontation that followed she said to him (so he writes) with laughable pompos-ity, 'How can you expect to comprehend the mystery and complication of that phenomenon which is Wanda Landowska?' Visiting a new teacher, Eta Harich-Schneider, in Germany early the following year, Kirkpatrick learned of a letter Landowska had written demanding that Harich-Schneider prevent him from playing in public. 'He looks nice and harmless,' her letter stated, 'but he is a narrow and conceited impudent upstart.'

Landowska was probably taken aback by Kirkpatrick's decision to play Bach's complete *Goldberg Variations* in a concert in Germany in late January 1933, three months before she gave her first public per-formance of the piece. It was then virtually unknown repertory, which Landowska would popularize later the same year in her record-ing for His Master's Voice – a poised, personal set of discs (the first ever of the complete work), her score a crosshatch of lines scattering the notes between fingers and keyboards, voices shared in impressive and imaginative contortions of the hand, articulation and regis-tration rich and varied, the whole performance unfolding with gentle grandeur and almost unbearable tension.

In 1932 teacher and pupil would have known they were shadowing each other, Landowska and Kirkpatrick simultaneously working on this staggering and difficult set of variations, but not in each other's

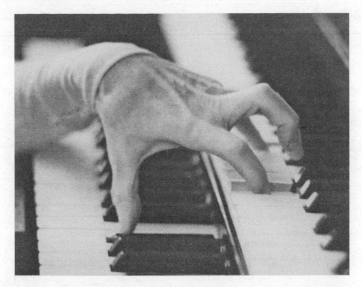

presence, not in classes or lessons, the piece an unspoken bond or source of friction between them. Their relationship was far more complex than either her teaching notes or his journal could ever capture.

Kirkpatrick's time in Europe inspired a series of fine and funny thumbnail sketches of some of the great figures in contemporary music, not just of Landowska. There are descriptions of Nadia Boulanger ('she looks like the geometry teacher in a middle west high school'); Stravinsky ('a slim sleek fellow in sweater and plus-fours, looking from a distance for all the world like a soda clerk in an ice cream parlour'); Dolmetsch ('Mr Dolmetsch plays the violin, descant viol, recorder, lute, harpsichord, all about equally badly'). They are a little like Picasso's caricatures in the previous three decades: quickly dispatched and hugely unfair, yet containing something recognizable.

Yet Kirkpatrick's response to the two most renowned Chopin pianists between the wars, Jan Paderewski and Alfred Cortot, offers more than mere caricature: he caught a key aspect of Chopin's performance history in France in the 1930s, one largely unexplored in Saint-Leu-la-Forêt. Attending a Chopin recital in June 1932, Kirkpatrick despaired at Paderewski's 'exaggerated romantic mannerisms' and distressing lack of strength and control, the fistfuls of wrong notes, the once-refined playing robbed by age, his concentration on pianism at the expense of music. 'It also seemed regrettable to see an old artist who ought to possess a marvellous mature serenity as a result of age vainly trying to warm over the unrest and romantic passions which make much of Chopin essentially the music of youth.'

Certainly by this time Paderewski could no longer play as before: he was seventy-one, his short term (1919) as Poland's Prime Minister and Minister of Foreign Affairs – awarded him in recognition of his wartime contribution to the campaign for Polish independence – more than a decade behind him. Many thought even then that his best years had passed. Paderewski had played Chopin all his life, of course, yet between the wars, in these early years of Polish nationhood, his Chopin performances attained deeper significance: they represented cultural equilibrium, a form of reparation. The Italian writer and journalist Curzio Malaparte witnessed the modern origins of this phenomenon when in Paderewski's year as premier he visited Warsaw's Brühl Palace (destroyed in 1944) and heard him play the Preludes. Afterwards he wrote touchingly of 'Paderewski's ghostly face, bathed in tears'.

Landowska admired how inextricably Paderewski was linked with Polish nationhood. 'Paderewski's art was as complete as his great nature,' she wrote in 1951 on the tenth anniversary of his death. 'Whether he spoke or played it was always with the same language, that of a proud and fearless soul. His passionate phrasing, his thoroughbred touch, the vehemence of his tempi, the nobility of his rubati, so profoundly Polish, were but a continuation of his speech.' Elsewhere she recalled with pleasure the oration he gave in what is now the city of Lviv in commemoration of the hundredth anniversary of Chopin's birth, how Paderewski spoke of Chopin the poet, magician and monarch, lifting up all social classes by his genius. 'It is thus that we hear in Chopin the voice of our whole race,' she remembered him saying, speaking without notes. 'It is thus that the greatest of men is neither above nor beyond his nation. He is the seed of it, the particle, the flower, the ear of wheat.' But Kirkpatrick either did not recognize or could not concede the significance of this aspect of Paderewski's character and affiliation with Chopin; the playing was all.

He was only slightly more generous about Cortot. Observing a class in Paris, Kirkpatrick was impressed by Cortot's manners, clarity of thought, sensibility, and the courteous way he treated his pupils as they played and discussed various Beethoven sonatas. He did not think Cortot's conception altogether matched that of Beethoven, however: there was something superficial in his approach, he decided – a hole in the sauce, a chef would say. 'His art, like most French music, seems a hothouse product, delicately flourishing in one corner of the human spirit, with none of the wholehearted surge of German music, nor the roots in the soil of popular dance and song.' It was an old argument, older even than the Romantic century that had initiated it: the great structuralist Germans versus the whimsical French (Huneker's attack at the turn of the century). It almost pained Kirkpatrick to rehearse this idea in his journal, so impressed was he by the way Cortot talked about Beethoven (in beautiful, refined French), yet so disappointed was he by the way he played him.

Kirkpatrick did not hear Cortot play the Preludes, which is both a shame and a surprise, for by the early 1930s they were more or less his exclusive territory, at least as far as the French public was concerned. Cortot had for some time performed the set complete in concert, a primacy he reinforced in 1926 with the release of his own edition of the work, with its careful fingering, phrasing and explications, which take up a page or so between each Prelude. In this edition Cortot also retraced von Bülow's steps, though with a more pessimistic heart, allocating to the Preludes titles that stressed illness and death as much as love and romance: 'Beside a grave' (No. 4); 'Prophetic voices' (No. 9); 'But Death is there, in the shadows . . .' (No. 15); 'The race to the abyss' (No. 16); 'Funeral' (No. 20); 'Blood, Passion and Death' (No. 24).

Cortot's interpretative advice was similarly laced with such imagery. 'Now, after a short and formidable silence, comes the dull thud of three muffled chords, which seem to gaze upon eternity from the threshold of an open tomb' – this for the cadence that ends No. 4, which Chopin employs to lever himself out of a tight harmonic spot. Even the miraculous middle bars of No. 13 he interprets as a maudlin dirge. 'It is a heart heavy with tears and regrets which finally reveals itself. Secret tears, regrets still breathing the happy ardour of the memories which inspire them, a feeling which touches the extreme limits of delicate sensibility, but whose nostalgia is all the more irresistible for the softness, the resignation, of its accent.'

The Polish pianist Arthur Rubinstein – one of the most renowned Chopin interpreters in the second half of the twentieth century – thought Cortot played this way because the idea of 'Chopin as the weak tubercular artist was still in public favour'. But there was something even more to it than the old trope of Chopin's sickliness shaping the music as he composed it; delicacy and sickliness were to govern interpretation too, Cortot seemed to be saying, his performances the guardian of a very weak flame. Such thinking helps explain Cortot's interpretative tack in his numerous recordings of the Preludes in these years: in 1926 for the first time, put down in HMV's studio in Hayes, Middlesex; then once more in 1927; 1928 (twice); and again in 1933. He would revisit them one last time in Paris in 1942, with German soldiers everywhere on the streets.

In his first recording the Pleyel sounds a little hollow in the bass and boxy in the middle, and there are occasional flubs (editing would only now become possible, and indeed a high art) and moments of distortion; overall, though, it is a pretty good sonic picture of an instrument difficult enough to capture well today, let alone in the pioneering days of electrical recording. But what is immediately apparent in these discs is that Cortot's titles and doughy explicatory notes were not merely for show: he believed these whimsical panto-mime images and scenarios – the fevers and meditations, the perfume and snow, the stormy seas, star-lit heavens, the dancing Naiads, the sickness and death. In No. 17 he lets Chopin's clock die away rather than chime eleven, since he viewed the Prelude as 'the delight of an unhoped for avowal'. His entry to the shimmering interior world in No. 13 is blazoned with a thumping great knock on the door, Cho-pin's subtlety and magic never more elusive. And the end of Sand's storm in No. 15 – the return of the gentler plops of rain on the mon-astery roof, or the stones in the garden, or on Chopin's chest – is forecast in a very loud voice.

It was at least a corrective to the Anton Rubinstein school of playing, and would earn Landowska's approval on these grounds alone. Yet there are still too many departures from the rhetorical effects Chopin stitched into the score and discussed with his pupils; next to Koczalski it seems all too obvious, hand-signals at every turn. This recording, however, and those that followed in 1933 and 1942, was quickly acknowledged as a twentieth-century benchmark. In these decades, as radio and gramophone fast achieved a wider reach and, in key ways, vied with the established authority and lineage of great masters and teachers (and of national schools of interpretation too), Cortot's discs exerted an enormous influence on how the Preludes were heard and played.

16

Saint-Leu-la-Forêt, Paris, Banyuls-sur-Mer, 1933–40

Hitler was appointed Chancellor of Germany on 30 January 1933 and two months later implemented a boycott of Jewish businesses and goods. By the end of the year more than 20,000 Germans had fled to France, escaping their splintering country, a number repeated each year until the end of the decade. They were wealthy or penniless, eminent or anonymous, though until 1938 – until the Anschluss, the German annexation of Czechoslovakia and the bloody recriminations of Kristallnacht – only a third of them were Jewish.

Neither their relatively small number nor their achievements prevented the re-emergence of the anti-Semitism that had remained a component of French intellectual life after the Dreyfus affair; at best it had been papered over, the paste none too strong. 'Paris has become the New Zion,' wrote the French author Paul Morand. 'First one, then ten, then a hundred, then fifty thousand' – the last figure more or less the number of Jewish refugees who would indeed make their way to France from Germany by the end of the decade.

Many of these émigrés were or would become distinguished artists: Bertold Brecht, Heinrich Mann, Walter Benjamin, Hannah Arendt and Arthur Koestler were just some who made France their home after Hitler's ascendancy to the position of Chancellor. ('Writers in abrupt exile,' Sybille Bedford labelled them plaintively, 'moved by revulsion, foresight and their sense of honour.') Their arrival triggered a cultural boom, an irony surely lost on the regime they had fled: almost 400 books by exiled writers were translated into French by the end of 1939. Exiled musicians integrated themselves into the Paris scene as best they could; opportunities were not limitless, but there was a common language, which helped all concerned overlook long-standing differences in style, tradition and artistic temperament, for a while anyway. Besides, these writers and musicians were part of an international constituency that for a century had treated Paris as its headquarters: they expected sympathy from their peers, even when, as the decade progressed and the national temperature cooled somewhat, the words 'Jew' and 'refugee' became synonymous.

They were certainly not missed back home, these artists and intellectuals, these dissenters and Jews. In a jerking-marionette speech at the opening of Munich's Haus der Kunst in July 1937, Hitler fulminated against artists who attempted to paint outside nature and promised that the courts and medical profession would intervene if good taste did not, the audience looking on politely askance, having not even yet encountered the kitsch inside the gallery. 'We will, from now on, lead an unrelenting war of purification, an unrelenting war of extermination, against the last elements which have displaced our Art.' As either warning or glance into the abyss, the *Entartete Kunst* exhibition opened a few days later, the improvised gallery's walls and floors lined haphazardly with the work of Dix and Baumeister, Kirchner and Schlemmer, and with other 'Jewish trash that no words can adequately describe' (as the catalogue put it), clumsy graffiti and sloppy labelling slapped on the walls to underline the intrinsically degenerate quality of it all.

There was opportunity in uncertainty, of course. German dealers needing to rid themselves of decadent art were met by French and American dealers with a good eye and no political baggage, happy enough to take it off their hands for a decent price or a prescient exchange. Such opportunism would go on quite late: Peggy Guggenheim came to Paris in 1940 vowing to buy a picture a day, leaving the capital only when the Germans started bombing the city's outskirts, having just convinced a panicked Brancusi to sell her *Bird in Space*. National Socialists soon recognized the commercial potential of such transactions, particularly Hermann Göring, who generally failed to distinguish between those transactions undertaken on behalf of the Reich and those on behalf of his own collection. The degenerate art purged from Germany's galleries by so-called confiscation committees – some 16,000 pieces, stored in a warehouse on Berlin's Kopernikusstraße – would be sold off to foreign dealers or exchanged for sanctioned works of art. Paying a peppercorn sum, Göring acquired a number of paintings from the Nationalgalerie collection – pieces by Munch, Marc, Cézanne and van Gogh – and had his agent sell them abroad at market rate, allowing him to indulge in purchases of Old Masters and tapestries for his own collection.

Although only a short distance from central Paris, Landowska was isolated from the capital's social and cultural shifts. She was aware of the sharp-changing winds – who would not be? – but considered her long-standing French residency, her fame and occupation, protection enough. In 1938 she took the extra precaution of obtaining French citizenship, nervous of what might befall Polish nationals if the storm clouds broke, memories of Berlin in 1914 remaining strong. With this one act she was secure, she reasoned: she was a Catholic in a nominally secular country, a 'sweet little Jewess' no more now than she had been forty years earlier when she so disappointed Moszkowski with her reply to his probe.

Germany's invasion of Poland at the beginning of September 1939 and the country's division and annexation a month later shook her confidence. She fell into despair, hiding once more in the company of Bach and Rameau, using the past to block out the tragic present. She started a new journal, but almost dared not: fear, grief and oppression overwhelmed her. She pasted in it a cutting from a serialized short story by her friend Colette, which would be published the following year as 'La Lune de pluie' ('The Rain Moon'). It concerns an encounter between an author and the secretary she has hired to type her manuscript, the writer discovering quite by chance, when dropping off a batch of pages, that she had once lived in the same apartment (the street name had changed, the facades altered) – a coincidence that draws her deeper into the secretary's strange, alluring world. The opaque familiarity of the place charms her and makes her think about involuntary memories, how they should act like blank pages between chapters in a book, which give order and punctuation to the narrative, how they should be like 'summer days, responsive to the light outside, in which relaxed and idle senses make chance discoveries'. Colette could be describing Landowska. Or Chopin, for that matter.

In October, Landowska listened to a broadcast of Cortot playing Chopin's Preludes, Cortot having first introduced the collection on air with commentary on its imagery and meaning. She told Restout that she 'would like to appropriate his absurd titles for the Chopin Preludes, if only to make fun of my titles for the Scarlatti Sonatas'.

In the last months of 1939 and the first one of 1940 she followed even more intensely what was happening in Poland: dissident families taken from their homes, separated, sent away for slave labour or worse, their property and chattels 'abandoned'; priests murdered, their churches sacked; gravestones erased and rewritten in German, the street signs as well; occupying soldiers forcing wealthy families out of their splendid city apartments so they might live there themselves; Warsaw's grand buildings and monuments left in ruins. It was all a rehearsal for the ideological and recriminatory destruction of Warsaw following the uprising of 1944, after which Hitler and Himmler ordered that the city be razed to the ground, Himmler adding the practical detail that it would thereafter serve only as a transport hub for the Wehrmacht.

Landowska would keep photos of this catastrophic destruction for the remainder of her life: long stretches of apartment blocks reduced to paper-lantern frames and endless mounds of rubble; an identical fate befalling the Saxon Palace, where Chopin had lived for the first seven years of his life while his father taught French to children of aristocrats at the Warsaw Lyceum within the palace; church after church demolished. German soldiers did not even bother to pillage priceless books and manuscripts from the city's great libraries before burning them to the ground.

Chopin posed these same Germans a problem. For the twenty years after Poland's emancipation in the conflagration of the previous war, Poles took their cue from Paderewski, rightly claiming Chopin as their own. Yet Germany was now determined to destroy not simply Polish buildings, but all traces of its culture.

One of Germany's own countrymen, a great artist himself, solved their conundrum. In 1837 Heine had written a series of ten letters addressing French arts, one of them about his friend Chopin. 'He is then neither Polish nor French nor German: he betrays a much higher origin, from the land of Mozart, of Raffael [sic], of Goethe; his true fatherland is the dream realm of poetry.' It was Chopin as a universal figure, unconstrained by mere national boundaries, one of only a handful of great artistic figures deserving this accolade. A hundred years after Heine, the musical theorist Heinrich Schenker constructed a far narrower and more decisive definition. 'For the profundity with which nature has endowed him, Chopin belongs more to Germany than to Poland.' He anticipated the terrific, biting line from John Kander and Fred Ebb's musical *Cabaret* (1966), set in the transition from decadent Weimar Germany to authoritarian Nazi Germany, about another of National Socialism's great enemies. 'If you could see her through my eyes . . . she wouldn't look Jewish at all.' To the conquering Germans, Chopin didn't look Polish at all. They had their cover for what followed.

In January 1940 Landowska entered a studio in Paris to record a disc of Scarlatti, including the Sonata in D (Kirkpatrick would later give it a catalogue number of 490), which marches along at a steady parade-ground step, the embellishments around the simple martial tune becoming more daring as it goes along. With uncanny timing, in the last two bars of the first half, as a bass-drum pedal note is beaten repeatedly in the left hand and a dramatic flourish unfolds in the right, French anti-aircraft guns fired at German planes over the outskirts of Paris. In the recording the artillery fire lasts only a few seconds (though there are additional soft rumbles), yet it strikes an eerily prescient note; the disc was Landowska's last European recording. Restout, in attendance, watched as technicians scrambled for cover, and saw Landowska concentrate even harder during the second half of the piece, the tape still rolling. All Restout wrote in her diary was 'Scarlatti (bombing)'. In this same month Landowska performed with Bronislaw Huberman in a concert at the Paris Opéra in aid of the French and Polish air forces, a gesture that would come back to haunt her.

There was an anxious calm to life in Saint-Leu-la-Forêt in the early months of 1940 as the household eked out a fantasy life on winter rations. Landowska worked away analysing Mozart keyboard fantasias, revising course notes, reading Rameau's *Traité de l'harmonie réduite à ses principes naturels* – his treatise of 1722 about the fundamentals of tonality and the primacy of the twenty-four major and minor keys, which he regarded simultaneously as a manual 'on everything that may be used to make music perfect'. In April at Salle Pleyel

Théâtre National de l'Opéra

Vendredi 12 Janvier 1940, à 20 heures 15

Soirée Exceptionnelle donnée au bénéfice des œuvres des

AILES FRANCO-POLONAISES

sous le haut patronage de

M. Albert LEBRUN, Président de la République Française
M. Wladyslaw RACZKIEWICZ, Président de la République de Pologne

avec le concours de

WANDA LANDOWSKA
BRONISLAW HUBERMAN

et

L'Orchestre du Théâtre National de l'Opéra

sous la Direction de **PHILIPPE GAUBERT**

◆

PROGRAMME

1. —	**Concerto**	J. S. BACH
	BRONISLAW HUBERMAN	
2. —	**Ouverture du Carnaval Romain**	BERLIOZ
	ORCHESTRE DE L'OPÉRA	
3. —	**Concert Champêtre** (dédié à Wanda Landowska)	Francis POULENC
	Les Viéleux et les Gueux	François COUPERIN le Gd (1668-1733)
	Ground	Henry PURCELL (1658-1695)
	Gigues en rondeau - Tambourin	Jean-Philippe RAMEAU (1683-1764)
	WANDA LANDOWSKA au Clavecin	

ENTR'ACTE

1. —	**Poème**	CHAUSSON
	BRONISLAW HUBERMAN	
2. —	**Prélude à l'après-midi d'un Faune**	DEBUSSY
	ORCHESTRE DE L'OPÉRA	
3. —	**Concerto**	SZYMANOWSKI
	BRONISLAW HUBERMAN	

Places de 20 à 100 fr. à l'OPÉRA et chez DURAND, Place de la Madeleine

she gave a recital, cramps stopping her during Couperin's unsettling Prelude in D minor, before she managed to pick up the thread.

Restout's diary entries lose their everyday quality as the months pass. Her urgency is apparent as Germany invades Holland and Belgium, as refugees spill into France, mostly on foot, the more affluent ones in cars, which they abandon on the roadside once the fuel is spent, and as Schunicke is interned in a camp near Fontainebleau (she had never naturalized), leaving Landowska frantically writing to friends who might help secure her housekeeper's release.

There is a pivotal moment early in *Suite Française*, the novel constructed from notebooks belonging to the French writer Irène Némirovsky, which became a best-seller sixty years after her death in

Auschwitz. A distressed Florence, mistress to an awful, egotistical writer, asks her manservant Marcel what the household should do, her urgency piqued by German soldiers having crossed the Seine. 'Madame should warn Monsieur,' he tells her after a moment's pause, not quite up to the task. He thinks to himself, though, that they should have left the night before, these rich people 'with no more common sense than animals! And even animals can sense danger . . .' He would have packed up the house an age ago, he knows: the silver, the furniture, the art, the clothing – all into cases and spirited away somewhere safe. Yet the inclination to stay was often as strong as the impulse to flee: Germany could falter, or the Allies prevail, after all, though such wishful thinking really ought to have died with the evacuations from Dunkirk. (Némirovsky remained in France when she needn't have, though she did organize her children's escape.) So madame puts a suitcase on her bed, places in it jewellery, underwear, spare blouses, an evening dress ('so she'd have something to wear once they'd arrived'), a dressing gown, her make-up bag, her husband's manuscripts. She cannot latch it, so she removes the manuscripts in order to retain the make-up bag, and thinks she will in any case be able to squeeze them into the hatbox, though they are already slipping from her mind.

Landowska and Restout were such characters, faced with the instinct to remain, the sudden urgency to flee, followed finally by the mad scramble to figure out where to go and what to take. They did not leave it quite as late as the fictional Florence, though they were still in Saint-Leu-la-Forêt on 3 June 1940 – six days before Field Marshal Rommel led his tanks across the Seine – when Luftwaffe planes bombed airfields, aircraft and factories around Paris. With their housekeeper Eugénie Fossoyeux they took refuge in a shelter in the garden ('Nini' complaining that her washing-up water will go cold). They decided in the days that followed to leave Paris, to join the exodus Némirovsky describes so well: cars with no lights, chock-full of suitcases, valuables, birdcages, clothes; trucks transporting people and furniture; horse-drawn traps carrying farmers, their cattle and children trailing behind.

'Mon mal vient de plus loin,' Phèdre says when confessing to the craven nurse Oenone her love for her stepson Hippolyte. *My ills began far earlier*. It was not simply the steady advance of German soldiers through France that imperilled these refugees. Rather it was a religious and cultural identity that went back generations and centuries, Germany granting no absolution to those who, like Landowska, professed no faith, or a different faith. Landowska's ills began with her Jewish parents, their parents, and their parents before them.

They were offered refuge in Blois, in the house of a friend's mother. On 10 June, Restout writes in her diary, 'to the sound of canon (the boches are at Pontoise) we gather up linen, clothes, books, leaving all Scarlatti, the Kolberg' – the thirty-three volumes of Polish folk songs and stories, riddles, proverbs and fairy tales, collected by the nineteenth-century folklorist and ethnographer Oskar Kolberg, whom Chopin had known when they were boys – 'the concertos of C. P. E. Bach, but I hold on to the course notes. At 11 in the morning Dia [Mathot, Landowska's secretary] drives by car to Blois. She turns around immediately and returns to Paris.'

In July, Mathot drove once more to Blois, and took Landowska to the internment camp in the Pyrenees to which Schunicke had been moved; here they effected her release. The three women then drove to Aristide Maillol's home in Banyuls-sur-Mer, the commune on the southernmost coast of France's *zone libre*, directly on the border with Spain. In August, Restout arrived at the small house the sculptor found for them. There for the moment they remained, nervously waiting to see what would unfold.

17

Saint-Leu-la-Forêt, Paris, Banyuls-sur-Mer, 1940–41

On around 20 September 1940 a small contingent of Gestapo officers forced open Landowska's home in Saint-Leu-la-Forêt, inspected the entire estate and contents, removed two wireless sets, applied seals to the doors (*Feldpostnummer* 032 65), then left. The officers were followed four days later by a team of music specialists from the Einsatzstab Reichsleiter Rosenberg (ERR), dressed in civilian clothing, and fifteen removalists from the French company TAM on the rue Balard in Paris. They worked methodically: the house and the collection had, over time, grown to accommodate each other and there was much to do.

It was a scene then playing out all over France. Before fleeing Paris the three branches of the French Rothschilds had done their best to circumvent it: they secreted away over 5,000 works of art from their collections, including a *Virgin and Child* by Memling, Vermeer's *Astronomer*, Ingres's portrait of James de Rothschild's wife Betty (to whom Chopin taught piano), along with pieces by Van Dyck, Titian, Watteau and Rubens. German procurement teams treated such attempts at camouflage and subterfuge as a mere *amusement*. With steely calculation they tracked down the family's art – to bank vaults in Paris and the Netherlands, to châteaux in Seine-et-Marne and the Calvados region, and to the Louvre's depots outside the capital – and brought it all to the Jeu de Paume. Napoleon III's indoor palm-ball court on the northern side of the Jardin des Tuileries, a short walk from the apartment that Chopin had kept in the Place Vendôme in his thirty-ninth and final year, was now an art clearing-house, filled with works supplied by agents, ERR officers, dealers, opportunists and crooks.

The palatial Rothschild residence on the rue Saint Florentin was looted by crisp-uniformed SS officers keen to avail themselves of *le goût Rothschild* – the Rothschild taste – all that tortoiseshell, ivory, mahogany and tulip wood. A photographer caught one officer with a gold-framed picture under his arm, another carrying a canteen's worth of silver cutlery, not the slightest hint of embarrassment evident in either. They had the law on their side in these private undertakings: anything left behind was considered *herrenlos* – abandoned – and ripe for the picking, destined mostly for the grand residencies or offices of senior party officials. As if to underline the extent of the abandonment, in July 1940 Marshal Pétain, Chief of Vichy France, stripped citizenship from every French person who had left the country between 10 May and 30 June 1940, and appointed the state the owner of their goods if they were not claimed in person within six months.

The number of acronyms of the various agencies involved in the state looting – ERR, AA, M-Aktion, NSDAP, GFP, RSHA, DBFU, RMWEV, RMVAP, MVF – almost matched the number of euphemisms given to their work. Acquisition. Sequestration. Confiscation. Aryanization. Purification. Curation. Nationalization. Repatriation. Restitution. Reclamation. Recuperation. Compensation. Liquidation. Capture. Dispossession. Exchange. Each was intended to lend the thievery an air of legitimacy.

There was a special task force for music, Sonderstab Musik, which was headed by the German musicologist Herbert Gerigk, an enthusiastic Nazi and expert on Verdi, who in 1940 co-authored the *Lexikon der Juden in der Musik*, an hysterical hatchet job on distinguished Jewish musicians, alive and dead. ('We have succeeded in purging all Jewish elements from both our cultural life and our music life,' Gerigk wrote in the preface.) Gerigk was tasked with acquiring

instruments from homes and collections in France, Belgium, Holland and Poland, but he was also to pursue important totems of Austro-Germanic music, and to overlook nationality in instances with wider significance. Hitler instructed that 'certain cultural items – mainly music manuscripts as far as Dr Gerigk is concerned – be confiscated and secured immediately, irrespective of the individual currently in possession of these items'. In such circumstances the manuscript of Strauss's *Elektra* would be found in the home of a Madame Hirsch (perhaps a relative by marriage of the music collector Paul Hirsch, Strauss's friend), along with fifty works of art, all of which were catalogued and packaged by the industrious ERR.

It was a strange, strained relationship, this rapport between the vanquishers and the high art of their homeland. Némirovsky caught it well in *Suite Française*. She has Lieutenant Bruno von Falk send his compliments to Madame Angellier and request with all good manners and an implicit shared culture that she hand over keys to the library and piano, assuring her that neither will be damaged. It is the same scenario described by Iris Origo a few years later at her villa in the hills of Fiesole outside Florence, now requisitioned by German troops, Origo pulling whatever strings she can for permission to remove valuable items. The first soldiers are already at the house when she arrives, installing a telephone in the former chapel. 'They are perfectly civil and ask for one piece of furniture only: the piano. "One of our officers," they say, *"ist ein berühmter Komponist* [famous composer]. He has composed an opera about Napoleon."' In exchange she is allowed to lock up the drawing room, with its gorgeous eighteenth-century Chinese wallpaper, and take away all her glass, china and linen.

This juxtaposition of high art and low deeds was not lost on those young men doing the ERR's heavy lifting. Early in the Occupation, Roland Weisshuhn, a Wehrmacht soldier, was part of the team responsible for stripping a well-appointed Paris house. The soldiers lifted art from the walls, took the oak table from the dining room, the walnut lawyer's cabinet from the library, a particularly fine piano from the salon. As the open-back lorry passed along the rue de Rivoli, the boulevard that dissects the Marais and runs parallel to the north wing of the Louvre, Weisshuhn lifted the piano lid and played some Chopin, a gentle riposte to his superiors and their monstrous edicts.

The officials in Landowska's house identified the Mozart and Handel collected editions, multiple volumes of Scarlatti sonatas, works by Schütz and Gluck, Gerber's rare manuscript copies of concerti by Carl Philipp Emanuel Bach, the original manuscript of Poulenc's *Concert champêtre*, and of course the complete Bach-Gesellschaft. Landowska's teaching notes – her detailed instructions to Curzon and Kirkpatrick on phrasing and interpretation and the sound and touch of old instruments – were no longer in the house: Restout had taken them when they fled. But there were manuscripts, article drafts, original compositions, first editions and gramophone pressings, and hundreds of letters, including Landowska's correspondence with Rilke and Tolstoy. The officers dismantled the instruments, packed the scores and 10,000 books, and drew up meticulous lists with descriptions, signatures, dates, addresses, catalogue numbers and file designations, ready for duplication and dispatch. They drank her wine (as rations, officials later claimed), stole her typewriters and soap (it was a dirty job), and sent to the Louvre the entire collection that Wanda Landowska had spent the previous forty years accruing.

Their typed inventory is gruesomely detailed: sixty crates containing correspondence, scores, books, manuscripts and gramophone records; modern Pleyel harpsichords and piano with long serial

Sonderstab Musik   Paris, den 19.2.1941
                                          Vg.

                    Notiz über Bezeichnung von Kisten
                    ═══════════════════════════════════

Wanda L a n d o w s k a , St. Leu la Foret

    P 1   Verschiedene Literaturwerke
    P 2   "   "   u.Noten
    P 3   "   "   u.Privatakten
    P 4   Korrespondenz
    P 5   Zeitschriften und Korrespondenz
    P 6   "   " " u.Noten
    P 7   "   " " " "
    P 8 - P 15   Noten
    P 16 - P 18   Literaturwerke
    P 19 - P 24   Literaturwerke und Noten
    P 25   Schallplatten
    P 26   "   und Bücher
    P 27   Noten
    P 28   Noten, teils Bücher
    P 29   Cembalo (79260/192406/48)
    P 30   Cembalo (30463/192665/51)
    P 31   Flügel   (73 K/144/189344)
    P 32 - P 37   s. Aufstellung Darius M i l h a u d

    P 38   Noten und Bücher
    P 39   Cembalo, 17. Jahrhundert
    P 40   Cembalo, 1642 v. Hans Buchers
    P 41   Spinett, Pleyel 1807
    P 42   Tafelklavier, Carl Jac.Mordquist,Stockholm
    P 43   Cembalo (innen Bild nach Verracchio)
    P 44   Füsse zu P 43
    P 45   Stumme Klaviatur
    P 46   Tafelklavier (Inschrift musica magnorum
                                 xi solanum dulce laborium).
    P 47   Füsse zu P 46
    P 48   Klavichord
    P 49   Tafelklavier (C.Granfeldt, Stockholm)
    P 50   Tafelklavier
    P 51   Ximbal
    P 52   Klavichord
    P 53   Untersatz zu P 51
    P 54   2 Niola d'amore
    P 55   Hausorgel 1757
    P 56   Piano (Joan Bauza, Palma)
    P 57   Klavichord
    P 58   Untersatz zu P 57
    P 59   Viola da Gamba, Clarinette, Flöte, Zither
    P 60   Korrespondenz

numbers; a Pleyel spinet of 1807; an unbranded harpsichord with an 'innen Bild nach Verrocchio' ('inside image after Verrocchio'); an early-nineteenth-century square piano by Carl Jacob Nordqvist of Stockholm, and another with the inscription 'Musica magnorem solamen dulce laborum' ('Music is a sweet solace for great labours'); two viola d'amores and a viola da gamba; a flute, a clarinet, a zither. In the fifty-sixth crate was the piano made by Juan Bauza, Palma.

The housekeeper Nini protested as much as seemed wise, but then simply kept her eyes on everything being taken from the house. Weeks later Restout heard from neighbours about the noise of packing cases being nailed shut, the echo of transport vans coming and going, of local residents trying to remain inconspicuous for the long days and weeks during which they observed the plunder of their eminent neighbour's property – first the instruments and library, later the furniture and personal items: two *vitrines en chêne de Hongrie*; three *grandes lampes sur pied*; six *chaises acajou Louis-Philippe* (mahogany keepsakes from the period of Chopin's sometime patron); two *fauteuils club*; one *table machine à écrire chêne de Hongrie*; and on and on.

At the time Landowska and Restout knew nothing about the sacking of their home. They knew of changes to French law, though. On 4 October 1940, once the last of the instruments had been taken to the Louvre and three days before the collection was transported to Berlin by lorry, a law was quickly passed concerning Jews in France. Foreign residents of Jewish descent (individuals with three Jewish grandparents) were now subject to internment, while all nationals of Jewish descent could be forced by the *Préfet* of any *département* to live where instructed. A day earlier Jews had been banned from positions in the civil service, military, judiciary and on political bodies, and forbidden from holding influential posts in French cultural life – teaching, journalism, broadcasting, film. Eventually their phone lines would be cut and their right of movement within Paris restricted: no access to cafés or concert halls, parks and public transport, no excursions at night. Some resourceful Parisian Jews would survive the war, hiding with the help of sympathetic friends, or with the assistance of the Resistance or the Communist Party. Most would not: they were arrested when ordered to report to police stations to

check on their status. Or they were rounded up in Jewish neighbourhoods – in the eleventh *arrondissement*, officers going from house to
house, or randomly checking papers in the street. Everything happened in stages: first the law, then the daily humiliations, finally
transportation and extermination.

By the time this new French internment law was introduced, Landowska had heard from Resistance contacts that her home had been
ransacked. Restout travelled to Saint-Leu-la-Forêt to see the damage
at first hand, and there experienced the chilling ghost-town atmosphere. 'I go to the house,' she wrote in her diary. 'There are seals
affixed to every door except the kitchen and cellar where Nini lives
with the dogs.'

On her return to Banyuls-sur-Mer she wrote in protest to the
Délégation Générale du Gouvernement Français dans les Terri-
toires Occupées. She included an inventory, urgently constructed from

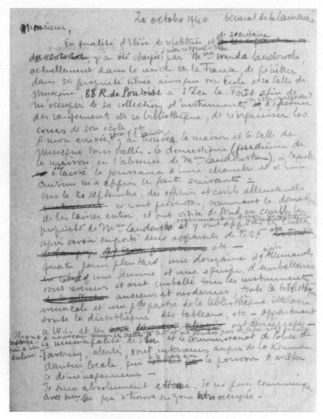

Nini's observations and her own memory. She listed the *épinettes* and *psaltérion*, the music library, manuscripts and books, the paintings and carpets, radios, wristwatch, bottles of champagne, soap, bolt of velvet intended for a concert dress, typewriter, portable gramophone, and oak table with two leaves. Of course she also listed '1 piano manufactured in Palma, which Chopin played during his time in Majorca'. It had all been taken with such cold precision, from the study inside the house, from the bedrooms and kitchen, from the concert hall in the garden.

Restout thought sense would prevail. Or that the *Statut des Juifs* would: it had passed a day before she drafted her letter, promising exemptions for Jews working in the arts or sciences who provided the state exceptional service, which she wrote out in her neat hand.

She also had an ally, M. de Boissieu of the Délégation Générale, who wrote on her behalf to the military command in France. 'The matter especially concerns CHOPIN'S piano and a score of instruments. Such a loss to the French artistic patrimony would be absolutely irreplaceable.' But the *Statut* was a smokescreen and Restout's complaint was effortlessly swatted away. The property had been abandoned by an anti-German Jewess whose passport, proving her Polish citizenship and suggesting her religion, was in possession of the police. 'The items confiscated from Landowska therefore cannot be considered French art property. Rather, these objects were confiscated at the time as abandoned Jewish property pursuant to the Führerbefehl [Führer's order].'

And so the sixty crates remained in Berlin – first in storage facilities of the transport firm Edmund Franzkowiak, then, from August 1941, in the headquarters of Sonderstab Musik in Oranienburger Straße, a little way along from the Neue Synagog, a splendid Moorish building that had survived Kristallnacht only through the courageous intervention of an Aryan police officer who dispersed the crowds. Chopin's piano was catalogued and highly prized – much as it had been when it first arrived at the *Altbau* that Landowska shared with Lew in the previous war, the apartment that Binder had photographed so beautifully, only a few miles from where it now sat.

While these statutes were issued and these disputes unfolded, André Gide was in Paris revising his *Notes on Chopin*. He had announced the book as far back as 1892 – Anton Rubinstein still alive and stating that music had ended with Chopin's death, that Romanticism was frozen in the scores he left behind and in the example and aesthetic he established – yet Gide would pick away at it until 1948, a year after he won the Nobel Prize in Literature.

He had lived with Chopin's music all his life – as an amateur pianist, but also as a keen agent of French culture – and happily rekindled arguments many considered settled. There was no music less Germanic than Chopin's, he wrote (*pace* Schenker): it could not be further from the enormousness of Wagner's works, with their strange, relentless excesses, their intrinsic mawkishness. Yet though Gide appreciated the Polish inspiration in Chopin's great scores, he was also able to identify what he called a French cut to this raw cloth. He thought Chopin's intrinsic identification was with French culture, with the sparseness and concentration of the Baudelaire of *Les Fleurs du Mal*, the two men sharing a horror of declamation, a distaste for vulgar rhetoric. 'His sole concern, it seems, is to narrow limits, to reduce the means of expression to what is indispensable. Far from charging his emotion with notes, in the manner of Wagner, for example, he charges each note with emotion, and I was about to say: with responsibility.'

Gide was of course captivated by the Preludes, those expressions of the essential, some of which he heard as charming, others terrifying, none indifferent. 'Each of them is a prelude to a meditation; nothing can be less a concert piece; nowhere has Chopin revealed himself more intimately.' He was echoing T. S. Eliot's Boston hostess from almost thirty years earlier, who thought the Preludes should be played only among friends. Yet even this was too much for Gide in No. 2: it is too full of private grief and torment to be performed to others, yet 'played in a whisper for oneself alone, its indefinable emotion can not be exhausted, nor that kind of almost physical terror, as if one were before a world glimpsed in passing, of a world hostile to tenderness, from which human affection is excluded'. Gide was not convinced by Ganche's explanation of the Prelude – of the church bells in his and Chopin's childhoods – but nor does he say (or even necessarily know) that Chopin composed the piece through his almost perverse fascination with the grim, discordant sounds in the lower octaves of the Bauza piano, a fairground cacophony he simply could not leave alone.

Film changed the way Gide heard Chopin's music. He thought the cinematic technique of slow motion allowed an appreciation of graceful gestures and identification of what had been lost in Chopin's music in the skirmish of contemporary life. Like Landowska, he thought virtuoso players of the day performed Chopin too fast and too loud, in order to make it sound more difficult than it is. 'Is there art more gentle/Than this slowness?' he wanted to print on every Chopin score, lifting the words from his contemporary, Paul Valéry. Without such slowness and subtlety, players were trampling on the element of surprise written into Chopin's music.

Inevitably, Gide thought this quality of surprise was linked to the spirit of improvisation that he identified in Chopin's music and considered imperative in performances of it, the single quality he thought contemporary players missed. 'We are told that when he was at the piano Chopin always looked as if he were improvising; that is, he seemed to be constantly seeking, inventing, discovering his thought little by little. This kind of charming hesitation, of surprise and delight, ceases to be possible if the work is presented to us, no longer in a state of successive formation, but as an already perfect, precise and objective whole.' It is the Chopin of Delacroix and Heine, Grzymała and Sand, of Mikuli and Koczalski.

*

In Banyuls-sur-Mer Landowska had no instruments, no money, and no means of earning any through teaching or performing – not solely in occupied France and the *zone libre* administered from Vichy, but in neighbouring Spain too, which was now (at least ideologically) an ally of Germany. In November she ordered from Pleyel a replacement harpsichord, which never arrived. In the same month she visited the Mexican consul in Marseilles and obtained a visa, listing real or fabricated offers of engagement from an American agent: the Pittsburgh Symphony Orchestra with Fritz Reiner, and the Los Angeles Symphony Orchestra with Bruno Walter. She applied for an American visa too, though this was less straightforward than it should have been: an ugly stream of anti-Semitism coursed through parts of the State Department, the sheer number of people trying to escape to America only quickening its flow. It made émigrés creative. 'We must get one of our bugger friends to marry Sybille,' Maria Huxley said of her friend Sybille von Schoenebeck whose Jewish ancestry and sharp criticism of Nazism ensured she could neither return to Germany nor renew her passport in a consulate abroad. Walter Bedford, one such bugger friend, stepped forward, granting Sybille a new nationality and name, under which she wrote some of the most beautiful English prose of the post-war years.

There were individuals determined to help Jewish refugees beached in France, people who used their position or generosity to undermine the institutional lethargy and hostility of the State Department. Throughout the winter, spring and then summer months of 1941 – as Riga fell to Germany, as the city's Jews were moved first to a new ghetto and then, later in the year, to the Rumbula forest for execution (24,000 Latvians and 1,000 Germans shot in two days) – Landowska was in contact with Varian Fry. He was a young American journalist, who in 1935 had written scathingly about German treatment of Jews in Berlin, and who moved to Marseilles after the fall of France as an agent of the newly founded Emergency Rescue Committee, which aided war refugees. In a touching letter to his wife Fry described the greatest living painters, sculptors and authors who were then in correspondence with him, and former prime ministers and cabinet members too. 'What a strange place Europe is when men like this are reduced to waiting patiently in the anteroom of a young American of no importance whatever.'

Fry was far too self-deprecating. Before he was forced to leave the city he helped more than 2,000 people, including Hannah Arendt, Wilhelm Herzog, Claude Lévi-Strauss, Marc Chagall, Heinrich Mann and Alma Mahler-Werfel, who had in her trunk her late husband's scores and the manuscript of Bruckner's third symphony, a delicious snook to the ERR. Their visas were signed by the enlightened American Vice Consul to Marseilles, Hiram Bingham IV, or his deputy Myles Standish, before Bingham attracted the ire of both Vichy and American officials and was moved to a less controversial posting.

When Baudelaire seasonably wished himself out of wintry Paris he thought of Lisbon. 'It is a city by the sea; they say that it is built of marble, and that its inhabitants have such a horror of the vegetable kingdom that they tear up all the trees.' A century after Baudelaire, Lisbon was the destination for distinguished Jewish artists and intellectuals seeking refuge and passage. They were first given sanctuary in or around Marseilles – which Chopin had once also gratefully accepted as he recovered from his winter in Majorca – before being smuggled over the border into Spain (those without full papers trekking over the Pyrenees), and from Spain to neutral Portugal where, in the capital, they awaited transit. As the war progressed and

Germany's likely fate became apparent, a new ingredient was thrown into this mirage city's heady mix of émigrés, hucksters and thieves: German officials desperate to get gold out of their homeland or France, arriving in Lisbon on Lufthansa flights from Berlin or Paris, their suitcases full, their valuable cargo to be sold on the Lisbon exchange or in South America.

In October 1941 sixty-two-year-old Landowska was photographed in Banyuls-sur-Mer with Aristide Maillol. It is the most melancholic of all her surviving photographs, the sculptor, a few months shy of his eightieth birthday, an impassive greybeard straight out of Tolkien, offering his friend whatever comfort he could. And then on 18 November, with an American visa in her passport and Restout at her side, Landowska made her way to Barcelona, then Madrid, and then Lisbon, where she obtained an export pass from the British Consulate General for her belongings – one case and five trunks containing 'personal effects, musics, one piano' (a Pleyel harpsichord belonging to her student). On 28 November she boarded the SS *Exeter*, a passenger ship operated by the American Export Lines Inc., bound for a world elsewhere.

18

New York City, Paris, Leipzig, Silesia, Raitenhaslach, 1941–4

Their timing was good, for it was becoming difficult to hide: midway through the following year the Paris police would round up 12,000 Jews and intern them in the most squalid conditions in the Vélodrome d'Hiver, before overseeing their deportation to Auschwitz. Yet their timing was also eerily bad: Landowska and Restout arrived in New York City around midday on 8 December 1941, a day after the Japanese attack on Pearl Harbor. Officials were twitchy and passengers were unsurprisingly anxious about how the attack might affect their entry into the country. Officers placed the *Exeter* in quarantine while they checked documentation, releasing most of the passengers, yet detaining Landowska: her American visa had expired during the time it had taken her to find passage. Restout elected to remain with her, and the two of them spent a cold, uncomfortable night on board. The following day they climbed down a ladder into a small boat, which took them to the dock at Ellis Island, home to New York's immigration station, the arrival point for passengers travelling steerage or without valid papers.

In the main immigration hall – a French Renaissance Revival building with polished terracotta floor and 28,000 white hound-tooth tiles on the vaulted ceiling, large American flags (with only forty-eight stars on them) suspended from two sides of the gallery tracing the four walls – Landowska and Restout encountered dazed, miserable, diseased immigrants wandering the floors, most of them having nursed seasickness for two weeks in bunks somewhere deep in their ship, and distressed, bewildered Japanese citizens shouting and gesticulating and begging for answers. Landowska found a dirty, battered upright piano, its keys covered in grime and soot, its tuning as terrible as Sand had found Bauza's instrument in Majorca.

Nonetheless she blocked out the noise and confusion, the fear and uncertainty, ignored her sudden communion with steerage passengers dressed in their Sunday suits (an 'X' chalked on the lapel or breast of those thought diseased), whose journey she had shared at several removes, and sat at the piano. 'We do not know how long we shall have to stay, but at least I can work!'

They were to have been met by Landowska's friend Henryk Kaston, a musician and former soldier in a Polish cavalry regiment of the French army, who had been captured by the Germans but escaped by dressing in the clothes of a local farmer, and who went on to find acclaim in America as a jeweller and bow maker. Realizing something was wrong when they did not disembark with the other first-class passengers, he scrambled to obtain letters of recommendation from eminent American musicians. With these in place, with the standard security questions answered ('Whether a polygamist'; 'Whether an anarchist'; 'Whether a person who believes in or advocates the overthrow by force or violence of the Government of the United States'), and after two nights' incarceration, they were required each to deposit a bond of $500, after which their passports were stamped and entry granted, Landowska on a temporary visitor's permit that would be upgraded only in August 1943.

In New York they moved about: first a hotel, then a house in Scarsdale, then an apartment at 123 West 44th Street, close to the noise and fast pace of Times Square. There were compensations in their fragile, patchwork lives: on West 44th they were only a short walk from the new Museum of Modern Art, which had opened with such fanfare only a few years earlier, its International Style architecture and Picasso retrospective garnering huge attention and affection. But so too were there restrictions: Landowska's permit did not allow her to receive foreign income – recording royalties, for example. ('We have previously made application to the Trading with the Enemy Department,' HMV would tell her in February 1943, the bureau's title equal to anything in Orwell.) Soon Restout would be issued with a ration book permitting them limited quantities of sugar and gasoline, a little later coffee and kerosene, bicycles and rubber. They had not left the war behind: they had simply traded it for a more benign version.

From West 44th Street they moved into a sixth-floor apartment at 50 Central Park West, a large block built in 1907, with candy-cane pillars at the entrance, a plain facade, high ceilings, and views from their corner position over the neighbouring church turrets to the Park, the distant buildings along Fifth Avenue then only a gentle clutter. They slowly kitted it out: a modest single bed for Landowska, covered in a fur spread quite out of place amidst the sombre panelling and parquetry; jade plants around the desk at which Restout would later photograph Landowska rapt in a score, a heavy magnifying glass next to the inkwell filled with purple ink; a few pots and pans in the kitchen, battered and borrowed, underlining the impression that Landowska was no gourmand: there simply did not seem to be time for anything but music.

The apartment was eight blocks from Steinway Hall – not the elegant showroom on 14th Street where William and Henry performed their magic, but its replacement on 57th Street, just down from Carnegie Hall and next door to the Buckingham Hotel, the handsome Beaux-Arts building where Paderewski used to stay whenever he was in town. It was here in 1928, three years after its inauguration (it was an almost exact contemporary of Landowska's recital hall in Saint-Leu-la-Forêt), that Rachmaninoff and Horowitz performed a duo piano recital; the quality of music-making thereafter never really let up. From Steinway & Sons Landowska obtained a grand piano for the apartment, in time adding a second.

This was her new American life. In photographs of the apartment's interior there are no books in sight, almost as though she could not face building a new library from scratch: surely her own collection was still intact somewhere in Germany? Or perhaps she was paralysed by loss, by financial deprivation too. In these early months she rekindled old friendships and associations from a time before Saint-Leu-la-Forêt, a time before her career bedded down in a commune north of Paris, its rhythm dictated largely by her activities there. She thought of concerts she might give, recordings she might make, grasping at anything, really, in an attempt to create some semblance of her old life.

Perhaps when Landowska sat at the immigration hall's barrelhouse piano she had worked on Bach's *Goldberg Variations*, for just two months later, in New York's Town Hall, the émigré Landowska played the piece in her first public concert in America in over ten years. It had not been performed on the harpsichord in New York since early in the previous century.

THE TOWN HALL

WANDA LANDOWSKA

BACH: The "GOLDBERG VARIATIONS"
In its complete and original form—
for the harpsichord with two keyboards.

Alfred Scott • Publisher • 156 Fifth Avenue, New York

The composer and critic Virgil Thomson wrote of the full house populated by the great and good of musical New York, who gave her a warm ovation after almost two hours, every repeat honoured; of beautiful phrasing and flawless execution; of her expert conception and analysis; of rhythm that not even Benny Goodman could better. 'A performance so complete, so wholly integrated, so prepared, is rarely to be encountered.' Thomson also enjoyed the whiff of cordite in Landowska's statement in *The New York Times* that, given the piece was composed for two keyboards, those who tried to perform it on the piano were fooling themselves: she was claiming it as her own. Thomson loved what he called the cut-throat world of contemporary harpsichord players (their antics exceeded only by those of singers, he thought), its constituents jealous of the vigour and life she brought to the piece. He loved too that she was a musician whom other soloists found profitable to study – a distinction he also afforded Josef Lhévinne, but never Jascha Heifetz or Yehudi Menuhin. Mostly he loved how her singular performance had generated such acclaim.

Restout loved it too. Her notebook for March that year lists the musicians and auditors now wanting to participate in private masterclasses: Gloria Scharff, Suzanne Bloch, Niula Schapiro, Leon Kuschner, Mrs Zaslawski, and other such beautiful Jewish names – including, on 13 March, Doda Conrad, son of a childhood friend of Landowska's, who would soon play an important role in her American life – a delicious smattering of émigré and Old World New York willing to pay ten dollars to perform for the great Landowska, or five dollars for the privilege of watching others do so. This one evening at the Town Hall had turned around her parlous financial position.

There was one further and ironic aspect to the recital. The printed programme included an advertisement for Schirmer's score of the *Goldberg Variations*, edited by none other than Landowska's former pupil and sparring partner, Ralph Kirkpatrick. The two musicians were once again juxtaposed, each warily staking a claim to this repertoire, each unwilling to cede ground to the other, proving Thomson right at every juncture.

At the end of 1942 – with the *zone libre* now occupied and renamed *zone sud*, with the Vichy administration muzzled and the distance between resistance and collaboration shorter than ever – Cortot, aged sixty-five, entered Studio Albert in Paris to make his sixth recording of the Preludes. His performance is gentler than in 1926. His reading of No. 1 is exactly what Gide had in mind when he criticized the frenzied, reckless tempo that pianists adopt in this Prelude and in Chopin in general. He still does his sudden rushes in No. 2, which he pulls back with as little ceremony as he begins them. His articulation in No. 3 is dry and clear, but hardly, as Chopin marks, *leggiermente* – lightly, delicately. He pulls off the cadential final chords of No. 4 without resorting to the pantomime thuds of fate and eternity he earlier invoked. In No. 6 he manages great contrapuntal voice leading and left-hand sonority, which underlines the main difference between Chopin's Preludes and Debussy's (Debussy tending towards harmonic voice leading, Chopin polyphonic). No. 8 is a bit loud and clangy, but in No. 11 he manages an engrossing spirit throughout. He enters the magical middle section of No. 13 without the booming, false portentousness of his 1926 recording, but there are still his heavy, secret tears once he is inside it. He plays No. 16 thrillingly as a mad, eccentric, silent-film chase, with some humour.

Yet his clock in No. 17 once more strikes eleven with diminishing power. He finds himself in a messy scramble in No. 18, the most episodic of the Preludes, each utterance outbid by the one that follows. He ignores the crescendo in the last bars of No. 20, dismissing the *forte* Chopin scribbled into the penultimate bar in the copy owned by his pupil Madame Dubois since it did not accord with his view that the 'piece is made still more impressive by the striking way in which the volume of tone gradually diminishes, calling up the vision of a funeral procession, slowly receding towards the terrible mystery of the unknown' (Anton Rubinstein's trick in Chopin's *Marche funèbre* in the previous century). No. 24 is scattered with more wrong notes, though it comes across powerfully, neither Chopin nor Cortot offering resolution, no neat bow on the grand package that has been assembled during the previous thirty-five or forty minutes.

There were certainly other musicians then navigating Nazism more enthusiastically than Cortot. Fully half the members of the Wiener Philharmoniker were card-carrying Nazis: the orchestra expelled thirteen Jewish players, five of whom later died in ghettos or concentration camps, and exiled others because they were married to Jewish women. It also awarded its Ring of Honour to Baldur von Schirach, Vienna's notorious Nazi governor, responsible for the deportation of many thousands of Jews to their near-certain death, and presented him with a replacement after his release in 1966 from Spandau Prison following a twenty-year sentence for crimes against humanity.

There were many other musicians who exploited ideology or opportunity in these years, throughout the darkest days and actions of the Third Reich. In 1933 Richard Strauss did not hesitate when asked to replace Bruno Walter on an international tour with the Leipzig

Gewandhaus Orchestra after Walter, a Jew, was publicly removed from his position. Herbert von Karajan looked on greedily as Wilhelm Furtwängler twisted and turned in his relations with the regime, joining the Nazi Party and conducting concerts to celebrate Hitler's birthday, happy enough to be Nazism's poster boy, at least for a while, when it could help his career. The Dutchman Willem Mengelberg conducted in Germany and in occupied countries throughout the war and allowed his name to be associated with Nazi organizations – so much so that in 1945 his homeland banned him from appearing there. The devout Catholic Olivier Messiaen perpetuated that ugly trope about the Jews having committed deicide, and as a prisoner of war in Lower Silesia was especially grateful to the music-loving German guards who gave him pencils, erasers and manuscript paper, along with extra rations and time in the afternoons to compose.

Yet there were also those who were not so opportunistic, those who turned their backs on the regime as quickly and as certainly as the Manns. Furtwängler wrote an open letter to Goebbels soon after Hitler gained power, stating his approval of the eradication of wider Jewish influence on German music before asking whether it would be possible to hold on to talented individual players. (He thereafter lobbied on behalf of many such musicians, using his position as cover, knowing the Reich was simultaneously using it for propaganda – a trade-off he was more than willing to make.) Strauss, illustrating the moral flux and complexity of the times (at least for some), insisted the name of his Jewish friend and librettist Stefan Zweig be included on the poster for *Die schweigsame Frau* at its premiere in Dresden in 1935, which infuriated the Nazi regime and ensured the opera's closure after only three performances. Charles Munch joined the Front National des Musiciens, a Resistance organization, and deflected various requests from Nazi officials for concerts or allegiance. And then there were those musicians who refused to return to Germany once the war was over: Arthur Rubinstein answered the oft-posed question of why he never played there after 1945 by saying that he had lost a hundred members of his family to Nazi pogroms and felt no need to perform in the country responsible for them.

Distinguished French artists and writers had their work cut out to resist the siren calls of German cultural attachés set on making ideological converts, or at least creating the appearance of conversion, which was enough for their purposes. (The anti-Semitic writer Louis-Ferdinand Céline needed no special grooming.) The authors Robert Brasillach and Drieu La Rochelle visited Germany and wrote positively about Nazism in their fiction and journalism. Both Edith Piaf and Maurice Chevalier toured there during the war, to the detriment of their post-war reputations. Other artists stepped gingerly on the tightrope stretched between their political convictions and the opportunities presented to them during the Occupation. But Cortot was different. His love of German music and culture left him blind to Nazism's actions and deaf to the ideological arguments against Germany's greed, militarism and cruelty, which were easily heard by those willing to listen. So at exactly the moment his old friend Landowska was fleeing Nazism, her life in danger, her possessions stored in sixty crates in a warehouse in Berlin, Cortot was rushing towards it.

In the quiet centre of one of his sonnets Shakespeare writes, 'How with this rage shall beauty hold a plea?' Perhaps this was Cortot's approach in these years, his recording of the Preludes a show of solidarity with conquered Poland, a claim staked for universal culture unsullied by nationalism or barbarism. Perhaps he saw himself as rising above the destruction playing out so savagely across Europe by the time of his sessions in Studio Albert. Yet this was the same man who could conduct *Tristan und Isolde* in Vichy in 1941, seemingly without moral equivocation, who could join Vichy France's anti-Semitic National Council, accept Pétain's invitation to become France's High Commissioner of Fine Arts (which would result in his brief arrest in 1944 for collaboration), and behave quite odiously towards Jewish colleagues.

There was a meanness in Cortot's outlook, a level of self-absorption he excused as the pursuit of high art. It is the same meanness he extended to George Sand, whom he thought unworthy of the artist with whom he associated himself so firmly and righteously. 'Already a woman of considerable experience,' he would write after the war, winking at her sexuality, 'imbued with vague philanthropic theories and half-baked libertarianism, which she made the excuse for her insatiable sexual appetite ... [Sand] was a powerful, vital machine incapable of discernment or discrimination. She was not repelled either by vulgarity or mediocrity.' It was more of the gloopy misogyny that coated Sand from the time of her relationship with Chopin onwards, connecting Custine to Cortot and ensnaring many nineteenth-century writers on Chopin along the way – some in the twentieth century too.

His sketch does something even worse than the expected misogyny. It robs Sand of an indispensable part of her character, a quality Cortot himself had trouble mustering during the Occupation: her immense loyalty, the characteristic that allowed Chopin the space to work and breathe, to compose without distraction, to write works that have long outlived him and anything Sand wrote during his lifetime or after his death.

Cortot published his short book as part of his post-war attempt at public rehabilitation, his effort to reassume the role of Chopin's conscience and best earthly representative. At times what he says is interesting. He writes that the only two books in Chopin's apartment in the Place Vendôme at the time of his death were an anthology of popular Polish poetry and Voltaire's *Dictionnaire Philosophique* (1764), open at the entry on Taste. ('Taste, the sense by which we distinguish the flavour of our food,' Voltaire writes, 'has produced, in all known languages, the metaphor expressed by the word "taste" – a feeling of beauty and defects in all the arts.') And occasionally he is amusingly prim, dismissing the very twentieth-century assertion that Chopin's fulsome and affectionate early letters to Tytus Woyciechowski were 'those of a lover rather than a friend'. He is fierce about the treatise on music that Chopin haphazardly attempted to write (whose manuscript he acquired in London in 1936), with its very bad French (so Cortot thought), its many clichés and crossings-out, and its lack of substance about the mystery of his art or even, more modestly, his teaching. Mostly, though, Cortot's pilgrimage is somewhat worthy, and a lost opportunity given his unique hold on the twentieth-century's perception of Chopin, the Preludes in particular. And he is wholly unfair to Sand.

The looting never seemed to stop. In the summer months of 1943 freight wagons containing 120 uprights and several grand pianos left France for Germany, the instruments intended for the Ostministerium. These were followed a week later by two wagons of pianos for victims of Allied air raids. Then twenty-four instruments and a mass of gramophone records, destined for the mid-eighteenth-century Cistercian monastery at Raitenhaslach – a small town a little over 100 kilometres east of Munich – that Sonderstab Musik used as a storehouse. Then forty pianos; then twenty; then twenty more; then three more wagon-loads for Raitenhaslach; then thirteen pianos for SS headquarters, to be used by soldiers for recreation; then 105 uprights and five grands for the submarine and air force bases. It is a repetitive and repellent but strangely hypnotic catalogue.

Some of the most notorious instances of plunder and redistribution of instruments in these later war years were carried out on behalf of the Reichs Bruckner-Orchester, which was dreamed up by Hitler, funded by Goebbels, and based in Saint Florian, a small Austrian town sixteen kilometres from Linz. (It was Goebbels who, in February 1943, presented the Japanese violinist Nejiko Suwa with a reputed Stradivarius, while the Japanese ambassador, representing Germany's staunch Axis ally, beamed away.) The orchestra, founded in 1942 as an adjunct to Berlin's Reichsrundfunk in honour of the great German composer (and to improve morale in his war-wearying homeland), was to own a complete set of quality instruments; to get them, it established a close relationship with the dealer Hamma & Company in Stuttgart. (Company invoices record the sale of sixty-seven stringed instruments, 'by order of the Reich Ministry for Propaganda and Public Enlightenment, Berlin'.) Although the relationship between

dealer and the Reich appears to have been, for once, commercial (as was the case with another supplier, Musikhaus Lüdemann of Köln), the provenance of so many fine instruments, many by seventeenth- and eighteenth-century Italian luthiers, many sourced in France, all exchanging hands in a short period of time, was by no means straightforward.

Such transactions led to a declaration in January 1943, signed by seventeen governments of the future United Nations, along with de Gaulle's Comité National Français, which brims with anger and disgust, its language pointedly undiplomatic: the systematic spoliation 'has taken every sort of form, from open looting to the most cunningly camouflaged financial penetrations, and it has extended to every sort of property – from works of art to stocks of commodities, from bullion and bank-notes to stocks and shares in business and financial undertakings'. Signatory countries therefore reserved the right to declare invalid any purchase undertaken in occupied territories, regardless of its apparent legitimacy.

The declaration noted that the war was shifting in favour of the Allies and that the campaign of looting was consequently intensifying, as Germany moved its plunder to neutral countries, where it persuaded citizens to 'act as fences or cloaks on behalf of the thieves'. But it was running out of neutral countries, and as 1943 progressed and Berlin was intensively bombed, so too was it running out of strategies. The careful lists, the secure locations, the grand plans for museums and conservatoria all took on a more desperate, improvised air. So in September 1943 Chopin's Bauza piano, along with the harpsichords and spinet, the clavichords and square pianos, and hundreds of other instruments stored in Oranienburger Straße, were all transported east to Leipzig. The catastrophic Allied bombing of Kassel in October proved British planes could make the long distances through German skies either undetected or without retaliation, and when in December 1943 the reach of the Allies extended still further east, many of those instruments moved to Leipzig for safekeeping were destroyed.

Landowska's collection was more fortunate. Before bombing could incinerate it, the majority of her library of precious books and manuscripts was moved to Schloss Langenau near Hirschberg in Upper Silesia, the border region endlessly fought over by Poland and

Germany, while her surviving instruments were moved from grossly disfigured Leipzig to the isolation of Raitenhaslach: to the cool stone rooms off the elegant rococo cloisters of the monastery – full of pretty altars and frescoes and lovely, plain headstones – where, for the moment, they were safe.

In this same year the Germans hid in Lower Silesia a Chopin relic of incalculable value, one intimately connected with the piano moved to safety in Raitenhaslach. In 1939 Professor Józef Michał Chomiński had discovered in the State Music Conservatory in Warsaw the autograph manuscript of the Preludes, the very score Chopin had sent to Julian Fontana near the end of his winter in Majorca – with its beautiful crossings-out and hypnotic detail, all in scratchy ink – instructing him to copy it for his French, German and English publishers. The manuscript's fate in the previous hundred years was unknown, the dots between Paris and Warsaw impossible to join. Chomiński requested that the National Library photograph it, which is where it was when war broke out. The library officially acquired it in 1942 and when a year later, in October 1943, the Nazis organized a Chopin exhibition in Cracow, the manuscript took pride of place. Almost inevitably, at the exhibition's close it disappeared; Schenker's assertion that Chopin belonged more to Germany than Poland was on this occasion taken literally. Miraculously, it would be discovered in 1947 in Kłodzko in Lower Silesia, after which it was returned to the National Library, where it remains.

*

During the Prussian siege of Paris in 1870–71 the photographer Nadar – who had captured Sand so well – founded the Compagnie d'Aérostiers Militaires. From his base in Montmartre he launched a series of 'siege balloons' – magnificent golden globes constrained in net webbing – which transported mail, military reports and tactical summaries through the sky and over the city walls, high above the fray. He named one balloon after Sand, another after Hugo – a perfect tribute to the author of *Notre-Dame de Paris*, with its chapter 'A Bird's-Eye View of Paris', in which Hugo imagines houses pressing upon each other, slowly piling up inside the city's wall until 'they gush forth at the top, like all laterally compressed growth, and there is a rivalry as to which shall thrust its head above its neighbours, for the sake of getting a little air'.

Resistance France, once more under siege, also looked to Hugo, the same Hugo whom Chopin had once played for in the apartment of his friend the Marquis de Custine, more than a lifetime ago. In 1944 a French underground newspaper described him as their 'epic poet of the free people becoming their voice and conscience', and then the French Committee for National Liberation explained exactly why: 'He reminds us of the great revulsion of the French people against an earlier form of fascism,' referring to Louis-Napoleon's *coup d'état* in 1851 and subsequent reign.

Yet the liberation was proving painful, as American and British bombing raids over Paris and its suburbs were now intense: sorties on railway yards and bridges; the Renault factory in Boulogne-Billancourt; a ball-bearing plant and aircraft-engine repair factory in Courbevoie; ever more specific military targets. The collateral damage was considerable: thousands of civilians were caught in this violent coda to the terrible strain and compromises of four years of German occupation. Throughout the country there were shortages of food and power, shortages even of young workers who either volunteered or were seconded to mandatory labour programmes in Germany. Those remaining in France were more often than not working on behalf of the Reich, their salaries funnelled over the border into the German treasury. Even the weather during the Occupation seemed to underline these strange inverted worlds: abnormally cold winters, alluringly warm springs, heatwaves during successive summers.

Meanwhile, in New York, Landowska did her bit. The U.S. Office of War Information asked permission for the Goldman Band to record her *Fanfare de la Liberation*, which it planned to broadcast via shortwave to Poland. Of course she obliged, as she did when asked to record an accompanying message of encouragement. 'Nostalgic but full of hope I send you this message of music. How sweet it would be for me to bring you some comfort, better still, some happiness!' She described how the fanfare contained the true spirit of France – a melody by Couperin, which evoked the flutes and bagpipes of a village festival in Taverny, the commune next to Saint-Leu-la-Forêt. Her piece was a celebration of a land unoccupied, a culture unblemished by murder, despoliation, repression, collaboration, Teutonic might. 'Danse . . .', she said in conclusion, the single word left hanging, capturing her hopes for normality.

How different was this Landowska from the woman in Banyuls-sur-Mer. There are wonderful photographs of her in New York City late in the war and in the early years of peace. In one she is coming offstage at the Town Hall in January 1947 beaming at Schunicke or whoever is behind the camera, the single standard lamp by which the recital was lit visible in the background. There is another of her in the green room flanked by glamorous fans; another of her in a tall-backed chair receiving the adulation of a large post-concert throng; another of her putting on a fur wrap, a handsome African-American porter smiling away at her side. There is a formal portrait of Landowska at the harpsichord in the Central Park apartment, her cat sitting on the music stand, an unlikely sentinel. And there is still another, this time onstage at Carnegie Hall, sitting at her two-manual, seven-pedalled Pleyel harpsichord, one of only two or three such instruments in the country.

On 26 August 1944 long lines of civilians lined the Champs-Élysées to watch the Second Armoured Division of de Gaulle's Free French Forces, under General Leclerc's command, pass through the Arc de Triomphe, then along the avenue – the same route Chopin and Delacroix had traced ninety-five years earlier, earnestly discussing harmony and Berlioz and Beethoven, Chopin with only months to live. Three days after Leclerc's arrival, the 28th Infantry Division of the U.S. Army marched down the Champs-Élysées in a Victory Day parade. It had been four years since dewy-eyed German soldiers had marched this same stretch, drum majors leading the pack, four years since bemused French civilians had watched military parades on the prestigious Avenue Foch, troops eighteen abreast passing by the grand Rothschild residence that the occupiers would soon empty, and by the charming three-storey house Arthur Rubinstein had bought just before the war, which they would also soon sack.

The journalist Janet Flanner chronicled the end of the Occupation. She was at a piano recital in May 1944, the programme featuring great French figures – Debussy, Fauré, Chopin – a repudiation as barbed as the Resistance quoting Hugo. ('Very fine,' her musician sister commented gnomically. 'The piano is a half tone low.') Flanner wrote of the average Parisian losing forty pounds throughout the Occupation, while peasants sold produce on the black market for huge profits. She noticed in December 1944 that physical intimacy had returned with de Gaulle's government and that seismic events playing out on the Continent had such local consequences. She described a Paris nourished by liberation, which was just as well as there was neither meat nor heat to nourish it. And she correctly depicted her country as the most blessed survivor 'of an Old World that is being destroyed into something new':

> For five years Europe has been the victim of cannibalism, with one country trying to eat the other countries, trying to eat the grain, the meat, the oil, the steel, the liberties, the governments, and the men of all others. The half-consumed corpses of ideologies and of the civilians who believed in them have rotted the soil of Europe, and in this day of the most luxurious war machinery the world has ever seen, the inhabitants of the Continent's capital cities have been reduced to the primitive problems of survival, of finding something to eat, of hatred, of revenge, of fawning, of being for or against themselves or someone else, and of hiding, like savages with ration cards. The desperate economic competition which will arrive with the peace will be scarcely less bloodthirsty.

It was a prescient analysis, as Allied troops positioned themselves in a country so recently occupied by their enemy and attempted to bring about a truce.

19
Paris, New York City, Munich, 1945

On the walls of the family house, and in his father's gallery too – attractive showrooms in the rue La Boétie (the same street in which Picasso lived) – hung paintings by Courbet and Corot, Matisse and Picasso, Braque and Laurencin, Ingres and Delacroix. His father was the French-Jewish art dealer Paul Rosenberg, who in 1939 and 1940 had moved around the paintings in his personal and business collections, hoping to circumvent what he sensed was coming. He sent some of the most valuable works to a small château in Floirac, in the Gironde district of south-west France, and made arrangements for them to be shipped to New York. While the removal company in Bordeaux obfuscated, citing new regulations and the need for more inventories and information and stressing the difficulty of obtaining requisite specialists to pack the paintings correctly, German officers prepared to strike. (Two Paris dealers had tipped off officials about this tranche of Rosenberg's collection, having first negotiated a 10 per cent commission.) In mid-September 1940 soldiers and police surrounded the château, questioned the staff, loaded the art into five vans, and returned to Paris, where they deposited everything in the German embassy. Rosenberg and his family had escaped to America a month earlier, by the route Landowska would later trace through Lisbon: as a consequence his collection was considered *herrenlos*.

Alexandre Rosenberg, Paul's eldest child, was a student when war broke out, soon afterwards an officer in the Free French Forces serving campaigns in Africa, Germany and France. As part of Leclerc's Second Armoured Division, Lieutenant Rosenberg marched into Paris in August 1944, through the Arc de Triomphe and along the Champs-Élysées, fêted as one of the capital's liberators. A day later he was ordered to secure a railway yard in Aulnay-sous-Bois, in the north-east suburbs of Paris, from which a train was attempting to leave for Germany. On opening its cargo wagons Rosenberg discovered hundreds of paintings, including works by Braque, Laurencin and Picasso, which he recognized immediately from his family home.

The recovery and restitution of looted art really began this haphazardly, a full nine months before the end of war in Europe. It mirrored the haste and confusion in the final weeks of the Occupation, when the German command closed down its offices and shipped home whatever art was close by in whatever manner it could. Rosenberg's paintings from the château in Floirac, kept throughout the Occupation by Ambassador Otto Abetz – Renoir's *Breton Woman*, say, or Degas's *Portrait of Gabrielle Diot* – were sent to Germany before the Second Armoured Division arrived in Paris, some to a castle in Wildenstein, others to Schloss Sigmaringen, a hundred kilometres south of Stuttgart, where Abetz, Pétain and his recently deposed head of government, Pierre Laval, were holed up, trying to determine their next move.

His father's paintings had been burned into Alexandre's childhood consciousness. It was a characteristic of many collectors who survived the war and then set about recovering their drawings and paintings, their sculptures and bibelots, that they remembered precisely where individual pieces had hung or sat, in villas or apartments they no longer had, alongside furniture swallowed up by the Reich, next to tapestries or above exquisite Chinese rugs. Big collectors like the Rothschilds possessed detailed inventories – for insurance, for resale, for when they loaned pieces or deposited them in vaults – and worked from these documents. But memory was an equally potent tool, as Restout discovered when in America she made an inventory of the contents of the house and hall in Saint-Leu-la-Forêt. When a full thirty years after German soldiers first marched into Paris, Alexandre Rosenberg flicked through a catalogue for an upcoming auction at Versailles's Rameau Hotel, he noticed straight away a listing for Braque's *Table with Tobacco Pouch* (1930), which had been in the château in Floirac, thereafter in the German embassy in Paris, and was now being offered for sale by Josée de Chambrun, Laval's daughter. Rosenberg arrived at the auction with police officers, who confiscated the painting. It was not the first time that Madame de Chambrun had found herself in this position.

A desire for justice, for the restitution of property, did not always align with a wish to return home. 'I'm not going back to that place – not now, not ever,' says Helen Mirren's character about Vienna in the film *Woman in Gold*, which chronicles Maria Altmann's recovery of Klimt's famous painting of her aunt, *Portrait of Adele Bloch-Bauer I*. The cellist Anita Lasker-Wallfisch, former member of the Women's Orchestra of Auschwitz, talks of a similar revulsion, how when she first returned to Germany after surviving the camp she found it impossible to look in the eye men above a certain age, as she would inevitably find herself wondering what they'd got up to between 1933 and 1945. 'I had once been the proud owner of a beautiful cello made by Ventapane,' she later wrote. 'God knows who plays on it now.'

Elisabeth de Waal, whose grandson Edmund would write so affectingly about his family's travails after the Anschluss, made a novelistic study of three individuals who returned to Vienna after the war. *The Exiles Return* captures in quick, straight brushstrokes the very mixed emotions of those who left and those who stayed behind. A Jewish antiques dealer once more sets up shop in the capital, honourably refusing to trade in looted artefacts – in counterpoint to the book's many unrepentant Nazis and sympathizers. Another character is asked why he is back, to which he shrugs, 'I came home. I am an Austrian. I belong here.' When another says of his return, 'People were still the same: they liked cakes – and probably music – and all the other pleasures of the senses', it is impossible not to think of different Austrian characteristics: the virulent anti-Semitism, the enthusiastic embrace of the Nazis, the lingering imprint of totalitarianism on postwar society – the noir world that director Carol Reed captured so brilliantly, in such murky shades of grey, in *The Third Man*. This same individual in *The Exiles Return* suggests as much when he notices two dark paintings in gold frames in a real estate agency in Vienna, which sends the agent into a spin about their provenance, talking too quickly, explaining in superfluous detail how he came by them, legitimately he stresses, at an auction after the war, their previous owner having died abroad, unfortunately, his heirs recovering and selling whatever they could – bluster and splutter outbidding each other. 'These returning émigrés all have illusions,' thinks another man as his wife recounts to an old friend, who had fled the war, some gruesome episodes from Russia's post-war occupation of its quarter. De Waal's even-handedness here is chilling.

Landowska had no such illusions. But nor was her dilemma that of Maria Altmann, unable to picture herself once more in her previous life. Landowska certainly shared some of Arthur Rubinstein's disdain for Germany and distrust of Europe, yet she could easily have cultivated thoughts of return any time after Germany's surrender of France. Ongoing hostilities made such planning difficult, of course, regardless of the direction the war was heading by the end of 1944; and when the war with Japan finally ended in September 1945, Landowska was sixty-six, which was old to be slipping back into a former life in which her house had been stripped bare. Yet it was not impossible.

Her reticence was in part because life in America, after a perilous start, was actually working out. Her accounts for 1945 list recitals in Princeton, two at the Metropolitan Museum, a return to the Town Hall in November (gross receipts $2,524), two concerts with the New York Philharmonic Orchestra in February ($600) and another two in December ($850), lessons ($3,787), masterclasses, private concerts ($4,500), and gramophone royalties ($1,804): her total income for the year was $16,813. This was at a time when the annual rent on the apartment at 50 Central Park West was $3,700 and Restout was drawing $650 as Landowska's secretary – the same year the Department of Commerce identified only 1.8 per cent of white urban residents on incomes over $10,000.

Louise Dahl-Wolfe, the celebrated photographer responsible for iconic images of great artistic figures of wartime and post-war America – W. H. Auden, Orson Welles, Carson McCullers, Christopher Isherwood and Lauren Bacall among them – photographed Landowska for *Harper's Bazaar* not long before her February appearances with the New York Philharmonic. They are clumsy photographs, Landowska looking old, a little dazed, the background cluttered, the lighting ramshackle. She had always carefully controlled her iconography – not just the velvet dresses she wore and the ghostly appearances and gloomy lighting at her

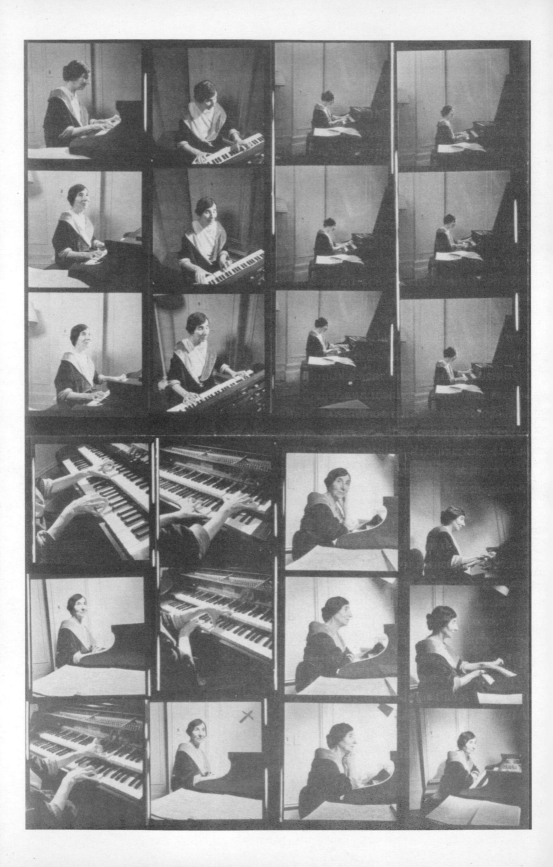

recitals that Kirkpatrick so derided, but also the relationship she had with the camera and the images she allowed to be published. A single X marks one frame on the contact sheet: in it Landowska looks like an ageing, imperious bird. These shots do not seem to be the work of a great photographer, nor portraits of a great artist in her prime.

And she really was in her prime. In spring 1945 she once more recorded Bach's *Goldberg Variations*, this version slower than in 1933, a little gentler yet simultaneously more rhapsodic, the finger articulation as careful and unrushed as ever, with each variation displaying the quality that Chopin brought to his playing – the ability to make the piece sound as though it was plucked from the air. The instrument is brighter than the earlier one, twanging only when both keyboards are coupled, and occasionally at the end of a long take when the sound droops. John (Jack) Pfeiffer, who would produce her RCA recordings in the 1950s, was hardly alone in describing these *Goldberg* discs as a superb achievement: 35,000 sets were bought in America alone within the first six years of release. 'It was totally unheard of at that time,' Pfeiffer later observed.

Although the Scarlatti discs she made in early 1940 – anti-aircraft fire flashing in the background – marked the beginning of Landowska's war, the *Goldberg* recording did not signal the end of it. There was too much unfinished business. She started to trace her belongings. First Restout wrote a report (quite for whom she was not yet sure) based on the letter of protest she had sent to the French Délégation Générale at the end of 1940, the draft and copy diligently kept. She rehearsed once more the terrible sequence of events: the arrival of the Gestapo officers; the visit a few days later of ERR officials and removalists who took the books and instruments, champagne and phonograph records; their return in the following weeks for the remaining paintings and furniture, files and personal effects. The territory by then was so wearyingly well traversed. List-making was now the activity of Jewish survivors, not the Germans who had persecuted them: lists of property, possessions, bank accounts, artworks, and family members missing or murdered. It was not about money and compensation, not initially; instead it was about Jewish survivors brushing themselves down after years of criminal indignity, recovering their identity, regaining whatever stature and self-respect they could.

In her attempts to find her precious instruments and expansive library, Landowska was blessed in a friend she had met in Berlin at the tail end of the nineteenth century, Marya Freund, a young Polish-Jewish soprano who later established a successful career specializing in contemporary music. (Freund sang the Wood Dove in the 1913 premiere of Schoenberg's *Gurrelieder* and later gave the first performances in France and Britain of *Pierrot Lunaire*, Schoenberg's hypnotic, moon-flecked cycle.) Her son, the bass Doda Conrad, had helped Landowska and Restout when they first arrived in New York, seven months before he joined the U.S. Army.

While serving in Berlin, Conrad met Lt. Col. Mason Hammond of the Monuments, Fine Arts, and Archives programme (MFA&A), which President Roosevelt inaugurated in June 1943, who suggested that the artistic Conrad join his team of so-called Monuments Men. On hearing of his new commission, Landowska asked him to look out for her Pleyel harpsichords. Perhaps she asked half in jest – such an impossible request – yet Conrad promised he would: it is what sons do for old friends of their mothers. He instructed his MFA&A colleagues to keep an eye out for a 'strange-looking piano'.

He soon had news. In December 1945 Conrad wrote to Landowska from a former Nazi administration building in Munich, which the MFA&A had transformed into a collection point for looted goods. Here there were numerous musical instruments in crates branded HA

(Halphen, from the estate of composer Fernand Halphen) and LA (Landowska), some of them found in the Salzkammergut area of Austria, others in the old Cistercian monastery at Raitenhaslach. He could not yet tell her precisely what was in them – the collection point was large and frantically busy, and a protocol was only slowly falling into place – but one day soon he hoped to be in the happy position of transporting to Paris her *instruments de travail*, the two modern Pleyel harpsichords.

Not long after this discovery Conrad received a call from Captain John Morey in Bavaria, who told him of a strange-looking piano in the recreation room of the headquarters of the Military Government in Altötting, which was unlike any instrument he had seen before. It was covered in beer bottles, its lock forced, evidently not well looked after by the soldiers who had plinked away on it during the dull hours they were not fighting or training. Could this be the instrument Conrad sought? Conrad told Morey to open its lid and see whether there were any identifying marks. Morey found something written inside, but in French, which he did not speak. Nevertheless, he could make out a name: Wanda Landowska. It was one of the missing Pleyels.

It is not always easy to disassociate objects from their context: things can adopt new meanings and take on the patina of their surroundings. Yet Landowska was able to separate the instrument from its recent associations, so overjoyed was she at its discovery. She telegraphed Conrad immediately, asking him to send it to New York, and two days later she followed up with an emotional letter. 'To describe to you the extraordinary emotion of your letter of 15 December would be impossible . . . Your account is like a miracle. It's this way that once more you have become my liberator. What a prodigious and unbelievable coincidence that is this discovery. But also, what vigilant and indefatigable affection you have shown.' She explained that, because Germany had compensated Pleyel for the theft by 'ces Messieurs' of the two harpsichords and single piano on loan to her at the time the house was looted, they effectively belonged to her. She had been without them for five years, she wrote, a deprivation that trapped her in New York, unable to accept engagements out of town lest her only instrument be damaged in transit.

She told him more good news, about a cold-call from a woman whose friend had been preparing records and documents for the

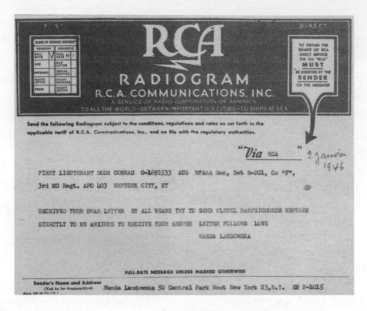

forthcoming war crimes trials in Nuremberg when he discovered, in Alfred Rosenberg's file, reference to Landowska's letters, a selection of which had now arrived in New York. Days later she wrote to Conrad's mother to tell her what a magnificent son she had raised. 'Do you remember our hours of making music together?' she asked from nowhere, suddenly picturing the two of them as students in Berlin almost fifty years earlier. Do you remember 'the "Moja pieszczotka" of Chopin that we worked on together? I often think of this with fondness.'

She had in mind Chopin's setting of a poem by his friend Mickiewicz, one of twenty extant songs he composed between 1827 and 1847, sixteen of which Fontana collected and published in 1857 as Chopin's Op. 74, another slipping into the collection once censorship allowed. 'Moja pieszczotka' ('My Darling'), written a year before Chopin and Sand travelled to Majorca, is a charming miniature that does not really sound like Chopin: its accompaniment is too plain, its melodic line too folky, its chromatic shifts clunky. Yet in New York in 1946 it served as a bond between Landowska and an old friend whose officer son had located her cherished harpsichord.

20

Los Angeles, Paris, Vienna, 1945–6

In these early days of miracles and recovery Columbia Pictures released *A Song to Remember*, which did for the image of Chopin and Sand in the twentieth century what Liszt's biography had done in the nineteenth. Chopin first appears as a handsome, toothy eleven-year-old, who sits at the piano playing Mozart as if riding a bull, noticing through the window Russian troops escorting Polish prisoners to Siberia. 'My dear boy,' his teacher Elsner comments, 'music and freedom are like one. They both belong to the world. A real artist wants freedom in every country.' At a Warsaw salon hosted by Count Wodzińska the twenty-year-old Chopin follows on from Paganini, performing on an ornate piano in an opulent dining hall, plates of pork and pheasant in plentiful supply. He stops when the Russian Governor-General of Poland arrives. 'I do not play before tsarist butchers,' he explains, a brave public snub from this rumoured member of the Polish Resistance. A girlfriend gives him a handful of soil before he rows to Paris, so it seems, his treatment of the Governor-General necessitating his escape. 'This is Polish earth, Frédéric,' she tells him, 'and don't ever forget it.'

In Paris he dresses like a sort of merchant sailor and eats at the Cafe de la Boheme, beneath portraits of Liszt, Hugo and Balzac, the latter settling into a good meal when Chopin enters. Sand, accompanied by Liszt, arrives wearing tails, top hat, red waistcoat and jodhpurs, as though straight from the Lido. 'The man is a woman,' Elsner says (Chopin's remark to Hiller all those years before). 'A little unusual, isn't it? Why does she wear pants?' Chopin is soon at her house on her Nohant estate – not in the gloomy garden Delacroix painted so well, but sitting at the piano saying, 'This melody is for you, George.' George is touched, though she is already calculating how to get him to come away with her. 'You could write miracles of music in Majorca,' she tells him before they kiss.

In Majorca, Sand writes in a huge study with tapestries, fireplaces, wood panels, upholstered chairs, plump quill pens, large inkwells, heavy drapes; it could not be further removed from the coffin-lidded rooms, modest sticks of furniture and charcoal-smoking brazier in their cell in Valldemossa. Chopin composes (though not the Preludes) on a beautiful instrument, nothing at all like Bauza's *pianino*, the sounds filling the room quite unlike Sand's descriptions of them in letters. After leaving the island he does an arduous tour to raise money for imprisoned Poles back home: Rome, Amsterdam, Vienna, London. But it is suddenly somehow the end of his life, a decade lost, and the sheer effort is evident. At Salle Pleyel he is puffy and sweaty, and he spits blood on the keys; death soon captures him. Sand remains an imperious bitch to the end.

The film's patriotic aspirations are simple to interpret and understand: it was released in January 1945 (though seven years in the making), the year whose great message would be the triumph of democratic principles over autocracy and occupations. The Warsaw Uprising of August 1944, when Polish Resistance fighters attempted to drive German troops from the city, and which ended in bloody ignominy, further underlined this political aspect of the film. Yet the real interest in *A Song to Remember* lies in what it says about the perception of Chopin halfway through the twentieth century. Despite director Charles Vidor's admirable efforts to frame the story in terms of national resistance, despite the genuine political resonances between Poland in the 1830s and 1940s, the film's writers and producers were actually banking on Romanticism as a worldwide currency. Chopin was not solely a Polish figure caught up in the disjointed narrative of nationhood: he was also an international symbol of high art and civilization, somehow outside the century in which he had lived. The German attempt to expunge Chopin of his Polish roots and claim him for Germany had failed: he emerged from the war an even more resilient and universal character – much as Heine had once described him.

This is also the message of Władysław Szpilman's touching memoir *The Pianist*, published in 1946, which covers his survival in Poland under the Occupation, where he scraped together a meagre existence and observed with a cool eye the ghetto collaborations between Lithuanians, Poles, Jews, Ukrainians and their German masters. In what could seem a mere narrative conceit in lesser hands, Szpilman punctuates his memoir with different performances of Chopin's Nocturne in C sharp minor, Op. posth. He is playing it live on Polish radio when, in September 1939, German tanks roll into Warsaw, the sound of shells penetrating the insulated studio walls, as they will only a few months later during Landowska's recording session. It is the work he plays to the kind German officer who later brings him food and a blanket when he is close to death. And it is the piece he performs again on Polish Radio when the war is over, as if nothing had changed in the intervening years, though of course everything had.

Szpilman studied with Landowska's adored teacher Michałowski and was fed a diet rich with Chopin's music and Michałowski's thoughts on how to preserve a particular performance tradition. So when he plays Chopin to the officer, after earlier being caught out following curfew by a German patrol and let go by the soldier who learns of his profession and tells him 'I am a musician too', it is because Chopin binds them together in humanity's highest cultural aspirations. It is the explicable though disconcerting pact that music forges between enemies, as Némirovsky and Origo describe so well.

It was also the experience of another Polish Jew. Returning to Paris soon after the war, before the Americans had gone home 'in search of central heating' (Nancy Mitford's words), Arthur Rubinstein was struck by the exceptionally warm reception for his Chopin recitals – a warmth not always so evident when Cortot ruled Paris, and one that would now last until his final performance in the city thirty years later. (At his house in the Place du Bois de Boulogne, off the Avenue Foch, he encountered the family renting it under one post-war decree or another, the damage done by the Germans who lived there during the Occupation evident in every room. 'They emptied it thoroughly like all the other houses,' the building's pre-war concierge tells him, a sinister grin on his face.) The French had long thought of Chopin as their own, of course, but here was a Pole, a Jew, playing his music and touching their hearts. Perhaps the war had altered Parisian audiences, made them more sensitive, less insular. Or perhaps they were just happy to have Rubinstein back in town, no questions asked, no admissions made.

Rubinstein was gracious but also strongly patriotic: for all his belief in Chopin as a universal figure, there were times when he needed him to be Polish, as both Landowska and Paderewski did. From the stage he berated delegates at the opening conference of the United Nations in San Francisco in 1945 ('[In this] Hall, where the great nations have gathered to make this world a better place, I don't see the flag of Poland, on behalf of which this cruel war was waged'), before sitting down and playing the Polish national anthem.

Rubinstein's single (and uneven) recording of the Preludes from 1946 is so different from Cortot's. It is far less whimsical, more concerned with structure than narrative, which is not so easy to achieve in such fleeting pieces. Every gesture underlines Rubinstein's pre-war instinct that Chopin was a muscular figure, regardless of his poor health and physical frailty. In his recording of Chopin's Polonaise in A flat, Op. 61, he plays the opening martial motif almost distractedly, not quite sure whether this one particular flavour is important in an appreciation of the whole. In the Nocturne in C minor, Op. 48, he initially gives the impression he has neither the strength nor intention to open the sluice gates at the halfway point; when he does, the impact is overwhelming. In these Chopin performances and recordings he is audibly attempting to wrest Chopin's crown from Cortot. Indeed to many observers,

Rubinstein after the war eclipsed Cortot as the century's pre-eminent Chopin interpreter, his frequent recordings and concerts generating new generations of music lovers and Chopin aficionados.

Cortot post-war had the good sense to put chauvinism aside and argue instead for 'a Chopin who existed in a world created by his imagination, who had no other existence save that of his dreams . . . who by the outpourings of his genius was able to immortalize the dreams and longings of countless human souls'. He is as flowery as you would expect, nonetheless his instinct here points to a Chopin for all humanity.

The messy poverty, unrelenting chaos and wholesale rebuilding of Europe in these early post-war years – cities and political ideologies and relationships and families all refashioned – ensured that there was both solace and opportunity to be found in great Romantic scores. On 30 April 1945, the day Hitler committed suicide, American soldiers came to requisition a villa in Garmisch-Partenkirchen, at the bottom of the Bavarian Alps. It was the home of Richard Strauss, who emerged from inside and said to Lieutenant Milton Weiss, 'I am the composer of *Der Rosenkavalier*', as though it afforded him immunity, which it actually did, for a while. To verify his claim he sat at the piano and played some excerpts (much like Landowska in Berlin thirty years earlier), after which the soldiers left him alone.

Strauss was old, and his training and identity were entrenched in the practices and political ideology of the united Germany that emerged from the bloody Prussian victory of 1871. How else to explain his *Vier letzte Lieder*, those impossibly Romantic orchestral songs – Strauss's very personal farewell to an artistic epoch – which really had no business being written as late as 1948. Yet the songs are emblematic of a wider cultural phenomenon after the war, one that ensnared Chopin and his Preludes too: a reluctance to kick over traces linking the post-war order to everything that had gone before. Heine's line about the new age following Goethe's death needing new art unconnected to the past did not apply here: high culture was to be Western society's unifying principle, so soon after being its pawn – an objective framework for spiritual renewal in the wake of destruction. In music this post-apocalyptic framework led to the founding of major festivals in Britain, the formation of a permanent opera company at Covent Garden, and the resumption of opera and symphony seasons throughout Europe, as soldiers returned home and the musicians among them slipped back into their former lives. Amidst all this there was an instinctive scramble towards important works of the nineteenth century, which acted almost as moral ballast. 'Romanticism was impregnated in post-war music making,' conductor Simon Kenway thinks. 'It promoted a civility in manners and arts.' And, usefully, an opportunity to paper over nationalist, cultural and political differences between allies and enemies.

Herbert von Karajan was both an architect and beneficiary of such thinking. He was the classic Romantic figure: individual, simultaneously progressive and reactionary. In his denazification tribunal in March 1946 (he had joined the party in April 1933) he was given a clean bill of health and soon afterwards conducted a concert in Vienna with its Philharmonic Orchestra, which earned from the occupying Soviet authorities a ban on further concerts there. After its lifting the following year von Karajan enjoyed a stellar career, notably as principal conductor of the Berlin Philharmonic Orchestra for more than three decades (1955–89). Although he did perform contemporary scores, his fame rested on his recordings and interpretations of the great milestones in the Romantic repertory. There was a public thirst for these works among the vanquished, but among the vanquishers

too. No other art form was so assiduously digging afresh in nineteenth-century mines: not literature, not the visual arts, certainly not cinema (adaptations aside). Yet Romanticism was fused into von Karajan's musical DNA as surely as it was into Strauss's: it was the basis of his training, in the blood of his mentors and those (few) conductors he admired (Rudolf Kempe, Carlos Kleiber and Arturo Toscanini), and offered a repertory he could colonize and perpetuate. He made this tradition his own – recording technology on his side – determined to keep alive the works and precepts of musical Romanticism, and continued to do so until late in the twentieth century.

21

New York City, Munich,
Saint-Leu-la-Forêt, 1946

Landowska and Restout now lived their lives with a scrappy urgency. In April 1946, as they awaited more news about the other keyboards Conrad had found, Landowska put a figure next to each missing instrument in her collection: $5,000 for the Ruckers harpsichord (over $65,000 today); $5,000–$6,000 for the *clavecin gothique*; $2,500 for the Italian instrument; $3,500 for the Ruckers spinet; and then, far down the list, 'Piano Chopin . . . relic, price impossible to determine'.

In mid-July she received a letter from Rose Valland, the unassuming Frenchwoman who had spent the war at the Jeu de Paume ostensibly working for the Germans, feigning ignorance of their language yet all the while understanding everything spoken and written, cataloguing the treasures that arrived daily, nightly making a detailed record of their provenance, a list that now formed the basis of the MFA&A's operations. More instruments bearing Landowska's name had been found, though they were not in uniformly good condition, and others were still missing. 'I hope to give you better news in February,' she added, 'great artist that you are.'

Yet the news was already good, for on a separate page of notepaper Valland listed the instruments recovered. The haul included the Ruckers harpsichord and spinet, two more historic harpsichords, two square pianos, the *psaltérion*, a chamber organ, a clavichord. Last, again almost an afterthought, as though no one really knew where to put it, was the 'piano de Chopin'.

Landowska responded at the end of the month, telling Valland of Conrad's discovery of the modern Pleyel harpsichord (though of course she already knew), of her immense gratitude and good fortune at the retrieval of some of her possessions. 'They are for me more than rare and precious antiques. These are living documents rather, priceless.' Her gratitude was still tempered by loss, for she asked Valland to keep looking for the other modern harpsichord, with the seven pedals and two keyboards, 'Pleyel' written on its fallboard.

From Saint-Leu-la-Forêt, Dia Mathot told Landowska of cherry-eating blackbirds in the garden, of a harvest of tomatoes and potatoes, of gooseberries eaten straight from the branch (there was no sugar to turn them into jam), of plums for compote. 'My dear, there is a terrible wind today, as if the house were haunted. Everything is making a noise.' In another letter she disclosed the extent of deprivation in post-war France: please send Nestlé milk chocolate or Hersheys, she wrote, Philip Morris cigarettes, boxes of powdered lemon, a warm winter coat, pairs of cotton gloves.

Landowska did not yet know about the letter Mathot had received from Max Unger concerning the wartime fate of Landowska's books and instruments: their removal from France to Berlin; their transportation to Leipzig for safekeeping after the extensive bombardment of Berlin; their storage there in a former Jewish school in Gustav Adolph Straße; the transfer of the library to Schloss Langenau, where in February 1944 Unger catalogued it. He emphasized how reluctant a participant he had been in the activities of the ERR, joining in 1943 only when there seemed no escape, and signed off with a neat shoulder-shrug. 'I am unsure as to what happened to the valuables following the occupation of Silesia by the Russians and Poles; hopefully they were well taken care of' – though of course he knew that the Russians looted almost everything they found there in February 1945, and that the Poles mopped up the rest. It was Landowska's first taste of the self-exoneration and shape-shifting of former Nazis that would thwart her attempts at restitution for the remainder of her life – and quite some years beyond it.

Under the headline 'Collection Found in Salt Mines', in October 1946 *The New York Times* reported the recovery of Landowska's stolen instruments: the single harpsichord in the officer's recreation room; the crates found in salt mines in Austria; the keyboards in the monastery in Raitenhaslach. (No mention was made of the clavichord that Valland discovered in a private home not far from Munich.) 'All of the early and modern keyed instruments of the collection have definitely been accounted for,' the journalist wrote, inaccurately, 'and only a few of the orchestral instruments are still missing.' There are some good descriptions of them – not least of the fifteenth-century harpsichord with its elaborate case carved of Flemish wood, the inside lid decorated with an old Italian painting – before the

COLLECTION FOUND IN SALT MINES

THE important collection of old instruments taken from Wanda Landowska, the eminent harpsichordist, when the Germans confiscated her estate at St. Leu-la-Foret, has been found and shipped to Paris. Much to Mme. Landowska's joy, her favorite modern harsichord, a Pleyel, which she used constantly for many years, also was discovered on enemy territory and is now en route to her in this city.

All of the early and modern keyed instruments of the collection have definitely been accounted for, and only a few of the orchestral instruments are still missing. Once again Mme. Landowska possesses the rare harpsichord made by Hans Ruckers of Antwerp in 1642, the seventeenth century Italian harpsichord, and the fifteenth century harpsichord with its elaborately carved case of Flemish wood and its old Italian painting.

Also recovered were her two Ruckers spinets, her sixteenth century Italian psalterion, two old clavichords, an organ of 1737, two early square pianos and the Spanish piano used by Chopin in Majorca.

journalist added a throwaway line about other parts of the find. 'Also recovered were her two Ruckers spinets, her sixteenth century Italian psalterion, two old clavichords, an organ of 1737, two early square pianos and the Spanish piano used by Chopin in Majorca.'

Salt, potash and copper mines in Germany, Austria and the Czechoslovak Republic were now added to the emerging vocabulary of restitution, the consequence of the MFA&A recovering collections such as Landowska's and newspapers writing about these finds with curiosity and enthusiasm. The public imagination was of course fired more by the grand hauls: 6,700 paintings, including the Ghent Altarpiece (attributed to Hubert and Jan van Eyck), recovered from the salt mine of Alt Aussee in the mountains near Salzburg, many of them stolen in Italy for Göring or the planned Hitler museum in Linz. The salt mine at Bernterode, in the northernmost part of the Thuringian Forest, housed death helmets, royal orbs, jewel-encrusted swords, and the coffins of important figures of Prussian history, Frederick the Great among them. Allied troops hauled the last of these above ground on VE Day while the 'Star-Spangled Banner' and then 'God Save the King' blared out from a radio close to the mine's mouth, a transmission on the Armed Forces Network of the celebrations in London. A copper mine in Siegen revealed, along with works by Gauguin, Renoir and Rembrandt, Vermeer's *Astronomer* (looted from Rothschild's collection), the manuscript of Beethoven's Symphony No. 6, and the stunning silver and gold reliquary bust of

Charlemagne, which enclosed the king's skullcap. A mine near Merkers in south-west Germany gave rise to one of the astonishing images of post-war recovery: an American soldier casually mounting guard in the gloom while officials inspect sacks of gold bullion, estimated to be 100 tonnes in total.

These discoveries continued as one Nazi official after another was tried and sentenced at Nuremberg, Göring reputedly unfazed by the extermination of six million Jews during the twelve years of Hitler's rule, yet indignant when accused of being a common art thief. Here, too, the enormity of Alfred Rosenberg's misdeeds was revealed: he was sentenced to death not just for crimes against humanity, but also for the 'organized plunder of both public and private property throughout the invaded countries of Europe'.

The Monuments Men were hindered by the cruel European winter of 1945–6, when impoverished Berliners chopped their way through the centuries-old woods in Tiergarten for fuel, when grounds froze over and made recovery from some sites beneath it impossible. They had to fight the hostility of army officers who considered their work inconsequential and inconvenient. And they were up against their own lack of resources, never more obvious than when dealing with priceless artefacts, which deserved greater care than their fly-by-night operation could offer.

Janet Flanner included an unguarded assessment of the grim conditions in which they did their work in a piece for *The New Yorker*, where she extracted a letter written by an MFA&A officer:

> How would you go about hauling up a close-to-life-size Michelangelo marble statue of the Virgin and Child from the bottom of a salt mine, in a foreign country, with the mine machinery kaput from our bombs, with nearly no help from our Army, since it was authorized to give nearly none, without proper tools, without trained handlers, and without even the tattered bed coverlets of the moving man's trade to use as padding?

Nonetheless their hauls were mesmerizing – because of the scale of the looting, the quality of the art, and Germany's craven determination to hold on to it all when its dreams of a thousand-year Reich were crumbling all around it.

Landowska's instruments had arrived at the Munich collection point from Raitenhaslach in September 1945, where they were eventually catalogued by Valland or another MFA&A officer, each keyboard carefully checked against inventories made before the war or during it, either by the rightful owner of the property or by those who had stolen it, its condition assessed and recorded on an English-language file card.

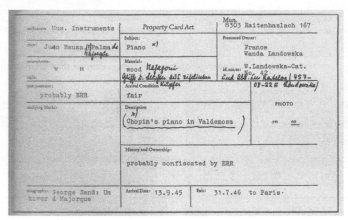

Chopin's piano is identified as the work of Juan Bauza, Palma de Majorque, the property of Wanda Landowska, and also as 'Chopin's piano in Valdemosa'. It states that the piano was 'probably confiscated by ERR'. And in the column headed 'Bibliography' the officer remarkably added 'George Sand: Un hiver à Majorque'. How civilized this cataloguer must have been to here invoke Sand, a bad-tempered ghost from a feast held a hundred years earlier, sitting out in the cloisters or the monk's burial plot, snatching time away from the children or the maid Amelia or her thieving neighbour, writing letters or scribbling notes for the books that would help immortalize Chopin's time in Majorca.

Restitution is complicated even when it seems straightforward. The latest owner of a painting or sculpture may have bought it in good faith, or considered that the purchase had helped the original Jewish owner liquidate his or her assets at a time when there were prohibitive taxes on those leaving the country, and precious few opportunities to do so. Or the new owner may have bought the piece from a dealer without really enquiring about provenance (there was much wilful amnesia), and certainly not been told it, perhaps even paying market price for it, whatever that then meant. Although the Inter-Allied Declaration of 1943 stripped away the nuances of art sold under duress, new owners of valuable paintings or instruments could and did counter that they had bought them legitimately. Why, therefore, should they return them?

These moral questions were undermined by more practical hindrances: Nazi records burned for heat (including files in Goebbels's office); instruments privately purchased; art works and instruments left unguarded in the repositories to which they had been whisked by desperate German soldiers (their world fast shrinking), which left them vulnerable to looting by locals and Allied and Soviet souvenir hunters. With these complexities, what chance of locating, identifying and returning the estimated 20,301 instruments given up before February 1944 by Jews and other deportees in Prague alone? Or the brass and woodwind instruments found in Auschwitz after its liberation: tenor and alto horns, a helicon, polished trumpets – the collection of an Alpine mountain band, surely, not of a concentration camp.

Long after the war Restout clipped out an article from *The New York Times* about the Service de la Protection des Oeuvres d'Art, which was based in what had once been Salomon Rothschild's residence on the rue Berryer in Paris, Rose Valland there in charge of an administrative staff and a team of ten full-time experts. In the article Valland mentions the major works still missing, the once wonderful collections broken up, the attempts to find works looted by U.S. Army personnel and taken home, the contrasting priorities and activities of art hunters in different countries, the willingness or otherwise of dealers and owners to be scrutinized. The article was intended to mark the twenty years since the Second Armoured Division marched into Paris, yet the complications of restitution were the same as they had been then.

Landowska's dilemma was more mundane. And it was one shared by many émigrés: she had moved far from where her possessions had been taken and to where they would be returned. Despite her success in America, she was without the resources to pay for their shipping, let alone the space to accommodate them. 'I have long reflected on the possibility of selling these instruments here (Met museum or elsewhere),' she told Mathot, 'but the complications, the enormous cost of transport and of customs etc. would put off a possible purchaser, which means I have abandoned the idea.' So at the end of July 1946 the Bauza piano and nine other keyboards, in varying states of disrepair, were transported from Munich to the Palais de Tokyo in Paris, which was then being used as a collection point.

She tried to work out what to do with them, what to do with the house and recital hall in Saint-Leu-la-Fôret. The best thing would be to sell the instruments in Paris, she wrote to Mathot, rather than pay to transport them the twenty miles to Saint-Leu. Yet for whatever reason they were returned to Saint-Leu, all except the Pleyel harpsichord Conrad had found, which was restored and then shipped to Landowska in New York, where it was burdened by the same issue of import duty that clung so resiliently to that other Pleyel keyboard caught up in customs, in Palma, a hundred years earlier.

A year later Landowska loaned the Chopin piano to the Conservatoire royal de Liège for its *Exposition d'art Romantique Chopin–George Sand*. It was in excellent company: the exhibition included photographs of Valldemossa; a copy of the letter Chopin sent Pleyel from Majorca on completing the Preludes; Chopin's death-mask and the cast Clésinger made of his hand; Kwiatkowski's painting of Chopin's deathbed, lent by Cortot; portraits of Chopin and Delacroix; an original edition of *Un hiver à Majorque* and various Sand manuscripts; an invitation to the *Théâtre des Marionnettes de Maurice Sand, à Nohant* and other such intimate pieces loaned by Aurore Sand, Maurice's daughter, which together provided a vivid evocation of two lives intertwined. Item 167 was the *Piano droit de Frédéric Chopin – on which he composed several famous compositions* (the catalogue announced), including Prelude No. 6 ('of such tragic emotion'), which is probably not the case. 'Removed by the Germans in 1940, the "Valdemosa piano" has just been recovered and restored to its owner, the great artist Mrs. Wanda Landowska, who was willing to allow this precious relic to be exhibited at the Royal Conservatory of Liège.' At the exhibition's close it was returned to Saint-Leu-la-Forêt.

22

MOSCOW, 1950

From behind the Iron Curtain, recordings of a young pianist slowly infiltrated the West: concerts in Prague and Sofia, Warsaw and Moscow, on labels like Melodiya, Praga and Muza. Born in the Ukraine in 1915, Sviatoslav Richter studied with Heinrich Neuhaus at the Moscow Conservatory and made his debut at the age of nineteen in a programme dedicated to Chopin's music. He would come to think more like a troubadour than a recitalist, travelling on tour whenever he could by rail or road, stopping off in small villages and towns along the way where, in a suitable church or town hall, he unloaded his piano and announced a performance that hour or night, mining repertory from his fabulously rich memory, afterwards finding accommodation in town or heading back on the road, another impromptu stop never far away. He did perform in large concert halls – not least in the West after 1960, when the terrifying Soviet culture minister Madame Furtseva allowed such appearances – but felt more at home in small venues, the stage sometimes lit by nothing more than a standard lamp (Landowska's trick) so as to encourage the audience's concentration.

In Moscow in 1950 he performed a solo Chopin recital, which itself was provocative: according to Prokofiev (on this occasion more disparaging of the state than of Chopin), Chopin's music had for a time been banned in the Soviet Union since its 'extreme sentimentality' was considered detrimental to the Russian populace. Richter would later admonish those who thought Chopin conceived the twenty-four Preludes as a complete cycle that should be performed as one; the sheer wealth of material would prevent listeners from appreciating the quality and majesty of each piece. So in Moscow he put together just twelve of them (and not sequentially), including six composed in Majorca. The recital was recorded (he preferred live performances to

studio takes), and his interpretation of the Preludes is unlike any other on disc: a spacious, spellbinding account of familiar works rendered utterly unfamiliar.

He opened with No. 4. Even if a pianist does not know that Chopin composed the piece after spending eighteen and a half hours aboard *El Mallorquin*, it is usually difficult to avoid hearing in the repetitive accompaniment the monotonous rhythmic chugs of a paddle-steamer. Not in Richter's hands. The performance is so uncommonly slow, with rubato applied to every shift in the train of harmonies left un-blurred by both tempo and pedal, the simple elongated aria in the treble stave given a wholly different sound from the accompaniment in the bass, the large vocal leaps spelled out almost gutturally, the whole thing aimless yet somehow also full of direction. Listening to it is disorienting. There is such a strange, lurching suspension of expectations, as though Richter is employing words that have long since dropped from usage.

His performance of No. 7, another composed on the Bauza piano, is similarly unsettling. It too is desperately slow: he takes close to a minute to play sixteen bars, whereas most pianists whip through them in about half that time. In No. 17 the castle clock tolls with all the depth and solemnity Baudelaire could have wished for, while the lacework in No. 8 (Liszt's favourite) sounds as though it could fray at any moment.

Richter probably then knew nothing of Valldemossa, nothing of the cell's lively acoustic or the distinct registers of the small piano on which some of the Preludes were written. Even so, he managed something so personal, so timeless, with rubato unconstrained by time signature or modern convention: it is a perfect re-creation of a sound and style lost in the wholesale shift in how Chopin had come to be played. Perhaps his affinity with Bach (another unfashionable composer in Soviet Russia) was key. He would later record *Das Wohltemperierte Klavier* in Schloss Klessheim in Salzburg – an effortlessly crystalline interpretation and execution, each moving part treated like the vital component of an intricate machine, which it is. 'I could detect something authentically Chopinesque about them,' he would later write of a recital in Tokyo where he played with equal imagination a different combination of Preludes, 'but it's highly unlikely that advocates of a sentimentalized Chopin will find anything to admire here.'

The best rubato is like a golf ball hovering on the lip of a hole for that interminable moment before it tips in. Everyone feels these hesitations, both the strange dislocation in time and the absolute rightness when the putted ball drops: the player, the commentators, those watching. It's the time it takes Alice to fall down the rabbit hole, a temporal dislocation easy to sense but difficult to analyse. Carlos Kleiber had this unforced, breathtaking quality when conducting Johann Strauss waltzes, which can sound so mundane in the wrong hands. So did Benjamin Britten playing Schubert.

Liszt famously likened Chopin's rubato in performance to a tree whose leaves are stirred into life by the wind, all the while the trunk remains immobile. Berlioz commented on this aspect of Chopin at the piano as early as 1833: 'His playing is shot through with a thousand nuances of movement of which he alone holds the secret, impossible to convey by instructions.' (He later teasingly modified this assessment, with good comic effect: 'In my opinion he pushed rhythmic independence much too far ... Chopin *could* not play in time.') Similarly, Charles Hallé, who maintained a cordial friendship with Chopin and heard him play often, wrote about plucking up the courage in 1845 or 1846 to ask why Chopin's Mazurkas sounded as though they were in 4/4 time when he played them, owing to how long he lingered on the first beat. Chopin strenuously denied it until Hallé made him play one while he counted along, out loud, four beats in each bar. (An earlier, identical conversation occurred between Meyerbeer and Chopin, though on this occasion Meyerbeer was more patronizing, Chopin more frigid, the meeting less successful.)

It takes courage to play this way: the results can sound forced or fake. But Richter managed it, turning the last bar of most of the eight waltz fragments in No. 7 into common time – four beats instead of the prescribed three. There are many other subtleties, much rubato in different shapes, an overarching sense of the whole, but it is through the insertion of these elongated bars that Richter achieves the piece's architecture. (In the live performance in Tokyo in 1979 these elongations are even greater.) It is such a simple yet audacious gesture, so right yet so unknown today when none but the most adventurous pianist dares to take what appears to be such a clumsy step. (In this Grigory Sokolov is Richter's direct heir: his performance of the Preludes in the 2008 Salzburg Festival is a phenomenal achievement.)

Cortot is nothing at all like this in his 1942 recording of the waltz: he relies instead on sudden rushes in an already brisk tempo, gentle lingerings over key moments, and the occasional dislocation between bass note and treble melody. Both pianists were dealing with Chopin's stubborn refusal on paper – as either protest, petulance or mischief – to push in any single way the somewhat limited instrument on which he wrote the Prelude, relying instead on the performer to create the magic, something he himself did without thinking. Richter does this, Cortot doesn't. And in these phrase-end bars, in this waltz, at this moment in Moscow in 1950, he made sixteen threes add up to much more than forty-eight.

They are a good match, Chopin and Richter, the Russian's dolorousness and poised musicality a perfect fit with the Chopin that Sand encountered late one night in the monastery after returning with the children from a nocturnal scramble: hair on end, face pale as the moon, eyes filled with dread, suddenly snapping out of his glum mood and offering to play for them whatever he had just composed, the outcome of whichever terrible obsessions had crept over him in his loneliness and sorrow, so Sand thought. In his many Chopin performances Richter perfectly captured the quality of improvisation and fragility that had been lost during the nineteenth century, the quality W. H. Auden would later describe so well:

> Listening to the *Études*
> of Chopin, entranced
> by such a love-match of Craft
> and Utterance, he forgot
> his Love was not there.

Richter was more attuned to this love match than any of his contemporaries and so many of his successors. He performed Chopin with such transparency and suppleness, perfectly capturing the timbre that in Majorca and then Paris helped make the arrival of the Preludes so completely unexpected.

23

Saint-Leu-la-Forêt, New York City, Lakeville, 1949–59

Wearying detail and frustratingly inconclusive conversations and correspondence about her home and property coloured Landowska's final decade, all the while Doda Conrad liaised with French lawyers and notaries, restitution officials and Pleyel. In 1953 he gave her advice about the condition and value of her home. The land alone was worth 1,400 to 1,500 francs per square metre, almost four million francs in total (around 90,000 euros today). The buildings would also be worth four million francs, he thought, or would be once she spent two million or so repairing locks, doors, windows, roof, plumbing and wiring. The contrast between the rooms Mathot was living in and those used merely to store returned items was painful. Landowska's office, with its beautiful outlook over the street, one of the few rooms Mathot heated when bitter winds rattled the windows, when snow carpeted the garden, retained her imprint, Conrad told her, but there was little else to connect the house with its vibrant incarnation of the interwar years. It was a place of both warmth and sadness, he said, almost as though he wanted to discourage her from thinking fondly of her past. 'Paris is sad: it's grey, it's cold,' he later wrote to her. 'All the world has left for Easter; I've never seen such an exodus. It's probably because the winter was so hard. People go towards the sun.'

In August 1953 Landowska wrote to him in the rue de Bruxelles, in Paris's ninth *arrondissement*, a short walk from Gare Saint-Lazare and the successive apartments on the rue de la Chaussée-d'Antin that Chopin had occupied for most of the 1830s before leaving for Majorca. A friend had offered to bring to America a few items from Saint-Leu and she had selected some paintings, one of a Spanish Virgin, another of a violinist. And then a postscript: 'As for the Chopin piano, that depends on where you end up. Have you decided?' It would seem she had promised the piano to Conrad, though in his reply he made no mention of it; Bauza's instrument had slipped down low on their lists as well.

The following year Denise Restout visited France, her first trip home since boarding the *Exeter* all those years before. In Saint-Leu-la-Forêt she saw the instruments that had made their way back to the house. 'All but the piano of Chopin were in terrible condition,' she would later write, though in 1960 she thought she might yet be able to restore these 'souvenirs of St-Leu times': the Ruckers spinet, the bottom of which was intact, as were its strings and jacks; a clavichord, which was missing only two strings; but not the historical harpsichords, which she acknowledged were beyond repair.

Landowska let these matters pass. She was working away at what she called her last will and testament: a recording of Bach's forty-eight Preludes and Fugues – the work Chopin had with him in Majorca. *Time* first wrote about this undertaking in June 1949, describing Landowska's arrival at RCA's Manhattan studio each Saturday and Sunday evening at half-past six, how Restout would then open her toolkit and attend to the harpsichord, tweaking all that complicated Pleyel machinery. Schunicke set out pillows, unloaded sandwiches and coffee from the hamper, and put horehound drops where they could be reached. Landowska then emerged from her dressing room in a loose smock, blue knee-length socks, red fur-trimmed bedroom slippers, and set to work. She had performed all of Book I at the Town Hall a year earlier, so they were under her fingers; in any case, she told the journalist, she had been playing Bach on the harpsichord in public for forty-six years: the pieces really ought to be within her grasp. 'Although she is as spry and sparkling eyed as ever ("I feel as young as a child"), Landowska has given up touring. In the last few years, she has also given up the idea of returning to her once-famed Ecole de Musique Ancienne at picturesque Saint-Leu-la-Forêt near Paris, from which she fled in 1940 before the Nazis took over.'

Time visited her once more, in 1952, in her new home in Lakeville, Connecticut, on the eve of RCA's release of the fifth album in the *Wohltemperierte Klavier* series, one still to come. It described her daily routine: the coffee and correspondence Restout or Schunicke brought to her bed at eight each morning; the bright-red corduroy

robe she slipped on for breakfast downstairs ('red is for violence, like Bach, sometimes'), where she nibbled away at figs, dates and lettuce, as though an elderly rabbit; the long days that followed ('I never practice, I always play'), which could end very late at night; the walks in the countryside, whether in rain or sunshine. *Time* noted her dislike of all those nineteenth-century pianists who put Bach and Handel and Mozart back on the loom, as if it was necessary to make them palatable to modern audiences: Bach-Liszt, Bach-Bülow, and the like. 'What would sculptors say if a mason undertook to cut away some marble from the Venus de Milo to give her a wasp waist, or if one tried to twist Apollo's nose in order to give him more character?' she asked. When the journalist mentioned the ghosts with which Landowska lived and communed daily, her eyes lit up. 'This small empress in exile from her time' – Landowska's own line, pressed into service by a journalist with a quick ear – 'has lived with them for most of her life. For her they are alive.'

One of these ghosts assumed flesh when in January 1959 her prized Bach-Gesellschaft was discovered in a house in Paris's rue de Richelieu, its boxes charting a heavy-inked trail back to West Germany. But at seventy-nine Landowska was almost too old to care about this latest flash from her past, and the discovery passed her by. She still received friends at home, but on 26 July 1959 she sat at the harpsichord for the last time, and then took her final walk in the nearby field. By the beginning of August she could only make it as far as an armchair on the first floor, unable to venture downstairs. This indomitable spirit became more and more a weak shadow of her fiery self. 'Several times I read in her face that she knew that she was ready and that she was abandoning herself to divine wishes,' Restout wrote to Conrad. On 16 August, at a quarter to eleven in the morning, she tried to gulp in air once or twice – violent spasms of desperation or release – before dying. 'This extraordinary heart stopped beating. It was finished.'

'How beautiful she was in her last sleep, so young, the line of her profile so pure, with a mysterious half smile, such a happy serenity emanated from her,' Restout told Conrad. It is much as people described her all her life. (It was also exactly how Clésinger wanted Chopin remembered.) Restout and Schunicke dressed her in a white silk tunic and a red jacket and laid her out in the music room, facing out on to the garden, close to one of her harpsichords. Two days later they accompanied her to New Haven, Connecticut, where she was cremated in accordance with her wishes. She had directed that her ashes be disposed in the grave of her brother Paul in Couperin's Taverny, the commune north of Paris directly next to Saint-Leu-la-Forêt.

Harold Schonberg wrote a nice appreciation in *The New York Times*, affectionately describing her performance of the first book of *Das Wohltemperierte Klavier* in the Town Hall – the five minutes it took her to walk the twenty feet onstage, palms pressed together as if in prayer, eyes cast to heaven hoping for further inspiration or Bach's last-minute instruction. For Schonberg, as for many, her concerts were the only time he heard Bach's keyboard works played with clarity. 'When she held on to a fermata (a held note), worlds tottered and breathing stopped until she continued the next phrase.'

Schonberg was also keen to place her in the century of her birth. 'She was born in an age of romantic playing – an age dominated by the figures of Liszt and Leschetizky and their pupils. She grew up with certain romantic traditions of performance, and those traditions remained with her to the end, whatever the stringency of her musical scholarship.' Her life did indeed map late Romanticism, this woman old enough to have played for Brahms, old enough to have met Anton

Rubinstein. 'If I am not mistaken,' she once wrote, Strauss perhaps in her mind, 'romanticism is departing with a noisy farewell in the person of a few pundits of progress who continue to exaggerate the Wagnerian genre; this, I should hope, will not prevent their creating masterpieces.' Yet in her final years she told Restout how sad she was that she would not be around for its inevitable return. 'Let us not say adieu, but *au revoir* to Romanticism because soon it will come back adorned with new attractions and under a changed name.'

She was talking about composition, not performance of course: concerts and careers after the war remained mired in Romantic habits and repertory, the territory that von Karajan and Georg Solti occupied for such a long time. Such traditions were bedded down in post-war American consciousness and culture – and to a lesser extent in Britain's – courtesy of the many émigré soloists, orchestral musicians, conductors, administrators, producers, scholars and audiences who, like Landowska, changed the way people came to think about art music in their adopted country.

Yet had Landowska lived she would have had her wish soon enough. 'The twentieth century never took in music,' Malcolm Gillies thinks, 'though we write the history of it as though it did. It is music in search of a tradition it never really found.' No defined musical period followed the Romantic era, he argues: there was no agreement on what style of music should prevail, just a series of trends – expressionism, serialism, neoclassicism, indeterminacy, *musique concrète,* minimalism, post-modernism, et cetera – that never took hold, never coalesced into a consensual tradition. In the field of composition, nineteenth-century musical Romanticism adapts and survives. Old forms are inhabited, established emotions excited. The long Romantic century might logically have ended with Strauss's *Vier letzte Lieder,* yet Romanticism's musical language and syntax are still passed on to young composers determined to emulate or improve on their predecessors' works, and who sometimes content themselves with ever grander and more extended versions of the repertory and traditions they inherited.

Innovation continues to come in waves, of course, which soon ebb to reveal the Romantic traditions that underline and support all the experimentation – not simply what is written, but how it is presented, who listens to it, where and when it is performed. It is as though these traditions are ringed by a great rubber band, which effectively pulls back those composers, performers and programmers who push too far or firmly against it. And in these revealing junctures, musicians, audiences and institutions are often not confident enough to confront the museum culture in which they find themselves moored.

*

CF 40872

Ceci est mon testament.

Je soussignée Wanda Landowska (veuve de Henri Lew) de nationalité française, domiciliée et résidant à Lakeville Connecticut, États Unis d'Amérique, institue pour ma légataire universelle de tous mes biens mobiliers et immobiliers en France au jour de mon décès (le présent testament ne visant que les biens en France) mon amie Elsa Schunicke, de nationalité Française, demeurant à Lakeville, Connecticut, États Unis d'Amérique. En cas de prédécès de cette dernière, j'institue pour ma légataire universelle, de tous mes biens mobiliers et immobiliers en France au jour de mon décès, mon amie Diana Mathot de nationalité Française demeurant à Saint Leu la Forêt, Seine et Oise, France.

Je révoque toutes dispositions antérieures relatives aux présentes, concernant mes biens en France.

Fait et écrit entièrement de ma main à Lakeville Connecticut, États Unis d'Amérique, le trente et un Juillet mil neuf cent cinquante trois Wanda Landowska

Je désire être incinérée. Déposer mes cendres dans mon caveau à Taverny auprès de mon frère Paul.

Restout and Schunicke divided up the possessions not specified in Landowska's American will. Restout kept linen, the lamb-fur coat, the painting of the Spanish Virgin, a drawing by Carpeaux, a ladder, a Magnavox recording machine, metronomes, a slide projector, phonographs, Blenko glassware, Landowska's music scores and books and documents, and all the normal possessions accumulated over a lifetime – though in reality they represented less than a quarter of one. These stayed with her in the house in Lakeville, which in time she renamed The Landowska Center, its letterhead featuring a silhouette profile of Landowska sitting in a high-backed chair at a two-manual Pleyel harpsichord, its lyre pedal board just evident. Schunicke took lamps and fans, a typewriter and air conditioner, a table and chairs: she would soon have to furnish a small house in Coral Gables. The American will allocated her the two Steinway pianos. Restout got the Challis clavichord, the Virgil practice keyboard, and the Pleyel harpsichord that Landowska had requested in Banyuls-sur-Mer all those years ago – before flight took command of her life – an instrument that finally caught up with her in America.

Landowska's French assets were covered by a separate will: the house in Saint-Leu-la-Forêt and its contents; the existing bank accounts; the royalties still issued by Les Industries Musicales et Electriques Pathé Marconi, all of which she left to Schunicke. She and Restout then drifted apart, lacking any adhesion beyond their shared history with a remarkable woman.

Five years later Restout wrote to Rose Valland and included a copy of the book she had edited containing Landowska's most important articles on music. In it are photos of some of the historical instruments Landowska never saw again, and 'which since her death have been once more dispersed'. Landowska remained immensely popular – she was invoked, improbably, in *Playboy* magazine in October 1968 in an advertisement for an eight-track car stereo – her legacy preserved in the many brilliant recordings she made in her fifties, sixties and seventies, her celebrity reaching far beyond the confines of the music world.

Restout told Valland that she wanted to write Landowska's biography but found the task so difficult without her books and scores. 'Do you think there is still a glimmer of hope of finding her library?' In

her response Valland rehearsed the whole grim tableau – during the war and after – before ending pessimistically. 'Given these conditions, there is very little chance that the annotated scores you are particularly interested in fell into the hands of people capable of understanding their interest and value. But perhaps I might be wrong to generalize thus. I hope an exception might be possible for some of these pieces. Who knows now, in the calm that has returned to the nation of Landowska . . .'

The calm in the nation of Landowska, the nation of Chopin, was uneasy. And it would only deteriorate as the decade progressed and the Cold War intensified. Yet Restout responded with dignity and gratitude, saying she would rely on luck, on chance encounters and coincidence, on the good will of humankind. It was a slim trunk for such heavy branches.

24

Washington D.C., Valldemossa, London, Saint-Leu-la-Forêt, 2015–17

There are long passages in *Moby Dick* when we're never quite sure Ahab will find the damn whale. On board the *Pequod* he obsessively charts winds and tides, monitors where the whale's food has come from, and calculates where the currents will take it. He is still shaken by terrible, vivid dreams, the whale haunting him even in his sleep, yet he rationalizes his quest in a way that even his crew – all but cynical Starbuck – can understand. Near the equator he delivers a rousing speech to his whalers, lightning striking the mast, typhoon waves lashing the hull. And throughout his many lectures and investigations, asides and conclusions, Herman Melville is courteous to his readers, never promising more than he can deliver, yet still clouding the narrative with dense wisps of uncertainty.

Hunting the Bauza piano feels a little like this. It did not seem so initially. In 2010 Martin Elste, the Landowska scholar and curator in Berlin's Musikinstrumenten-Museum (where in the 1890s Landowska began her odyssey), published *Die Dame mit dem Cembalo*, which reproduces Binder's photograph of Landowska in front of the Chopin piano, the caption asserting that after her death Elsa Schunicke inherited the instrument. 'Diese Nahm es mit nach Coral Gables, Florida, wo sie ihren Lebensabend verbrachte, und wo sich das Instrument noch heute in einem Museum befinden soll.' ('She took the piano with her to Coral Gables, Florida, where she spent her remaining years, and where today the instrument is said to be found in a museum.') The Bauza instrument, midwife to some of the greatest nineteenth-century piano music, which travelled first those winding miles from Palma up the Serra de Tramontana to Valldemossa, from there to Berlin, then on to Paris, then Saint-Leu-la-Forêt, then back to Paris (the Louvre), from there again to Berlin, then Leipzig, then to a monastery not far from Munich, then to Munich itself, and from there once more to Paris and back to Saint-Leu: this most resilient piano is now, apparently, in a museum in Florida.

But I have missed some of the nuance in Elste's caption, the hint of speculation in the German subjunctive, as he soon tells me. 'But had I known in which museum the piano is now, I would have written it! Perhaps you can find out and then tell me.' He was attempting to lay down a piece of a very large puzzle, but his proposition was more hopeful than analytical; Ahab monitoring the tides and currents, calculating where they will take his whale, it is not.

Carla Shapreau is a bright American lawyer, academic, cultural property researcher, violin maker, and indisputably the person today doing the most important work on music restitution. She represents claimants, investigates individual instruments, writes pithy articles in *The New York Times* or dense papers with titles like 'The Loss of French Musical Property During World War II'. She can only speculate about the fate of the Bauza piano today. 'I have not yet found any evidence that Landowska brought this piano to the U.S.,' she writes. 'I'm sorry I don't have an answer to the question regarding the current whereabouts of the Chopin piano,' she adds, feeling some sympathy for me, 'but sometimes not finding what you are looking for isn't a bad place to end a story.'

Yet Skip Sempé is not so sure the instrument never made it to America. 'About the "Chopin piano", I have also heard that Elsa had it in Florida when she died. But I have no trace of this. Perhaps Teri would know.' 'Teri' is the New York lawyer and harpsichord enthusiast Teri Noel Towe, who grew up on Landowska discs. These include the second *Goldberg Variations* recording and her *Wohltemperierte Klavier* series, of course, but also her thrilling reading of the Toccata in D, BWV 912 – Bach's magical, improvisatory trek through a small handful of stunningly distinct landscapes, its final page containing twelve bars of whirlygig figurations, almost impossible to play at the speed at which they need to be played but which Landowska tosses off apparently effortlessly. Teri first met Restout when he was a freshman at Princeton, forty years before her death in 2004. He says categorically, lawyerly, that Skip is mistaken, that it was not in the house in Lakeville when he started visiting Restout in 1967 and was not talked of in the context of Schunicke's cottage in Coral Gables. More pertinently, he adds, Landowska's record producer Jack Pfeiffer never mentioned it, nor did harpsichordist Irma Rogell, both of whom knew the Lakeville house well when Landowska was alive. 'My "gut reaction" is that, like the other instruments, the Chopin piano did not make it to the USA.'

Ten years before her death Restout wrote to Pfeiffer about the instruments that had been in the house at Saint-Leu-la-Forêt. 'In general, have you any idea what dispositions – if any – Elsa made regarding Mamusia's memorabilia? for instance: Chopin's piano? I know that the little Swiss organ was sold and "electrically-restored" . . . that one of the harpsichords is in Australia and that a spinet happily found its way to the Bruxelles Museum. Etc . . .' It was the letter of a real musician, determined that all these instruments should be together in one place to complete the portrait of the greatly missed Mamusia. Pfeiffer wrote back, discouragingly: 'Elsa, of course, left everything to [her sister] Trudi with whom I lost contact some years ago. It was her decision based on some strange feeling she had that I was not a devoted friend . . . At any rate, I have no idea what happened to anything Trudi had from Elsa.' Restout responded sympathetically, saying that she had long experience with the offhandedness of the Schunickes.

At the Library of Congress in Washington D.C. I sift through thousands of pages of Landowska's and Restout's papers hoping to find a clue, believing after a week of this that I can speak fluent French. There is a particular technique to this: from the hundreds of long letters in bad cursive writing, and from typed sheets (often carbon) with acutes and graves added by hand in blue ink, you forage for certain words: *instruments*, *repatriation*, Pleyel, Chopin, *restitution*, Nazi, Majorca, Saint-Leu-la-Forêt, *Clavecin*, Bauza. You then place page after wearying page on to an overhead document scanner, express surprise when you are told this service is free ('You pay your taxes, don't you?' asks the librarian. 'Yes, but not here'), and retreat to the home of a smart and helpful linguist friend, Sue Hackett.

There you have to mine all the correspondence between Restout and Valland and between the various parties seeking restitution and recompense, and other documents that miraculously survived the war: old passports and visas, shipping tickets, letters from the Pleyel firm, voluminous correspondence between Mathot and Landowska, and the doting letters and postcards from Conrad who wanders the Continent on an urgent commission from his master. There is one sad, black moment when Sue translates out loud Landowska's French will. ' "Je désire être incinérée": I wish to be incinerated – sorry, cremated . . .' It takes her only a second to make the correction, based on the right word for a person rather than an inanimate object, but that chilling second seems to hold the history of European Jewry between 1933 and 1945.

In Washington a librarian arranges for me to see one of the two Pleyel harpsichords recovered after the war, perhaps the one Captain Morey discovered in the officers' recreation room, which was restored in 2009 by Barbara and Thomas Wolf in The Plains, Virginia. I have had good fortune with American curators. A week earlier, having been shown round the Met's collection of musical instruments by its associate curator Jason Dobney, discussing the Bauza piano as we went, I asked a young security guard if I was allowed to take photographs. He nodded assent then asked, disconcertingly, 'Have you thought about the temperament of the Chopin piano in Majorca?' (I hadn't.) It was a very New York thing to happen: the guard has a master's degree in guitar and has had to think deeply about how temperament governs his own repertory. It was he who suggested Ross Duffin's book *How Equal Temperament Ruined Harmony: And Why You Should Care* ('The book is not quite as good as its title'), which set me thinking about the role of temperament in Chopin's Preludes, No. 15 in particular.

Landowska's Pleyel was in poor condition when it went to the Wolfs, the stage manager at the Coolidge Auditorium tells me. Photos show it in the house in Lakeville littered with cats, its legs serving as scratching posts, fur everywhere. We pull off the cover and it is once more the handsome instrument the Pleyel firm constructed to Landowska's specifications in the year she travelled to Majorca. I play a little of Bach's Toccata in D, BWV 912, one of the pieces Teri knew so well from Landowska's recording, with the impossible sewing-machine coda. The harpsichord hasn't been used for a while and the tuning sounds positively modal; it is all right on the eight-foot stop on the upper keyboard, but terrible on the lower one. I'm not sure in these moments that the ghost of Landowska is with me, let alone Bach's, but it is a privilege, for a few minutes, to follow in her fingerprints. And it makes me think more kindly about Cortot, who once wrote of the honour he felt playing Chopin on one of Chopin's own pianos, how his spirit seemed to infuse the performance with a unique quality.

Months later the young harpsichordist Christopher D. Lewis – a canny and passionate advocate of Pleyel instruments and the music written for them – sends me a series of photographs of Landowska taken in Lakeville in 1951 by the Jewish émigré Hermann Landshoff. In one she is tucked up in bed, her make-up perfectly applied, every bit the old grandma in 'Little Red Riding Hood' that Ralph Kirkpatrick described on their first meeting. The images could not be further from the Landowska of New York Town Hall and Saint-Leu-la-Forêt, of *Das Wohltemperierte Klavier* and *Time* magazine.

The photograph suggests her sense of humour, which Kirkpatrick never saw or at least never admitted. 'They think that I'm a Pole, or that I'm French, or that I'm American,' Landowska often said to Conrad, 'and the only thing I am really is an old Jewess, crazy about music. *Juire fou de musique.*' She had written her own epitaph.

Then I read about a newly discovered Chopin grand piano, a Pleyel, that was for a while in the apartment at 9, Place d'Orléans. It has been missing for years – or perhaps hiding in plain view. Using the ledgers Camille Pleyel kept so meticulously in the 1840s, Alain Kohler has identified the piano as the one on loan to Chopin between November 1844 and June 1845, which Edwin Beunk in the

Netherlands restored quite beautifully in 2009 without knowing its provenance. It could be the mahogany grand in the watercolour of Chopin's drawing room (the same model as the Chopin piano in the collection at Hatchlands), the painting looted during the Nazi occupation of Poland: it has the same legs and music rest, the same lyre pedals as the instrument in the painting.

Kohler is entirely at home in this world: he writes passionately about all the Pleyels in Chopin's possession in Paris and at Nohant between June 1839 and July 1847. Working as detective and scholar, musician and enthusiast, he has identified twenty-two such instruments, fifteen of them grands. This Beunk piano is the seventh surviving Chopin Pleyel, all of which are in museums or collections throughout Europe and Great Britain, from Valldemossa to Hatchlands. Surely Kohler knows about Chopin's Bauza piano? But his sole focus is on Pleyel instruments and he can only speculate that the Bauza is in an American collection.

So I ask Christophe Nebout, whose family firm has been restoring pianos since 1912, a year after Landowska first attempted to buy the Bauza instrument, a year before she succeeded. Christophe and his team – artisans and apprentices, carpenters and technicians – work in an old atelier tucked into the Passage de Clichy, close to the Gare Saint-Lazare. Here they undertake the delicate, intricate work required to resuscitate old Pleyels and Bechsteins, replacing the soundboard and hammers, blasting the frame, stripping the case, reapplying varnish and polish. If anyone in Paris wanted to have work done on an old piano at any time between the 1950s and today, Pianos Nebout would be the obvious place to go. Client privilege would no doubt prevent Christophe from saying whether Chopin's Bauza had ever found its way to his family's workshop, but this turns out not to be a concern, more's the pity: he seems genuinely torn when he writes, 'Unfortunately we never had the chance to meet this piano. I'm afraid we won't have much more to say than you might already know.'

Carla Shapreau introduces me to Willem de Vries, author of the detailed study of the ERR's Sonderstab Musik bureau. ('Perhaps Willem knows where Chopin's piano has gone.') He grew up in a southern neighbourhood of Amsterdam populated by Jews who had managed to work their way out of the poor quarters of the city. When war broke out Willem's father joined the Resistance group 'South 2' and put his craftsman's skills to good work: making false passports, re-creating German stamps and letterheads, hiding Jews and then helping them escape with forged documents in their pockets. ('His hands could make what his eyes saw,' Willem says of his father.) In 1942 Jews remaining in the neighbourhood were rounded up and sent to camps, never to return. Willem was too young to remember much of this: he was born in 1939, a year before the German invasion of Holland. His father seldom spoke about his wartime activities, but the boy Willem (assiduously recording in a notebook the first American and British cars on Amsterdam's streets after the war: Fords, Chevrolets, Hudsons and Rileys) knew of the decoration he received for his Resistance work, and of the students at his school in the early 1950s without a single uncle or aunt between them, with names like Huberman, Diamand, Borenstajn, Lichtenstein.

Working in the 1990s on the Landowska theft, Willem began corresponding with Denise Restout, carefully articulating his discoveries, asking for clarification of details and assumptions. She told him about her long battle for compensation from the German government, of the case 'Schunicke et al. versus the German Reich' in the early 1970s, every bit as tortuous as Dickens's Jarndyce versus Jarndyce. At one point Schunicke is ordered to state:

a) Where the musical instruments returned after the end of the war are at the present time;

b) What in her opinion constitutes the reduction in the value of these instruments mentioned under sub a) which was indicated by her in her statement of February 6, 1971 (description of nature and scope of the damage, if necessary by submission of photographs of the instruments).

But there is no record of her response.

Quite odious witnesses appear at this trial, on precisely whose behalf it is sometimes difficult to tell. 'I can only faintly recollect the steps taken in the Landowska case,' Herbert Gerigk says under oath, lying through his teeth. 'The duties of the unit included among other things the securing of property of fugitives ... My duties included, among other things, the handling of objects of importance.' But then the dissembling: 'I was not personally present . . . I cannot indicate . . . It is possible there were fifty-three crates . . . I personally had neither access to or control over the instruments . . . I did not know . . . I am not able to give any information . . . All I know . . . To my knowledge . . .' et cetera. It is completely commonplace ex-Nazi stuff.

'For ten days, I have been trying to recall the circumstances,' Gerigk told a different investigation a decade earlier, and only 'vaguely remembered shipments arranged through the alleged M-Aktion, as well as through Baron von Behr, involving massive numbers of grand and upright pianos and other instruments to the eastern territories.' Finally he could recall a workshop in Paris in which instruments were refurbished by a team of thirty-six craftsmen and technicians (a microcosm of Pleyel's factory in Chopin's time), since 'many music instruments found in French homes had been in very poor condition,' he observed ungallantly. It was precisely such obfuscation, indignation, amnesia, buck-passing, collective guilt, arrogance, superiority and guile that accounted for the difficulties in restitution and compensation for so many victims of Nazi plundering in the decades following the war. The judge found in Schunicke's favour (though not Restout's) and put a figure on the missing instruments.

Years later another court case, which indirectly touched on the Landowska collection, took place under a very different jurisdiction and set of circumstances. Its crux is captured in a postcard that Doda Conrad sent Landowska from Majorca in the 1950s. It is of the Celda

53 VALLDEMOSA   Cartuja – Celda de Chopin   Ediciones Distribuciones
                      La Chartreuse – Cellule de Chopin   Antonio VICH –Mallorca

de Chopin in Valldemossa, sparse furniture along walls on which hang large paintings, and at one end of the room a small Spanish upright piano surrounded by framed certificates and documents. Except it wasn't the real Chopin cell, and the owners of the authentic apartment, number four, in which Chopin's Majorcan Pleyel was on display – along with keepsakes and manuscripts, photographs and Teofil Kwiatkowski's romanticized *Chopin on his Deathbed* – wanted the other cell (number two) to stop taking the money of tourists and pilgrims who made their way to Valldemossa from Palma – through those thirteen tunnels in the Serra de Tramontana, over the lovely viaduct and the series of narrow bridges – to pay their respects.

The court ruling of October 2011 is beautifully considered. It outlines the history of the Cartuja and of Chopin and Sand's stay there, and it spells out the dispute between the owners of the two cells, each of whom had long laid claim to the eminent artists in Valldemossa in that bitter winter of 1838–9. It dissects the tourist industry and incomes that have grown up around the two cells, how there was little to detect in this regard until the 1930s. It introduces sketches of the courtyard done by Maurice Dudevant as evidence that Chopin and Sand stayed in the fourth cell, not the second, the judge ruling that the distinctive chimney and stove depicted could belong to no other apartment (though not before the other family's solicitor had criticized Maurice's reliability as a witness and his skill as a draughts-man, as evinced by his drawings of Palma Cathedral, its steeples disproportionately high).

Finally, judgement on the piano. Having examined the cabinet and mechanics, having dated various bits of patented technology incorp-orated into the instrument, having counted the number of keys and inspected the joinery work and allocation of strings per hammer, the court expert testified that the piano could not possibly have been built before 1840. It is more likely to belong to the second half of the century, he added, imagining the circumstances of its construction, how Oliver y Suau Hermanos likely visited Madrid, inspected a piano made by the Slocker firm in or after 1846, which on his return to Majorca he copied as best he could. Surely if Chopin had encountered this piano in 1838, the judge suggests – with its range a quarter octave greater than that of the Pleyel he eagerly awaited, with three strings per note instead of the Pleyel's two – he would have been amazed at his good fortune, rather than ridicule the instrument so heartily.

The judge makes reference to Landowska having acquired the orig-inal Spanish instrument, but does not know its whereabouts. He then orders the owners of cell number two to stop advertising their prop-erty or the piano inside as being in any way connected with Chopin's winter in Majorca; those privileges are now the sole right of the own-ers of cell number four.

The court's ruling is about tourism and money and souvenirs and a piano, but the essential reason the stakes were so high, the edict so judicious, is because of the pieces composed in Majorca that winter. Cedric Tiberghien, preparing the Preludes for recording, sends me a photograph of himself and his son in the garden adjoining the gen-uine Chopin cell, a few steps from where George Sand's son Maurice set up his stool, took out his sketch pad, and drew the monastery roof tiles and chimney, a couple of paces from where Landowska once sat and posed for Henri Lew or whoever was travelling with her. It reminds me of a conversation a year or so earlier, Cedric telling me how for much of his life he resisted the pull of Chopin, which most French pianists experience from a young age, and that he was drawn instead to the structure and substance of Beethoven. Pianists as young as Cedric are still grappling with the nineteenth century's battle between sound and form. But with maturity comes the ability to tackle the elusive, and Cedric now feels ready to take on the Preludes, to trust his instinctive response to colour alongside structure. Later he gives me a first edit of his recording, which is full of such beautiful shades and glorious shapes, of both menace and tenderness, the whole thing underlining his belief in the overriding architecture of the collection.

These qualities are in short supply in Maurizio Pollini's performance of the Preludes one evening at London's Festival Hall. It is a sad reading from a giant of the keyboard not knowing his time has passed – Kirkpatrick's comment about Paderewski all those years ago. He seems mesmerized by fourth-finger melodies, uninterested in the textures and counterpoint beneath; he rams one Prelude into the next without any space at all, as though a gifted teenager impatiently playing them to his teacher for the first time; he makes everything sound the same, each piece too loud, no rubato whatsoever, cold, fuddled, terrible.

At the end the audience stands, rapturous looks on their faces. 'Are they applauding their idea of him,' my editor asks, 'or their memory of past performances?' It is both, I reply. Pollini clearly earned his stripes in other decades, not least as winner of the Warsaw Chopin Competition in 1960, Rubinstein a juror and, thereafter, a great admirer; he should have been better. Yet those in the hall were merely valuing his stature over his playing, which left them immune to his infelicities. But they were also acknowledging the unique stature of the Preludes, 180 years after these very pieces had left audiences wholly bemused. And this is worth celebrating: in the intervening years the Preludes have become tiny-great monuments of Western art music.

Jean-Jacques Eigeldinger writes to me with more discouraging news. In April 1958, having just turned eighteen, he visited the house in Saint-Leu-la-Forêt: Landowska had a year to live, and this was his pilgrimage at one remove. In the house he found the two early square pianos that *The New York Times* had written about in 1946, and the chamber organ too, back in its rightful spot inside the hall. But there was no trace of the Bauza piano, nor of any other instrument. It would seem that, some time between Restout's visit in 1954 and Jean-Jacques's pilgrimage four years later, the returned instruments bled from the house: into collections, offered as gifts, perhaps even destroyed – through neglect or intent – their intrinsic value no match for either the restorative work required or a fast-changing world. Whether or not Conrad in these years accepted Landowska's offer of the Chopin piano, it seems that it was never Schunicke's to give away. And that, for now, is that.

Perhaps the piano will one day show up; it seems impossible that an instrument of such hardiness and cultural potency should have been destroyed. Yet its disappearance is symbolic of a Chopin performance tradition that has vanished alongside it and which thoughtful musicians today attempt to track down. We must be patient on both counts – like Landowska in those final years, confidently anticipating Romanticism's return.

Carla sends me a new piece of hers in *The New York Times*. It concerns a 1706 Guarneri violin that Felix Hildesheimer bought in 1938 from Fridolin Hamma of Stuttgart, the same dealer who would soon be sourcing instruments for the Reich Bruckner Orchestra.

'Unable to escape from Nazi Germany, Mr. Hildesheimer committed suicide in 1939 and his family's property was confiscated.' Hildesheimer's grandsons, represented at a hearing by the Holocaust Claims Processing Office of New York, had tracked down the violin – now worth $158,000, valuers would soon estimate – and asked for its restitution. The Limbach Commission, a panel formed to mediate such cases, recommended that the heirs be compensated for two-thirds of the instrument's value, but that it remain with the family and foundation which purchased it in the 1970s in good faith.

Germany takes seriously the ongoing nature of such work. (It is only a few years since over 1,500 looted artworks were discovered in a Munich apartment: reminders of wartime looting can flash at any moment.) And Carla likes a happy resolution, which she wishes for me too. 'Until I next hear from you, I will imagine the lost Chopin piano with its candle holders from another era, and sending you best wishes for discovering its current whereabouts and perhaps one day playing it. And when you do, please let me know!' She attaches an image of Bauza's piano, one of the poor photos that Schunicke took for an inventory at the house in Saint-Leu-la-Forêt, so different from the warm-shadowed artistry of the Binder prints. It is the most oblique treasure map imaginable, with no further clue in sight.

Envoi

Vienna, 1952

At lunch in London one warm July day in 2013 my friend Ruth tells
me a story that sets me thinking about why we know so much about
plundered art, but next to nothing about looted instruments. It's a
tale that leads me eventually to Chopin and Sand, Landowska and
Cortot, to a small piano made by an unknown Spanish craftsman, to
Carla and Willem, Malcolm and Jean-Jacques, to the changing sound
and meaning of music over time – all of it on my trek through music's
Romantic centuries.

In 1950 Ruth's diplomat father Arieh Eshel, born Leopold Chill in
Berlin, accepted a position as Consul in Israel's new mission in Vienna.
Ruth reminds me that the Jewish population there was annihilated
after the Anschluss, along with their synagogues and other evidence
of their culture: in 1946 it numbered only 25,000, down from 185,000
eight years earlier. Although the nascent state of Israel was then
dispatching diplomats to countries all round the world, Eshel's appoint-
ment as the first Israeli consul to Austria was something more than
international diplomacy: it was also a moral rejoinder to a civilized
society that had acted with such unimaginable barbarity towards its
Jewish citizens. Eshel took with him his wife, Adele, and their two
children. They settled in Vienna's British sector, though the children
were schooled in the American one. They spoke Hebrew at home,
German most other places. Ruth was only five when they arrived,
already a piano prodigy, having aped (by ear) her older brother's diligently learned scores.

When Ruth was seven her parents decided to buy her a decent instrument. With Aida Barenboim, mother of Daniel and a family friend
from Eshel's previous posting in Buenos Aires, Adele visited a warehouse full of pianos. There she found a 1914 rosewood Bösendorfer,
with fat, square, art deco legs, and an even, singing sound. 'Of course,'
Ruth tells me at lunch, 'such instruments were then ten a penny.' In a

savage quirk of music history, in a city where beautiful pianos were left behind by Jews fleeing for their lives, or were systematically looted by terribly efficient Nazis, Vienna in the late 1940s and 1950s was a buyer's market.

Ruth played the Bösendorfer unceasingly: Bach, Beethoven, Chopin. 'It's a good pleasure to play on it, because it has a good tone,' she wrote to her father in Bad Goisern in the Salzkammergut in Austria, which following VE Day had surrendered so many valuable artworks and instruments, not least keyboards belonging to Landowska. A surviving recording of Ruth as an eight-year-old performing a Dittersdorf concerto with the orchestra of the Konservatorium der Stadt Wien demonstrates intense, natural musicality. She won a prize performing a piece by the teenage Richard Strauss, which earned both the congratulations and ire of the Israeli press: what was a Jew doing playing the music of a Nazi sympathizer? She was photographed at the piano at around the time of the Dittersdorf performance, looking entirely enchanting.

Years later she married Peter Kraus, whose grandparents had bribed the right officials to obtain exit papers for their daughter and grandson. With these in their pockets, in the final weeks before the beginning of the war, they caught one of the last trains from occupied Czechoslovakia – first to Enschede, the Dutch frontier station on the

German border, then Rotterdam, then on to England, arriving in London a week after they set off.

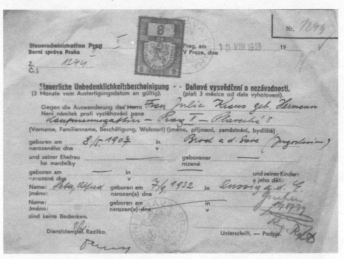

On her marriage to Peter, Ruth took the Bösendorfer with her to London.

'If only they could talk, these instruments,' she says of the looted and abandoned pianos we discuss over lunch. 'Their stories would fill books.'

This is only one book, and it concerns only one such instrument. But I dedicate it nonetheless to my dear friends Ruth and Peter Kraus.

Notes

The spelling of Valldemossa has been made consistent throughout, while the name Frédéric Chopin is given in the French spelling. Artur Rubinstein used the American spelling of his first name (Arthur) when writing in English, which is used here.

CPT   Jean-Jacques Eigeldinger, *Chopin: Pianist and Teacher as Seen by his Pupils*, trans. Naomi Shoehet, with Krysia Osostowicz and Roy Howat (Cambridge, 1988).

SCFC   Bronislaw Edward Sydow (ed.), *Selected Correspondence of Fryderyk Chopin*, trans. Arthur Hedley (New York, 1963).

WLDR   Wanda Landowska and Denise Restout Papers, 1843–2002, Music Division, Library of Congress, Washington D.C.

WM   George Sand, *A Winter in Majorca*, trans. Robert Graves (Barcelona, 1998).

CHAPTER 1

p. 3   *There were belly-men*: George Dodd, *Days at the Factories* (London, 1843), pp. 390–406; Arthur Loesser, *Men, Women and Pianos: A Social History* (London, 1955), p. 388.

p. 4   *A double-page spread*: 'Industrie française – Fabrication des pianos – M. Camille Pleyel', *L'Illustration* (9 June 1855), pp. 364–5.

CHAPTER 2

p. 6   *'First Class'*: Luis Ripoll, *Chopin's Winter in Majorca 1838–1839*, trans. Alan Sillitoe, 2nd edn (Palma, 1961), p. 5.

p. 6   *The paddle-steamer's beds*: Juan Cortada, *Viaje en la isla de Mallorca en el estío de 1845*. Entry for 19 July 1845.

p. 9   *Laurens re-created*: Jean-Joseph Bonaventure Laurens, *Souvenirs d'un voyage d'art à l'île de Majorque* (Paris, 1840); Brian J. Dendle and Shelby Thacker (eds.), *British Travellers in Mallorca in the Nineteenth Century: An Anthology of Texts* (Newark, NJ, 2006), p. 47.

p. 9   *Each of Laurens's lithographs*: Charles Wood, *Letters from Majorca* (London, 1888), p. 21.

p. 10   *Dressed entirely*: WM, pp. 103–4.

p. 10   *'The fact that'*: Charles Baudelaire, *My Heart Laid Bare and Other Prose Writings*, trans. Norman Cameron (London, 1950), p. 184.

p. 10   *Matthew Arnold*: Elizabeth Harlan, *George Sand* (New Haven, CT, 2004), p. xiii.

p. 10   *Some commentators*: Ibid., p. 128.

p. 10   *'a woman'*: George Sand, *The Story of My Life*, trans. Dan Hofstadter (London, 1984), p. 15.

p. 10   *Alexis de Tocqueville*: Alexis de Tocqueville, *The Recollections of Alexis de Tocqueville*, trans. Alexander Teixeira de Mattos (Westport, CT, 1979), p. 149.

p. 11   *'France is sinking'*: Harlan, *George Sand*, p. 307.

p. 11   *'although she had'*: Meirion Hughes (ed. and trans.), *Liszt's Chopin* (Manchester, 2010), p. 120.

p. 11   *Oscar Wilde*: Sand, *The Story of My Life*, p. 9; *'Madame Sand'*: Harlan, *George Sand*, p. 7.

p. 11   *'When, in Venice'*: Cole Porter, 'The Leader of a Big-Time Band', in Robert Kimball (ed.), *The Complete Lyrics of Cole Porter* (London, 1983), p. 231. Sand and Chopin never visited Venice together.

p. 12   *'a personal clash'*: WM, p. xi.

p. 12   *The passport*: Alfred Cortot, *In Search of Chopin*, trans. Cyril and Rena Clarke (Mineola, NY, 2013), p. 9.

p. 12   *He was worryingly slight*: Ibid.

p. 13   *'the portrait'*: Harlan, *George Sand*, p. 273.

p. 13   *Chopin's first biographer*: Frederick Niecks, *Frederick Chopin: As a Man and Musician*, vol. 2 (London, 1888), pp. 10–11.

p. 13   *'Chopin at first'*: Hughes, *Liszt's Chopin*, p. 122.

p. 13   *'What an unattractive person'*: Kornel Michałowski and Jim Samson, 'Chopin, Fryderyk Franciszek', *Grove Music Online. Oxford Music Online*. Oxford University Press, accessed 13 January 2017, http://www.oxfordmusiconline.com/subscriber/article/grove/music/51099.

p. 13   *'Consumption has taken possession'*: Adam Zamoyski, *Chopin: Prince of the Romantics* (London, 2009), pp. 160–61.

p. 13   *'You are ill'*: Marquis de Custine to Chopin [May 1837], SCFC, p. 146.

p. 15   *'No soul'*: Sand, *The Story of My Life*, p. 241.

p. 16   '*So far as*': Frédéric Chopin to Tytus Woyciechowski, 25 December 1831, *SCFC*, p. 107.

CHAPTER 3

p. 17   '*The district*': Luis Ripoll, *The Majorcan Episode of Chopin and George Sand 1838–1839*, trans. W. Kirkbride (Palma, 1969), plate.

p. 18   *To his Polish friend*: Frédéric Chopin to Julian Fontana, 15 November 1838, *SCFC*, p. 162.

p. 18   '*Oh, my dear fellow*': Chopin to Fontana, 15 November 1838, *SCFC*, pp. 162–3.

p. 18   *Sand thought the climate*: WM, p. 24.

p. 18   *most of the needle windows*: Brian J. Dendle and Shelby Thacker (eds.), *British Travellers in Mallorca in the Nineteenth Century: An Anthology of Texts* (Newark, NJ, 2006), p. 48.

p. 19   *the remains of two kings*: Arthur Foss, *Majorca* (London, 1972), p. 90.

p. 19   '*this huge*': WM, p. 45.

p. 19   *She was dismissive*: WM, p. 24.

p. 19   '*I dream of music*': Chopin to Camille Pleyel, November 1838, *SCFC*, p. 163.

p. 20   '*In Majorca*': WM, p. 33.

p. 20   '*neither donkey*': George Sand to Wojciech Grzymała, 3 December 1838, *SCFC*, p. 164.

p. 20   '*in a country*': WM, p. 104; *rancid oil*: WM, p. 16.

p. 20   *And despite temperatures*: Chopin to Fontana, 3 December 1838, *SCFC*, p. 164.

p. 20   *A succession of doctors*: WM, p. 35.

p. 20   '*It is all*': Chopin to Fontana, 3 December 1838, *SCFC*, p. 164.

p. 20   *Before leaving Paris*: Chopin to Fontana, 14 December 1838, *SCFC*, p. 165.

p. 21   '*The lack*': Sand to Grzymała, 3 December 1838, *SCFC*, pp. 163–4.

p. 21   '*stabbed at her*': Hélène Choussat, unpublished memoirs, Celda de Frédéric Chopin y George Sand, Cartuja de Valldemossa, Majorca.

p. 22   *1853, the year Steinway*: Cyril Ehrlich, *The Piano: A History*, revised edition (Oxford, 1990), p. 27. Ehrlich calls 1853 'the annus mirabilis' in pianoforte history for this reason.

p. 22   '*In its span*': *CPT*, p. 20.

p. 22   *Saint-Saëns*: Ehrlich, *The Piano*, p. 23.

p. 22   *Mr Pickwick's escape*: Charles Dickens, *The Pickwick Papers* (London, 1905), p. 609.

p. 23   *Sand wrote that the damp*: WM, p. 35.

p. 23   *'boorish Gómez'*: WM, p. 35.

p. 23   *'a wonderful monastery'*: Chopin to Fontana, 15 November 1838, SCFC, p. 162.

p. 23   *'It is a huge'*: Chopin to Fontana, 3 December 1838, SCFC, p. 164.

p. 23   *'Tomorrow I am going'*: Chopin to Fontana, 14 December 1838, SCFC, p. 165.

p. 24   *'roads are made'*: Chopin to Fontana, 28 December 1838, SCFC, p. 166.

p. 24   *The village of Valldemossa*: William G. Atwood, *The Lioness and the Little One: The Liaison of George Sand and Frédéric Chopin* (New York, 1980), p. 109.

p. 24   *peddling a barrow load*: WM, p. 16.

p. 25   *not the alluring pinks*: WM, p. 51.

p. 25   *Sand too was enraptured*: WM, p. 70.

p. 25   *'Palma. 28 December'*: Chopin to Fontana, 28 December 1838, SCFC, p. 164.

p. 26   *which Sand likened*: WM, p. 73.

p. 26   *the meat*: WM, p. 15.

p. 26   *'Doomed to eat'*: WM, p. 89.

p. 26   *in the most vulgar taste*: WM, p. 77.

p. 28   *and quilted coverlets*: Atwood, *The Lioness and the Little One*, p. 109.

p. 29   *Sand was dismissive*: Bartomeu Ferrá, *Chopin and George Sand in the Cartuja de Valldemosa*, trans. James Webb (Palma, 1932), p. 27; *'for its weight'*: WM, p. 76.

p. 29   *In the mountains*: WM, p. 74.

p. 29   *The afternoon shadows*: Luis Ripoll, *Chopin's Winter in Majorca 1838–1839*, trans. Alan Sillitoe, 2nd edn (Palma, 1961), p. 72.

p. 29   *'one of the coldest'*: WM, p. 12.

p. 30   *often under a tree*: WM, p. 132.

p. 30   *Amelia's indolence*: WM, p. 102.

p. 30   *Village children*: WM, p. 110.

p. 30   *'I can't send you'*: Chopin to Fontana, 28 December 1838, SCFC, p. 166.

p. 30   *Maurice determined*: WM, p. 80.

p. 30   *On a walk*: WM, p. 115.

p. 31   *On another occasion*: WM, p. 81.

p. 31   *rancid oil and garlic*: WM, p. 83.

p. 31   *On another day*: WM, p. 85.

p. 32   *'Why attempt'*: WM, p. 80.

p. 32   *who asked about*: WM, p. 86.

p. 32   *In Valldemossa*: WM, p. 132.

p. 32   *'That consumptive'*: WM, p. 121.

p. 33   *'cowards, hypocrites'*: J. M. Quadrado, 'To George Sand: A Refutation', *La Palma* (5 May 1841), in *WM*, p. 138.

p. 33   *'We nicknamed'*: WM, p. 107. Graves adds as a footnote, 'Indians seldom meet chimpanzees, which are natives of West Africa; and have to visit the East Indies for a view of the orang-utang.'

p. 33   *'George Sand'*: WM, p. 146.

CHAPTER 4

p. 34   *'a member of my family'*: WM, pp. 19, 20, 103, 109.

p. 34   *Jane Austen's*: See *Pride and Prejudice*.

p. 34   *Graves wrote . . . in the preface*: Robert Graves, *Good-Bye to All That: An Autobiography* (New York, 1995), p. xii.

p. 34   *'delicate both in body and mind'*: Meirion Hughes (ed. and trans.), *Liszt's Chopin* (Manchester, 2010), p. 108.

p. 35   *'She has treated'*: Benita Eisler, *Chopin's Funeral* (New York, 2003), p. 164.

p. 35   *'Chopin is playing'*: George Sand to Carlotta Marliani, 15 January 1839, George Sand, *Correspondance 1812–1876*, vol. 2 (Paris, 1883), p. 120.

p. 35   *'the most difficult'*: Théodore and Hippolyte Cogniard, *Pauvre Jacques*, trans. Richard Ryan, *Cumberland's Minor Theatre*, vol. 10 (London, n.d.), p. 11.

p. 36   *'It was there'*: George Sand, *The Story of My Life*, trans. Dan Hofstadter (London, 1984), p. 240.

p. 36   *Chopin had been thinking*: Maurice Brown, 'The Chronology of Chopin's Preludes', *Musical Times* (August 1957), p. 423.

p. 36   *In 1837 Chopin asked Fontana*: Brown, 'The Chronology of Chopin's Preludes', p. 423.

p. 37   *For his 2004 edition*: Jean-Jacques Eigeldinger (ed.), 'Preface', Fryderyk Chopin, Préludes, Op. 28 (London, 2004). See also Eigeldinger, 'L'achèvement des Préludes op. 28 de Chopin. Documents autographes', *Revue de Musicologies* 75 (1989), pp. 229–42, and 'Twenty-Four Preludes op. 28: Genre, Structure, Significance', in Jim Samson (ed.), *Chopin Studies* (Cambridge, 1988). In this chapter Eigeldinger makes reference to the attempts by earlier scholars to date the Preludes, notably Ludwik Bronarski, Maurice Brown and Gastone Belotti, basing some of his conclusions on 'a study of Chopin's graphological habits'. Yet Eigeldinger also cautions: 'This is not the place to go into the controversy about how many and which pieces were composed or completed in Majorca – is in any case almost insoluble for lack of sound evidence.' (Samson, *Chopin Studies*, p. 168.) He saved his analysis of the chronology for his later edition of the Preludes, though strangely did not include No. 15 in this list, contradicting his earlier assessment.

p. 37   *It was the intrepid*: Eigeldinger, 'Twenty-Four Preludes Op. 28', p. 174.

p. 37   *'It is never'*: CPT, p. 181.

p. 38   *'how to unite'*: Carl Czerny, introduction to Bach's *Das Wohltempierte Klavier* (Vienna, 1838).

p. 38   *where pupils learned*: CPT, p. 61; *Beethoven was obsessed*: Eugène Delacroix, *The Journal of Eugène Delacroix*, trans. Lucy Norton (London, 2006), p. 91. Entry for 2 February 1849.

p. 39   *Although Breitkopf*: *Thematisches Verzeichniss der im Druck erschienenen Compositionen von Friedrich Chopin* (Leipzig, 1852).

p. 40   *'Chopin is the greatest'*: Roy Howat, 'Chopin's Influence on the *fin de siècle* and Beyond', in Jim Samson (ed.), *The Cambridge Companion to Chopin* (Cambridge, 1994), Kindle edition, ch. 12.

p. 43   *'Chopin can hardly'*: Robert Schumann, review, *Neue Zeitschrift für Musik*, 9 (1838), in Rose Rosenberg Subotnik, 'On Grounding Chopin', Richard Leppert and Susan McClary (eds.), *Music and Society: The Politics of Composition, Performance and Reception* (Cambridge, 1987), p. 115.

p. 43   *unprecedented harmonic freedom*: Paul Dukas, 'A propos du monument Chopin', in *Les écrits de Paul Dukas sur la musique* (Paris, 1948), pp. 514–15.

p. 45   *'the most crushing'*: Sand, *The Story of My Life*, p. 245.

p. 45   *'He alters'*: Joseph Filtsch to his parents, 8 March 1842, *SCFC*, p. 217. Eigeldinger is sceptical about the authenticity of the Filtsch letters, though generally he considers the editor of Chopin's collected correspondence scrupulous.

p. 45   *'No! one does not spoil'*: Delacroix, *The Journal of Eugène Delacroix*, p. 183. Entry for 20 April 1853.

p. 45   *'a finished building'*: Ibid.

p. 46   *neurologists would much later*: Charles J. Limb, 'Your Brain on Improv', TED Talk, November 2010. https://www.ted.com/talks/ charles_limb_your_brain_on_improv?language=en. Limb's study shows that different areas of the brain light up when a pianist goes off on some fabulous tangent, indicating deactivation in the lateral prefrontal cortex (the part to do with self-monitoring) and activation in the medial prefrontal cortex (self-expression).

p. 46   *They negotiated*: Sand writes '400' francs in *WM* but '300' in a letter at the time.

p. 46   *The return trip*: *WM*, pp. 118–19.

p. 47   *'genius was filled'*: Sand, *The Story of My Life*, pp. 240–41.

p. 48   *'What rays'*: *CPT*, p. 281. Eigeldinger thinks that at least some of this Prelude was composed in Paris.

p. 48   *Czerny, a former pupil*: Carl Czerny, *A Systematic Introduction to the Improvisation on the Pianoforte, Opus 200*, trans. Alice L. Mitchell (New York, 1983), p. 6, in Jeffrey Kallberg, 'Small "Forms": In Defence of the Prelude', Samson, *The Cambridge Companion to Chopin*, Kindle edition, ch. 6.

p. 48   *He was toying*: Mackenzie Pierce to Paul Kildea, 23 November 2015. See Mackenzie Pierce, 'Chopin's Opus 28 and the Published Prelude Collection' in Massimiliano Sala (ed.), *Piano Culture in 19th-Century Paris* (Turnhout, 2015), pp. 291–311.

p. 49   *Édouard Manet*: Colin Bailey, 'The Floating Studio', *The New York Review of Books* (23 April 2015), Kindle edition.

p. 49   *'It maintains'*: Sand, *Impressions et Souvenirs* (Paris, 1873), in Richard Taruskin, 'Music in the Nineteenth Century', *The Oxford History of Western Music*, vol. 3 (Oxford, 2010), p. 368.

p. 50   *'filled the lofty'*: *WM*, p. 104.

p. 50   *'I write'*: Sand to Marliani, 22 January 1839. http://en.chopin.nifc. pl/chopin/life/calendar/year/1839.

p. 50   *'Dear friend'*: Frédéric Chopin to Camille Pleyel, 22 January 1839, *SCFC*, p. 168.

p. 51   *'and then politely'*: Chopin to Julian Fontana, 22 January 1839, *SCFC*, p. 167.

p. 51   *'We were treated'*: Sand to Marliani, 15 February 1839, *SCFC*, p. 169.

p. 52   *Much later*: Sand, *The Story of My Life*, p. 242.

p. 52   '*Another month*': Sand to Marliani, 26 February 1839, in Adam Zamoyski, *Chopin: Prince of the Romantics* (London, 2011), p. 170.

p. 52   *They boarded*: WM, p. 101.

p. 52   *his slight frame*: Chopin to Fontana, 7 March 1839, SCFC, p. 171.

p. 52   '*I have gone*': Chopin to Wojciech Grzymała, 12 March 1839, SCFC, p. 173.

p. 53   '*In response*': Pleyel to the Canut family, 23 September 1953, Celda de Frédéric Chopin y George Sand, Valldemossa, Majorca.

p. 53   '*let them wait*': Chopin to Fontana, 12 March 1839, SCFC, p. 172.

p. 54   *He went on to tell*: Chopin to Fontana [end of March 1839], SCFC, p. 173.

p. 54   '*his whole being*': Sand to Marliani, 28 April 1839, SCFC, p. 177.

p. 54   '*he would never*': Hughes, *Liszt's Chopin*, p. 126. In 1751 Carolus Linnaeus planned a garden full of different plants – goat's beard, chicory, and the like – that opened and closed at specific times of the day.

CHAPTER 5

p. 56   *His directions to Fontana*: Frédéric Chopin to Julian Fontana, 25 September 1839, SCFC, p. 184.

p. 56   *He asked that Fontana*: Chopin to Fontana, 1 October 1839, SCFC, p. 185; *Sand told*: George Sand to Wojciech Grzymała, 20 September 1839, SCFC, p. 183.

p. 56   '*for the boy*': Sand to Grzymała, 20 September 1839, SCFC, p. 183; '*with no blacksmiths*': Chopin to Fontana, 1 October 1839, SCFC, p. 185.

p. 57   *Balzac observed*: Honoré de Balzac and Madame Honoré de Balzac, *The Love Letters of Honoré de Balzac, 1833–1842*, trans. D. F. Hannigan, vol. 2 (London, 1901), p. 302.

p. 57   *From Dupont*: Chopin to Fontana, 3 October 1839, SCFC, p. 186.

p. 58   *who visits Staub*: Honoré de Balzac, *Lost Illusions*, trans. Herbert J. Hunt (London, 2004), p. 182.

p. 58   '*man who is rich*': Charles Baudelaire, *The Painter of Modern Life and Other Essays*, trans. Jonathan Mayne (London, 2012), p. 26.

p. 58   '*see to it*': Chopin to Fontana, 8 October 1839, *SCFC*, p. 188.

p. 58   *its sixty-odd toll barriers*: Eric Hazan, *The Invention of Paris: A History in Footsteps*, trans. David Fernbach (London, 2010), p. 138.

p. 59   '*some great fiery*': Julian Barnes, *Keeping an Eye Open: Essays on Art* (London, 2015), p. 48.

p. 59   *Galignani's popular guide*: *Galignani's New Paris Guide* (Paris, 1830), p. 22.

p. 60   '*Here, in the vast*': Heinrich Heine, *French Affairs: Letters from Paris*, trans. Charles Godfrey Leland (27 May 1832), in Hazan, *The Invention of Paris*, p. 33.

p. 60   '*I have found*': Chopin to Dominik Dziewanowski [second week of January 1833], *SCFC*, p. 114.

p. 60   '*Once you have*': Hazan, *The Invention of Paris*, p. 77.

p. 61   '*Flânerie is a science*': Ibid., p. 315.

p. 61   *Rich tradesmen*: *Galignani's New Paris Guide*, p. 23.

p. 61   *But move away*: Ibid., pp. 23–4.

p. 61   *The* deuxième: Ibid., p. lviii.

p. 61   *The Café de Paris*: William G. Atwood, *The Parisian Worlds of Frédéric Chopin* (New Haven, CT, 1999), p. 18.

p. 61   '*You cannot*': Henry Wadsworth Longfellow to Stephen Longfellow, Jr, 23 July 1826, in Adam Gopnik (ed.), *Americans in Paris: A Literary Anthology* (New York, 2004), pp. 51–2.

p. 64   '*perfect stream*': Hazan, *The Invention of Paris*, p. 39.

p. 64   '*The carriage drives*': Baudelaire, *The Painter of Modern Life*, p. 39.

p. 64   '*Now and then*': Jim Harter, *World Railways of the Nineteenth Century: A Pictorial History in Victorian Engravings* (Baltimore, MD, 2005), p. 142.

p. 64   *Industry was changing*: See T. J. Clark's *The Painting of Modern Life: Paris in the Art of Manet and his Followers* (Princeton, NJ, 1999).

p. 66   '*to the right*': Hazan, *The Invention of Paris*, p. 111.

p. 66   *The fire was lit*: Chopin to Józef Elsner, 14 December 1831, *SCFC*, p. 104.

p. 66   *the epidemic in 1832*: Jill Harsin, *Barricades: The War of the Streets in Revolutionary Paris, 1830–1848* (New York, 2002), p. 57.

p. 66   '*the multitude*': Hazan, *The Invention of Paris*, p. 250.

p. 66 '*as numerous*': Antoni Orlowski to his family, spring 1832, *SCFC*, p. 110.

p. 67 '*It stole rapidly*': George Sand, *The Story of My Life*, trans. Dan Hofstadter (London, 1984), p. 216.

p. 67 '*I remember that*': Gustav Karpeles (ed.), *Heinrich Heine's Memoirs: From his Works, Letters, and Conversations*, trans. Gilbert Cannan, vol. 1 (London, 1910), p. 273.

p. 67 '*the passersby*': Hazan, *The Invention of Paris*, p. 81.

p. 67 *On Christmas Day*: Chopin to Tytus Woyciechowski, 25 December 1831, *SCFC*, p. 105.

p. 68 *a wall of gruesome masonry*: Sand, *The Story of My Life*, p. 219.

p. 69 '*Oh, God*': Chopin's journal [after 8 September 1831], *SCFC*, p. 91.

p. 69 '*Among Poles*': Chopin to Woyciechowski, 12 December 1831, *SCFC*, p. 101.

p. 69 '*people who*': Joseph Filtsch to his parents, 29 November 1842, *SCFC*, p. 224.

p. 69 '*I am tortured*': Chopin to Woyciechowski, 25 December 1831, *SCFC*, p. 108.

p. 70 '*at once delicate*': Edmund de Waal, *The Hare with Amber Eyes: A Hidden Inheritance* (London, 2011), Kindle edition, ch. 9.

p. 70 '*Oh, it's untranslatable!*': Meirion Hughes (ed. and trans.), *Liszt's Chopin* (Manchester, 2010), p. 105.

p. 70 *Berlioz wrote*: Hector Berlioz, concert review, *Revue et Gazette Musicale* (8 January 1841), in Atwood, *The Parisian Worlds of Frédéric Chopin*, p. 180.

p. 71 *Sophie Gay*: Ibid., p. 192.

p. 71 *According to Alexandre Dumas*: Alexandre Dumas, *The Count of Monte Cristo*, trans. Robin Buss (London, 1996), pp. 514–17.

p. 71 '*the monstrous*': Harold C. Schonberg, *The Great Pianists* (New York, 1964), p. 92.

p. 71 *from the salons*: Concert review, *Courrier des théâtres* (24 November 1831), in James H. Johnson, *Listening in Paris: A Cultural History* (Berkeley, CA, 1995), p. 256.

p. 72 '*high Cs*': Hector Berlioz, *Evenings with the Orchestra*, trans. Jacques Barzun (Chicago, IL, 1999), p. 109.

p. 72 '*No one will*': Chopin to Woyciechowski, 12 December 1831, *SCFC*, p. 101.

p. 73   '*There is*': François Fétis, concert review, *Revue Musicale* (3 March 1832), in William G. Atwood, *Fryderyk Chopin: Pianist from Warsaw* (New York, 1987), p. 219.

CHAPTER 6

p. 74   '*The Preludes*': Jean-Jacques Eigeldinger, 'Twenty-Four Preludes Op. 28: Genre, Structure, Significance', in Jim Samson (ed.), *Chopin Studies* (Cambridge, 1988), p. 177.

p. 75   *Ignaz Moscheles (whose playing)*: CPT, p. 273.

p. 75   *Meyerbeer recorded*: Ibid., p. 157.

p. 75   '*I love it*': Ibid.

p. 75   *It seems*: Mackenzie Pierce to Paul Kildea, 22 November 2015. Pierce thinks Chopin's crazy workload and publication record during and after his stay in Majorca was driven in part by his need to pay for the trip.

p. 76   '*I did not . . . Schlesinger*': Frédéric Chopin to Julian Fontana, 12 March 1839, *SCFC*, pp. 171–2.

p. 76   '*Jews will*': Chopin to Wojciech Grzymała, 12 March 1839, *SCFC*, p. 173.

p. 76   '*Jews, vomited*': Edmund de Waal, *The Hare with Amber Eyes: A Hidden Inheritance* (London, 2011), p. 92.

p. 76   '*sordid Jew*': George Sand, *The Story of My Life*, trans. Dan Hofstadter (London, 1984), p. 242.

p. 76   *Heine encountered*: Gustav Karpeles (ed.), *Heinrich Heine's Memoirs: From his Works, Letters, and Conversations*, trans. Gilbert Cannan, vol. 1 (London, 1910), p. 266.

p. 77   '*when the big*': Hector Berlioz, 'Feuilleton' in *Journal des Débats* (27 October 1849), in Adam Zamoyski, *Chopin: Prince of the Romantics* (London, 2011), p. 116.

p. 77   '*ebb and flow*': Meirion Hughes (ed. and trans.), *Liszt's Chopin* (Manchester, 2010), p. 89.

p. 78   *Or they merely*: Léo's wife Sophie wrote of the singularity of Chopin's playing. 'He was not a pianist of the modern school, but, in his own way, had created a style of his own, a style that one cannot describe.' *CPT*, p. 279. Fanny Mendelssohn was initially unimpressed by Chopin's playing. Ibid., p. 268.

p. 78   '*The idea*': Ibid., p. 83.

p. 78   '*where clocks*': Charles Baudelaire, *Paris Spleen*, trans. Louise Varèse (New York, 1970), p. 32.

p. 79   *Chopin even managed*: Jeffrey Kallberg, 'Chopin's Music Box', in Artur Szklener (ed.), *Chopin's Musical Worlds: The 1840s* (Warsaw, 2008), p. 196. The description is by Élisa Fournier.

p. 81   *'The interior'*: Ackbar Abbas, 'Walter Benjamin's Collector: The Fate of Modern Experience', in Peter Osborne (ed.), *Walter Benjamin: Critical Evaluations in Cultural Theory*, vol. 2 (London, 2005), p. 214.

CHAPTER 7

p. 83   *rue Rochechouart*: The rue de Rochechouart is today a narrow strip of apartments over restaurants, jewellery stores, hotels, *tabacs*. The splendid early nineteenth-century facades have survived, though they have a shabby air and rub shoulders with twentieth-century buildings displaying little familial resemblance.

p. 84   *'A great'*: George Sand to Pauline Viardot, 18 April 1841, *SCFC*, p. 193.

p. 85   *'So many things'*: Ibid.

p. 85   *'A little spiteful'*: Marie d'Agoult to Henri Lehmann, 21 April 1841, *SCFC*, p. 193.

p. 85   *Liszt wrote*: Franz Liszt to d'Agoult, 14 January 1841, *SCFC*, p. 193.

p. 85   *'the most elegant'*: Liszt, concert review, *Revue et Gazette Musicale* (2 May 1841), in William G. Atwood, *Fryderyk Chopin: Pianist from Warsaw* (New York, 1987), p. 231.

p. 86   *'Is not the'*: Ibid., p. 234.

p. 86   *'Oh yes'*: Alfred Cortot, *In Search of Chopin*, trans. Cyril and Rena Clarke (Mineola, NY, 2013), p. 128.

p. 86   *'They are not'*: Atwood, *Fryderyk Chopin*, p. 233.

p. 87   *probably in April 1840*: Eigeldinger (*CPT*, p. 274) concludes that this visit was in either April 1840 or April 1841, though the former seems more likely given how cool things had become between the two men by early 1841.

p. 87   *'a work replete'*: *CPT*, p. 274.

p. 88   *'it is likewise'*: Meirion Hughes (ed. and trans.), *Liszt's Chopin* (Manchester, 2010), p. 62.

p. 88   *'Literature which achieves'*: Stephen Cushman et al. (eds.), *The Princeton Encyclopedia of Poetry and Poetics*, 4th edn (Princeton, NJ, 2012), p. 1,081.

p. 89   *'A book'*: Georg Christoph Lichtenberg, *Aphorisms*, trans. R. Hollingdale (London, 1990), p. 73.

p. 89   *'Nothing can'*: Ibid., p. 67.

p. 89   *'He marvelled'*: Ibid., p. 108.

p. 89   *This conflict*: Malcolm Gillies interview, 18 November 2014.

p. 90   *When in the following century*: Édouard Ganche to André Gide, 2 January 1932, in Thomas Higgins, *Chopin Interpretation: A Study of Performance Directions in Selected Autographs and Other Sources* (PhD thesis, University of Iowa, 1966), p. 161.

p. 91   *In just twenty-three*: See Rose Rosengard Subotnik's terrific essay, 'On Grounding Chopin', in Richard Leppert and Susan McClary (eds.), *Music and Society: The Politics of Composition, Performance and Reception* (Cambridge, 1987), pp. 105–31.

p. 91   *'I indicate'*: CPT, p. 128.

p. 91   *Italianized*: Ibid., p. 111.

p. 92   *'You wouldn't believe'*: Frédéric Chopin to Tytus Woyciechowski, 5 June 1830, *SCFC*, pp. 47–8.

p. 93   *'She breathes'*: Ibid., p. 48.

p. 93   *'Suddenly'*: See, for example, the opening chapter of *Bleak House*: 'Suddenly a very little counsel, with a terrific bass voice, arises, fully inflated, in the back settlements of the fog, and says, "Will your lordship allow me? I appear for him."' Charles Dickens, *Bleak House* (London, 2003), p. 19.

p. 95   *silvery colour in the treble*: Claude Montal, *L'Art d'accorder soi-même son piano* (Paris, 1836), in *CPT*, pp. 91–2.

p. 95   *'When I am'*: Reginald Gerig, *Famous Pianists & Their Technique* (Bloomington and Indianapolis, IN, 2007), p. 165.

p. 96   *'The hand'*: Karol Mikuli, *CPT*, p. 49; *'Why, she plays'*: Chopin on Arabella Goddard, Ibid., p. 57.

p. 96   *Elise Peruzzi*: Gerig, *Famous Pianists & Their Technique*, p. 161.

p. 96   *Émile Gaillard*: CPT, p. 276.

p. 96   *Custine told*: Marquis de Custine to Chopin, 27 April 1841, *SCFC*, pp. 193–4.

p. 96   *Mendelssohn compared*: CPT, p. 267.

p. 96   *Balzac called*: Ibid., p. 284.

p. 96   *Berlioz wrote*: Ibid., p. 272.

p. 96   *'for the most part'*: Ibid., p. 172.

p. 97   *later writing about*: Ibid., p. 97.

p. 98   *Antoine-François Marmontel*: Ibid., p. 128.

CHAPTER 8

p. 99   '*What must it*': Léon Escudier, concert review, *La France Musicale* (27 February 1842), in William G. Atwood, *Fryderyk Chopin: Pianist from Warsaw* (New York, 1987), p. 239.

p. 99   '*one cannot help*': Ibid.

p. 99   '*pour forth*': Ibid.

p. 100   '*a certain*': Ibid., p. 240.

p. 100   '*Just look!*': Ibid., p. 243.

p. 100   '*But since*': Joseph Filtsch to his parents, 30 December 1842, *SCFC*, p. 226.

p. 101   '*Everything you do*': Frédéric Chopin to George Sand [3 November 1843], *SCFC*, p. 232.

p. 101   '*as white as*': Chopin to Sand [2 December 1844], *SCFC*, p. 243.

p. 101   '*I imagine*': Chopin to Sand, 5 December 1844, *SCFC*, p. 245.

p. 101   '*Go and look*': Sand to Marie de Rozières, beginning of November 1843, *SCFC*, p. 231.

p. 101   '*After the first*': Chopin's mother to Sand, 13 June 1844, *SCFC*, p. 234.

p. 102   *Chopin asking him*: Chopin to Wojciech Grzymała, beginning of October 1843, *SCFC*, p. 230; *Franchomme*: Chopin to Auguste Franchomme, 20 September 1844, *SCFC*, p. 240; *Léo*: Chopin to Auguste Léo, 8 July 1845, *SCFC*, p. 247.

p. 102   *for which she paid*: Dumas then commanded 100,000 francs a novel, Liszt 10,000 francs a recital.

p. 102   *A watercolour*: Unsigned painting, which went missing from the collection of Chopin's grandniece Laura Ciechomska during the Nazi occupation of Poland.

p. 102   *by Théodore Frère*: *CPT*, p. 99.

p. 103   *at Hatchlands Park*: At Hatchlands it rubs shoulders with instruments owned or played by Mozart and Mahler, Haydn and Beethoven, Elgar and J. C. Bach, collected over time by artist and designer Alec Cobbe, each in excellent condition and working order, together forming a beautifully illustrated scrapbook history of Western art music.

p. 103   '*I already have*': Chopin to his mother, 11 February 1848, *SCFC*, p. 305. Chopin took the piano with him to England in April 1848 and sold it to Lady Trotter on leaving for Scotland. It remained in Trotter's family until the late 1970s when it was acquired for the Cobbe Collection. Cobbe has recorded Liszt's favourite Prelude on the instrument, Chopin having perhaps provided him with the spiritual template.

p. 103   *Patrons who successfully*: Concert review, *Revue et Gazette Musicale* (20 February 1848), in Atwood, *Fryderyk Chopin*, p. 244.

p. 104   *'The papers'*: Sand to Maurice Dudevant, 7 February 1848, *SCFC*, p. 303. Solange was then staying in Nérac.

p. 104   *for Delacroix's liking*: Eugène Delacroix, *The Journal of Eugène Delacroix*, trans. Lucy Norton (London, 2006), p. 75. Entry for 12 March 1847.

p. 104   *'You see how'*: Sand to Grzymała, 12 May 1847, *SCFC*, p. 283.

p. 104   *'every superstitious'*: George Sand, *The Story of My Life*, trans. Dan Hofstadter (London, 1984) p. 245.

p. 105   *the two came to blows*: Sand to de Rozières [summer 1847], *SCFC*, p. 291.

p. 105   *'This misfortune'*: Chopin to Sand, 24 July 1847, *SCFC*, p. 293.

p. 105   *'Adieu, my friend'*: Sand to Chopin, 28 July 1847, *SCFC*, p. 294.

p. 106   *'I shook'*: Sand, *The Story of My Life*, p. 247.

p. 106   *'I do not like'*: David Bellos, *The Novel of the Century: The Extraordinary Adventures of Les Misérables* (London, 2017), p. 8.

p. 107   *'What is there'*: Victor Hugo, *Les Misérables*, trans. Julie Rose (New York, 2008), p. 686.

p. 107   *'poverty'*: Ibid., p. 689.

p. 108   *In June 1848 Alexis de Tocqueville*: Alexis de Tocqueville, *The Recollections of Alexis de Tocqueville*, trans. Alexander Teixeira de Mattos (Westport, CT, 1979), pp. 160–61.

p. 108   *Blood slicked*: Eric Hazan, *The Invention of Paris: A History in Footsteps*, trans. David Fernbach (London, 2010), pp. 287–9.

CHAPTER 9

p. 109   *the abyss*: Frédéric Chopin to Adolf Gutmann, 6 May 1848, *SCFC*, p. 315.

p. 109   *He thought*: Chopin to Wojciech Grzymała, 13 May 1848, *SCFC*, p. 317.

p. 109   *'Whatever'*: Chopin to Grzymała, 8–17 July 1848, *SCFC*, p. 326.

p. 109   *'whom I have'*: Chopin to his family, 10–19 August 1848, *SCFC*, p. 339.

p. 109   *'He refuses'*: Chopin to Marie de Rozières, 1 June 1848, *SCFC*, p. 318.

p. 106   *He was miserable*: Chopin to Grzymała, 8–17 July 1848, *SCFC*, p. 324.

p. 109   'If only I were': Chopin to his family, 10–19 August 1848, *SCFC*, p. 339.

p. 110   'as smooth': Chopin to Grzymała, 4 May 1848, *SCFC*, p. 315.

p. 110   'I can well': Chopin to his family, 10–19 August 1848, *SCFC*, p. 333.

p. 110   'Old Mme Rothschild': Chopin to Grzymała, 2 June 1848, *SCFC*, p. 320.

p. 110   'The performer': Concert review, George Hogarth, *Daily News* (10 July 1848), in *CPT*, p. 294.

p. 112   *His wit*: Chopin to Auguste Franchomme, 11 August 1848, *SCFC*, pp. 327–8.

p. 112   'look at their hands': Chopin to Grzymała, 21 October 1848, *SCFC*, p. 348.

p. 112   'There are fine': Chopin to de Rozières, 2 October 1848, *SCFC*, p. 346.

p. 113   'such a one': Chopin to Grzymała, 4–9 September 1848, *SCFC*, p. 341.

p. 113   *he could not breathe*: Chopin to Grzymała, 4–9 September 1848, *SCFC*, pp. 340–41.

p. 113   'No one plays': Chopin to Julian Fontana, 18 August 1848, *SCFC*, p. 330.

p. 113   *stuck at the dinner table*: Chopin to Grzymała, 1 October 1848, *SCFC*, p. 344.

p. 113   'We are a couple': Chopin to Fontana, 18 August 1848, *SCFC*, p. 329.

p. 113   'Mr. Chopin': Concert review, *Illustrated London News* (18 November 1848), in William G. Atwood, *Fryderyk Chopin: Pianist from Warsaw* (New York, 1987), p. 260.

p. 113   'This world seems': Chopin to Grzymała, 30 October 1848, *SCFC*, p. 349.

p. 114   *He plotted*: Chopin to Grzymała, 17–18 November 1848, *SCFC*, p. 351.

p. 114   'I have never': Chopin to Grzymała, 17–18 November 1848, *SCFC*, p. 351.

p. 116   'Where Beethoven': Eugène Delacroix, *The Journal of Eugène Delacroix*, trans. Lucy Norton (London, 2006), p. 100. Entry for 7 April 1849.

p. 116   'The fact of the matter': Ibid., p. 100. Entry for 7 April 1849.

p. 116   'of her strange': Ibid., p. 90. Entry for 29 January 1849.

p. 117   *There were good, lucid days*: Chopin to Ludwika Jendrzejewicz, 25 June 1849, *SCFC*, p. 360.

p. 117　　*'the unbearable'*: Delacroix, *The Journal of Eugène Delacroix*, p. 101. Entry for 14 April 1849.

p. 117　　*Chopin died*: There have long been disputes over the cause of Chopin's death. In recent decades scientists have proposed cystic fibrosis as an alternative diagnosis, yet in 2017 a number of Polish medical specialists, having inspected Chopin's heart, dismissed this possibility. 'On the basis of this visual analysis,' they write, 'it can be stated with high probability that Frederic Chopin had long-lasting tuberculosis as the primary disease, which was the cause of progressive deterioration of his physical condition and numerous symptoms, mainly from the airways. Tuberculosis pericarditis, rapidly progressing within a rather short period of time, a relatively rare complication of diffuse tuberculosis, might have been the immediate cause of his death.' Michał Witt et al., 'A Closer Look at Frederic Chopin's Cause of Death', *American Journal of Medicine*, vol. 130, no. 10 (October 2017), pp. 211–12.

p. 118　　*Grzymała lashed out*: Grzymała to Auguste Léo, October 1849, *SCFC*, p. 374.

p. 119　　*Ludwika insisted*: Alex Ross, 'Chopin's Heart', *The New Yorker* (5 February 2014). http://www.newyorker.com/culture/culture-desk/chopins-heart.

p. 119　　*The funeral*: J. W. Davison, *Frederic Chopin: Critical and Appreciative Essay* (London, 1927), pp. 19–20. Davison, a grumpy critic during Chopin's lifetime, was present at the Madeleine service.

CHAPTER 10

p. 120　　*six million visitors*: Cyril Ehrlich, *The Piano: A History* (Oxford, 1990), p. 56.

p. 120　　*In his memoirs*: Dallas Kern Holoman, 'Introduction' to Robert Winter, 'Keyboards', in Howard Mayer Brown and Stanley Sadie (eds.), *Performance Practice: Music after 1600*, vol. 2 (New York, 1990), p. 324.

p. 121　　*'seminaries of revolution'*: Colin Jones, *Paris: Biography of a City* (London, 2006), p. 341.

p. 121　　*But the Emperor's vision*: Ibid., p. 349.

p. 121　　*'Alas, Old Paris'*: Eric Hazan, *The Invention of Paris*, trans. David Fernbach (London, 2011), p. 17.

p. 122   *'it must make'*: Adam Gopnik (ed.), *Americans in Paris: A Literary Anthology* (New York, 2004), p. 131.

p. 122   *'The deadly'*: Ibid., pp. 131–2.

p. 125   *Alpheus Babcock*: Ehrlich, *The Piano*, p. 32.

p. 126   *French polish*: Samuel Wolfenden, *A Treatise on the Art of Piano-forte Construction* (Old Woking, 1975), p. 83.

p. 127   *In the 1860s*: Ehrlich, *The Piano*, p. 117.

p. 127   *according to the editor*: Ibid., p. 144.

p. 128   *The Great Exhibition*: Ibid., p. 28.

p. 128   *In 1910*: Ibid., p. 222.

p. 128   *At the end of the century*: Ibid., pp. 40–41.

p. 129   *'All Europe'*: Walter Benjamin, *Charles Baudelaire: A Lyric Poet in the Era of High Capitalism*, trans. Harry Zohn (London, 1973), p. 165.

p. 129   *Marcellin Desboutin*: Anka Muhlstein, 'Degas Invents a New World', *The New York Review of Books* (12 May 2016), Kindle edition. 'He's a zinc or copper plate blackened with printer's ink, and plate and man are flattened together by his printing press whose mechanism has swallowed him completely.'

p. 129   *'This predominance'*: Arthur Loesser, *Men, Women and Pianos* (London, 1955), pp. 415–16.

p. 130   *their salons decorated*: *The Musical Courier* (11 September 1895), in Ehrlich, *The Piano*, p. 125.

p. 130   *Chopin grew*: Malcolm Gillies interview, 18 November 2014.

p. 131   *'register life'*: Malcolm Gillies, *Bartók Remembered* (London, 1991), p. 136.

p. 131   *'Chopin would'*: Stephen Hough, 'Why Was Josef Hofmann Considered the Greatest Pianist of All?', *Daily Telegraph* (17 September 2009).

p. 132   *'Are we to believe'*: *CPT*, p. 127.

p. 132   *'Here is a'*: Uli Gerhartz interview, 28 May 2015.

p. 132   *wrote to Tytus*: Frédéric Chopin to Tytus Woyciechowski, 12 October 1830, *SCFC*, pp. 59–60.

p. 133   *'You never feel'*: Peter Roennfeldt interview, 20 July 2015.

CHAPTER 11

p. 135   *'The collection'*: Mary Elizabeth Adams Brown to The Trustees of the Metropolitan Museum, New York, 16 February 1889. http://www.metmuseum.org/about-the-museum/museum-departments/curatorial-departments/musical-instruments/of-note/2014/mary-elizabeth-brown-collection. In a nice bit of serendipity, the collection, in which the path from Chopin to Steinway is carefully demarcated, is only minutes from the gallery housing Delacroix's painting, *George Sand's Garden at Nohant*.

p. 136   *Wild West*: Jayson Dobney interview, 21 September 2015.

p. 137   *'harmonious and possessed'*: Ross Duffin, *How Equal Temperament Ruined Harmony: And Why You Should Care* (New York, 2008), Kindle edition, ch. 7.

p. 137   *Equal temperament*: Ibid., ch. 8.

p. 137   *As late as 1972*: Ibid., ch. 10.

p. 138   *'terrible resonance'*: Cyril Ehrlich, *The Piano: A History* (Oxford, 1990), p. 61.

p. 138   *Advocates of older*: See Duffin, *How Equal Temperament Ruined Harmony*.

p. 138   *'All those with'*: Frédéric Chopin to Julian Fontana, 18 August 1848, *SCFC*, p. 330.

p. 139   *A conceptual flaw*: Tinne Mannaerts to Paul Kildea, 10 December 2015.

CHAPTER 12

p. 141   *'He was as'*: Obituary, *Revue et Gazette Musicale* (21 October 1849), in William G. Atwood, *The Parisian Worlds of Frédéric Chopin* (New Haven, CT, 1999), p. 408.

p. 141   *'This talent'*: Henri Blanchard, 'Obsèques de Frédéric Chopin', *Revue et Gazette Musicale* (4 November 1849), in Jeffrey Kallberg, *Chopin at the Boundaries: Sex, History, and Musical Genre* (Cambridge, MA, 1996), pp. 248–9.

p. 141   *Liszt took*: Meirion Hughes (ed. and trans.), *Liszt's Chopin* (Manchester, 2010), pp. 35, 98–9.

p. 141   *'a jewel-box'*: Hippolyte Barbedette, *Chopin: Essai de critique musicale*, in Thomas Higgins (ed.), *Frédéric Chopin, Preludes, Opus 28: An Authoritative Score: Historical Background: Analysis: Views and Comments* (New York, 1973), pp. 33, 65–6.

p. 142   *'something which is'*: Charles Willeby, *Frédéric François Chopin* (London, 1892), p. 190.

p. 142   *Cortot in the following century*: Alfred Cortot, *In Search of Chopin*, trans. Cyril and Rena Clarke (Mineola, NY, 2013), p. 29.

p. 142   *'Any pianist'*: Concert review, *Scotsman* (10 October 1848), in William G. Atwood, *Fryderyk Chopin: Pianist from Warsaw* (New York, 1987), p. 255.

p. 143   'The Parisian public': Joseph Filtsch to his parents, 16 February 1842, *SCFC*, p. 216.

p. 143   *Late in life*: Anton Rubinstein, *Lectures on the History of Piano Music*, in Philip Taylor, *Anton Rubinstein: A Life in Music* (Bloomington and Indianapolis, IN, 2007), p. 13.

p. 143   *Chopin had performed*: *CPT*, p. 139.

p. 144   'If, unfortunately': Anton Rubinstein, *Music and its Masters: A Conversation*, trans. Mrs John P. Morgan (London, n.d.), p. 20.

p. 145   *he predicted that*: Gustav Karpeles (ed.), *Heinrich Heine's Memoirs: From his Works, Letters, and Conversations*, trans. Gilbert Cannan, vol. 1 (London, 1910), pp. 270–71.

p. 145   *Madame von ——*: Rubinstein's biographer Philip Taylor thinks that the pianist possibly invented Madame von —— as a literary device.

p. 145   'its last': Rubinstein, *Music and its Masters*, p. 58.

p. 145   'With the excess': Ibid., p. 67.

p. 145   'a false road': Taylor, *Anton Rubinstein*, p. 219.

p. 146   'Whether the': Rubinstein, *Music and its Masters*, pp. 55–6.

p. 146   'the first of which': Ibid., p. 56.

p. 147   *He dedicated*: James Methuen-Campbell, 'Chopin in Performance', in Jim Samson (ed.), *The Cambridge Companion to Chopin* (Cambridge, 1994), Kindle edition, ch. 9.

p. 147   'rushed and raved': Robert Philip, *Early Recordings and Musical Style: Changing Tastes in Instrumental Performance 1900–1950* (Cambridge, 1994), p. 217.

p. 147   *who first programmed*: The American Carl Wolfsohn is credited with performing all of Chopin's solo works in Philadelphia a few years before Tausig.

p. 148   *grilling Wilhelm von Lenz*: *CPT*, p. 155.

p. 148   'In his hands': Edward Blickstein and Gregor Benko, *Chopin's Prophet: The Life of Pianist Vladimir de Pachmann* (Lanham, MD, 2013), p. 24.

p. 148   'If the Germans': James Gibbons Huneker, *Mezzotints in Modern Music* (London, 1900), p. 212.

p. 148   *By the time he wrote*: Kornel Michałowski and Jim Samson, 'Chopin, Fryderyk Franciszek'. *Grove Music Online. Oxford Music Online.* Oxford University Press, accessed 9 December 2015, http://www.oxfordmusiconline.com/subscriber/article/grove/music/51099.

p. 149   'drew carefully': Philip, *Early Recordings and Musical Style*, p. 217.

p. 150   '*This music*': Alan Walker (ed.), *Frédéric Chopin: Profiles of the Man and the Musician* (London, 1966), p. 140. Baudelaire is here paraphrasing Delacroix's words.

p. 150   '*A night moth*': Harold C. Schonberg, *The Great Pianists*, revised and updated edition (New York, 1987), p. 137.

p. 150   '*It takes*': Ibid., p. 137.

p. 151   *as a cycle*: Jeffrey Kallberg, 'Small "Forms": In Defence of the Prelude', in Samson, *The Cambridge Companion to Chopin*, ch. 6.

p. 151   '*Chopin played*': Jean-Jacques Eigeldinger (ed.), 'Preface', *Fryderyk Chopin, Préludes, Op. 28* (London, 2004), p. vii.

p. 152   *On the back*: Jean-Jacques Eigeldinger, 'Twenty-Four Preludes Op. 28: Genre, Structure, Significance', in Jim Samson (ed.), *Chopin Studies* (Cambridge, 1988), p. 170. The first suggestion is built around two different tonics, a fifth apart, E and B, to which Chopin allocated Preludes in both the major and minor key: nos. 9 (E), 4 (E minor), 6 (B minor), 11 (B). His second grouping is of Preludes in major keys – nos. 15 (D flat), 21 (B flat), 13 (F sharp), 17 (A flat) – in which the interval of the fifth is employed as a structural and motivic device.

p. 152   *His teacher Liszt*: Kenneth Hamilton, *After the Golden Age: Romantic Pianism and Modern Performance* (Oxford, 2008), p. 67. Rubinstein's pupil Annette Essipova was probably the first pianist to programme all twenty-four Preludes as a set, performing them in a concert in 1876. Erinn E. Knyt, 'Ferruccio Busoni and the "Halfness" of Frédéric Chopin', *Journal of Musicology*, vol. 34, no. 2 (spring 2017), p. 272.

p. 152   '*All-Chopin programs*': Frédéric Chopin, *Preludes*, ed. Rafael Joseffy, with a biographical sketch and prefatory note by James Huneker (New York, 1915–18), p. iii.

p. 152   '*by a hedge*': Chopin, *Études for the Piano*, revised and fingered by Arthur Friedheim, with a general prefatory note by James Huneker and introductory remarks by Friedheim (New York, 1916), p. 1.

p. 153   *Friedheim's way of thinking*: Ibid., p. 2.

p. 153   '*a few of*': Chopin, *Preludes*, p. vi.

p. 153   '*To a certain*': Chopin, *Études*, p. 2.

p. 153   '*greedily absorbed*': Ibid., p. 1.

p. 154   '*The Chopin best*': Hughes, *Liszt's Chopin*, pp. 35–6.

p. 155   '*in his Life*': George Sand, *The Story of My Life*, trans. Dan Hofstadter (London, 1984), p. 243.

p. 155   '*Dans les arts*': Rubinstein, *Music and its Masters*, p. 78.

CHAPTER 13

p. 159   *Her party*: Wanda Landowska's date book, 27–28 January 1911, WLDR, 102/8. Landowska uses abbreviations of *le matin* and *le soir* for a.m. and p.m. The diary mistakenly prints the year 1910 on this page.

p. 161   *'The harpsichord is'*: Wanda Landowska, 'Keyboard Aristocrat', *Grolier Encyclopedia Yearbook* (New York, 1949), p. 333.

p. 164   *'The Prelude in C'*: Jan Kleczyński, *Chopin's Greater Works (Preludes, Ballads, Nocturnes, Polonaises, Mazurkas): How They Should Be Understood*, trans. Natalie Janotha (London, *c.* 1895), pp. 47, 48.

p. 164   *'Besides these'*: Landowska's journal, 9 June 1894, WLDR, 100/2. All translations of the original Polish were commissioned by Denise Restout in preparation for her planned biography of Landowska.

p. 164   *citing her daughter's*: Ibid., 31 March 1895, WLDR, 100/4.

p. 165   *'Why are you'*: Ibid., June 1896, WLDR, 100/8.

p. 165   *She tells how she transposed*: Ibid., 28 March 1895, WLDR, 100/2.

p. 165   *'Bach is'*: Ibid., 10 March 1895, WLDR, 100/2.

p. 165   *'my good'*: Ibid., 7 January 1895, WLDR, 100/2.

p. 165   *'Why does Wanda'*: Ibid., 13 October 1896, WLDR, 101/1.

p. 165   *'How could I'*: Ibid., 11 January 1895, WLDR, 100/2.

p. 166   *'Making a'*: Ibid., 6 October 1895, WLDR, 100/6.

p. 166   *'A woman'*: Ibid., June 1896, WLDR, 100/8; *'Jews have'*: Landowska's journal, 1 August 1896, WLDR, 101/1.

p. 166   *'And am I'*: Ibid., 1 August 1896, WLDR, 101/1.

p. 167   *'The tone'*: Ibid., March 1895, WLDR, 100/6.

p. 168   *'aroused in me'*: Landowska to Éduoard Ganche, 1 January 1933, WLDR, 154/1.

p. 169   *'One day'*: Landowska draft, WLDR, 154/3.

p. 169   *'As a matter'*: Landowska to Ganche, 1 January 1933, WLDR, 154/1.

p. 173   *'They say'*: Harold C. Schonberg, *The Great Pianists*, revised and updated edition (New York, 1987), p. 415.

p. 173   *'We have been'*: T. S. Eliot, *Prufrock and Other Observations* (London, 1917), pp. 17–18.

p. 174   *'When he had'*: Marcel Proust, *Remembrance of Things Past*, trans. C. K. Scott Moncrieff, vol. 1 (Ware, 2006), p. 318.

p. 174   *Nor that Proust*: Marcel Proust, *By Way of Sainte-Beuve*, trans. Sylvia Townsend Warner (London, 1984), p. 143.

p. 175   *'If you place'*: Wanda Landowska, 'How Chopin Played Chopin', *Musical Standard* (8 March 1913), p. 197.

p. 176   *Here and elsewhere*: These criticisms are from a later published translation (1926) of Landowska's original article.

p. 176   *'The Chopin'*: Denise Restout (ed.), *Landowska on Music* (London, 1965), p. 404.

p. 176   *'M. de Bertha says'*: Wanda Landowska, 'Chopin's Nationality', *The Musical Leader* (May 1915), p. 3.

p. 177   *Auguste Mangeot*: Auguste Mangeot, 'A propos de la nationalité de Chopin', trans. Sue Hackett, *Le Monde musical* (? July 1911), p. 209.

p. 177   *Her aim*: Restout, *Landowska on Music*, p. 99.

p. 177   *'My dear Pau'*: Teri Noel Towe, 'Pablo Casals and Johann Sebastian Bach – A Personal Reminiscence' (unpublished, 1998).

p. 177   *Skip Sempé thinks*: Skip Sempé, 'Bach and the Landowska Legacy', lecture-recital, Library of Congress, 12 April 2013.

p. 177   *for their habit*: Restout, *Landowska on Music*, p. 374.

p. 178   *'Chopin', she would write*: WLDR, 154/3.

p. 178   *'sustained soliloquies'*: Restout Landowska on Music, p. 277.

p. 178   *'It is an actual'*: Landowska, 'How Chopin Played Chopin', *Musical Standard*, p. 197.

CHAPTER 14

p. 179   *In her journal*: Wanda Landowska's journal, 30 November 1914, WLDR, 103/3.

p. 179   *He asked*: Ibid.

p. 180   *'The Germans'*: Ibid.

p. 180   *She writes of more humane weaponry*: Ibid.

p. 180   *She analyses*: Ibid.

p. 180   *She writes how the Busonis*: Ibid., 3 January 1915, WLDR, 103/3.

p. 181   *She relates*: Ibid., March 1915, WLDR, 103/3.

p. 181   *'It sounded'*: Ibid., 15 January 1915, WLDR, 103/3.

p. 181   *'It is like'*: Ibid., 22 March 1915, WLDR, 103/3.

p. 181   *'After the war'*: Ibid., 20 December 1914, WLDR, 103/3.

p. 181   *'terror of'*: Charles Baudelaire, *Paris Spleen*, trans. Louise Varèse (New York, 1970), p. 94.

p. 181   *he was hit and killed*: Landowska later told a student the accident occurred in Paris, but her memory for dates and places was sometimes inaccurate. Lew's passport contains no stamp for France or Paris at the time of his death.

p. 182   *Landowska drafted*: Landowska's correspondence book, 20 April 1919, WLDR, 73/13.

p. 182   *She obtained a passport*: Landowska's Polish passport, 1919, WLDR, 202/2.

p. 185   *'dinners, soirées'*: Adam Gopnik (ed.), *Americans in Paris: A Literary Anthology* (New York, 2004), p. 335.

p. 186   *nearly every book*: Restout to Mary-Lou McGuire, 28 June 1966, WLDR, 175/4.

p. 186   *'To judge Romanticism'*: Denise Restout (ed.), *Landowska on Music* (London, 1965), p. 55.

p. 187   *'I had to'*: Wanda Landowska, 'Keyboard Aristocrat', *Grolier Encyclopedia Yearbook* (New York, 1949), p. 335.

CHAPTER 15

p. 188   *'Holy jumping'*: Ralph Kirkpatrick, *Early Years* (New York, 1985), p. 68. Journal entry for 13 October 1931.

p. 189   *And he was seeing*: Ibid., p. 87. Journal entry for 18 April 1932.

p. 189   *'Don't do an'*: Wanda Landowska teaching notes, 8 July 1932, WLDR, 163/3.

p. 189   *And she emphasized*: Ibid.

p. 189   *'glided on'*: Kirkpatrick, *Early Years*, p. 87. Journal entry for 3 May 1932.

p. 190   *'I have never'*: Ibid., p. 92. Journal entry for 10 July 1932.

p. 190   *'How can'*: Ibid., p. 92. Journal entry for 19 July 1932.

p. 190   *'He looks'*: Ibid., p. 101. Journal entry for 24 January 1933.

p. 191   *'she looks'*: Ibid., pp. 70, 78, 93. Journal entries for 20 October 1931; 25 December 1931; 19 July 1932.

p. 192   *'It also seemed'*: Ibid., p. 91. Journal entry for 27 June 1932.

p. 192   *'Paderewski's ghostly face'*: Philippe Sands, *East West Street: On the Origins of Genocide and Crimes Against Humanity* (London, 2016), Kindle edition, ch. 96.

p. 192   *'Paderewski's art'*: Wanda Landowska, 'Recollections of Paderewski', *Saturday Review* [June 1951], page proof, WLDR, 155/3.

p. 193   *'It is thus'*: Landowska, 'Paderewski Orator', WLDR, 155/2.

p. 193　*'His art'*: Kirkpatrick, *Early Years*, p. 92. Journal entry for 6 July 1932.

p. 194　*'Now, after'*: Frédéric Chopin, *24 Preludes*, Op. 28, Student's Edition by Alfred Cortot, trans. David Ponsonby (Paris, 1930), p. 11.

p. 194　*'It is a heart'*: Ibid., p. 37.

p. 194　*'Chopin as the'*: Arthur Rubinstein, *My Many Years* (London, 1980), p. 123.

p. 195　*'the delight'*: Chopin, *24 Preludes*, p. 53.

CHAPTER 16

p. 197　*more than 20,000 Germans*: Eugen Weber, 'France: From Hospitality to Hostility', in Peter Hayes (ed.), *How Was it Possible?: A Holocaust Reader* (Lincoln, NB, 2015), p. 194.

p. 197　*'First one'*: Ibid.

p. 197　*'moved by'*: Sybille Bedford, *Quicksands: A Memoir* (London, 2005), pp. 278, 279.

p. 198　*'We will'*: Lynn H. Nicholas, *The Rape of Europa: The Fate of Europe's Treasures in the Third Reich and the Second World War* (London, 1994), p. 20.

p. 198　*'Jewish trash'*: Ibid., p. 21.

p. 198　*Peggy Guggenheim*: Ibid., p. 87.

p. 198　*Göring acquired*: Ibid., p. 23.

p. 200　*'would like'*: Denise Restout's diary, 15 October 1939, WLDR, 107/10.

p. 200　*dissident families*: Nicholas, *The Rape of Europa*, pp. 64–5.

p. 200　*'He is then'*: *CPT*, p. 284.

p. 201　*'For the profundity'*: Jim Samson, 'Chopin Reception: Theory, History, Analysis', in John Rink and Jim Samson (eds.), *Chopin Studies* 2 (Cambridge, 1994), p. 7.

p. 201　*'Scarlatti (bombing)'*: Restout's diary, January 1940, WLDR, 201/1.

p. 201　*Landowska worked*: Ibid.

p. 203　*'Madame should'*: Irène Némirovsky, *Suite Française* (London, 2007), p. 18.

p. 203　*'so she'd have'*: Ibid., p. 19.

p. 203　*'Nini' complaining*: Restout's diary, 3 June 1940, WLDR, 201/1.

p. 203　*Némirovsky describes*: Némirovsky, *Suite Française*, p. 42.

p. 204　*'to the sound'*: Restout's diary, 10 June 1940, WLDR, 201/1.

CHAPTER 17

p. 206 *they secreted away*: Hector Feliciano, *The Lost Museum: The Nazi Conspiracy to Steal the World's Greatest Works of Art* (New York, 1997), p. 44.

p. 206 *With steely calculation*: Ibid., p. 47.

p. 207 *As if to underline*: Willem de Vries, *Sonderstab Musik: Music Confiscations by the Einsatzstab Reichsleiter Rosenberg under the Nazi Occupation of Western Europe* (Amsterdam, 1996), p. 102.

p. 207 *The number of acronyms*: Ibid., p. 85. AA: Auswärtiges Amt, Von Ribbentrop's Foreign Office; M-Aktion: Möbel-Aktion, responsible for taking household furniture and fittings; NSDAP: National-sozialistische Deutsche Arbeiterpartei, the full name of the Nazi Party; GFP: Geheime Feldpolizei (Secret Military Police of the Wehrmacht); RSHA: Reichssicherheitshauptamt, the Reich security headquarters; DBFU: Der Beauftragter des Führers für die Überwachung der gesamten geistigen und weltanschaulichen Schulung und Erziehung der NSDAP (Commissioner of the Führer for the Supervision of the Entire Intellectual and Ideological Schooling and Training of the NSDAP); RMWEV: Das Reichsministerium für Wissenschaft, Erziehung und Volksbildung (Ministry of Science, Education and Popular Culture), Reich Minister Rust's organization; RMVAP: Das Reichsministerium für Volksaufklärung und Propaganda (Ministry of Public Education and Propaganda), Goebbels' department; MVF: Militärverwaltung in Frankreich (Military Command in France).

p. 207 '*We have succeeded*': Jane Gottlieb, 'The School Receives Arthur Rubinstein Collection', *Juilliard Journal* (November 2007).

p. 208 '*certain cultural items*': de Vries, *Sonderstab Musik*, p. 128.

p. 208 *In such circumstances*: Ibid., p. 136.

p. 208 '*They are perfectly*': Iris Origo, *War in Val D'Orcia: A Diary* (London, 1985), p. 113.

p. 209 *As the open-back*: Christopher Pike interview, 29 January 2014. Weisshuhn was Pike's uncle.

p. 209 *They drank*: de Vries, *Sonderstab Musik*, pp. 228, 220–21.

p. 211 *two vitrines*: 'Liste des objets non identifiables', WLDR, 175/4.

p. 211 *On 4 October*: Irène Némirovsky, *Suite Française*, trans. Sandra Smith (London, 2007), p. 370.

p. 212 *Restout travelled*: de Vries, *Sonderstab Musik*, pp. 220–21.

p. 212 '*I go to*': Restout diary, 5 October 1940, WLDR, 175/8.

p. 213 *She listed*: 'Liste revisée', WLDR, 175/8.

p. 213 '*1 piano manufactured*': 'Inventory of stolen instruments, October 1940', WLDR, 175/8. Her hurried note for this inventory words it slightly differently: 'The piano made in Palma, Majorca and owned by Chopin.'

p. 213 '*The matter especially*': de Vries, *Sonderstab Musik*, p. 221.

p. 213 '*The items*': Ibid., p. 223.

p. 214 *a French cut*: André Gide, *Notes on Chopin*, trans. Bernard Frechtman (Westport, CT, 1978), pp. v–vii.

p. 214 '*His sole*': Ibid., p. vii.

p. 215 '*Each of them*': Ibid., p. 33.

p. 215 '*played in a*': Ibid., p. 46.

p. 215 *He thought*: Ibid., p. 38.

p. 215 *Like Landowska*: Ibid., pp. 36–7.

p. 215 '*Is there art*': Ibid., p. 38.

p. 215 *Without such slowness*: Ibid., p. 28.

p. 215 '*We are told*': Ibid., p. 21.

p. 216 *In November*: Restout notes, 23 November 1940, WLDR, 175/8.

p. 216 '*We must*': Sybille Bedford, *Quicksands: A Memoir* (London, 2005), p. 324.

p. 216 '*What a strange*': John K. Roth, Elisabeth Maxwell et al. (eds.), *Remembering for the Future: The Holocaust in an Age of Genocide* (London, 2001), p. 347.

p. 217 '*It is a city*': Charles Baudelaire, *Paris Spleen*, trans. Louise Varèse (New York, 1970), p. 99.

p. 217 *As the war*: Neill Lochery, *Lisbon: War in the Shadows of the City of Light, 1939–1945* (New York, 2011), pp. 210–11.

p. 218 '*personal effects*': Export Pass No. 1333, British Consulate General, 27 November 1941, WLDR, 202/2.

CHAPTER 18

p. 220 *midway through*: Colin Jones, *Paris: Biography of a City* (London, 2006), p. 483.

p. 220 *Landowska and Restout encountered dazed*: Arthur Rubinstein, *My Many Years* (London, 1980), p. 477. This description is based predominantly on Rubinstein's account, though it also incorporates information from Landowska's and Restout's later memories. Rubinstein practised on the same upright while awaiting his interview.

p. 221   '*We do not*': Denise Restout, 'Wanda Landowska's Aide Recalls U.S. Arrival on Morning of Dec. 7', *Lakeville Journal* (5 December 1991). Restout dates this incorrectly in the article, as her diary and immigration records establish.

p. 221   '*We have previously*': Leonard Smith to Wanda Landowska, 10 February 1943, WLDR, 176/8.

p. 223   '*A performance*': Virgil Thomson, *The Musical Scene* (New York, 1945), p. 201.

p. 224   *their antics*: Tim Page and Vanessa Weeks Page (eds.), *Selected Letters of Virgil Thomson* (New York, 1988), p. 177.

p. 224   *He loved too*: Thomson to Mark Levine [1942], in ibid., p. 190.

p. 224   *Her notebook*: Restout's notebook, March 1942, WLDR, 107/13.

p. 225   '*piece is made*': Frédéric Chopin, 24 *Preludes*, Op. 28, Student's Edition by Alfred Cortot, trans. David Ponsonby (Paris, 1930), p. 65.

p. 225   *It also awarded*: For a detailed study of the relationship between the Vienna Philharmonic and Nazi Germany, including photographs of Baldur von Schirach receiving the Ring of Honour, see Fritz Trümpi, *The Political Orchestra: The Vienna and Berlin Philharmonics During the Third Reich* (Chicago, IL, 2016).

p. 227   '*Already a woman*': Alfred Cortot, *In Search of Chopin*, trans. Cyril and Rena Clarke (Mineola, NY, 2013), p. 199.

p. 228   *In the summer*: Willem de Vries, *Sonderstab Musik: Music Confiscations by the Einsatzstab Reichsleiter Rosenberg under the Nazi Occupation of Western Europe* (Amsterdam, 1996), pp. 145–6.

p. 229   *It was Goebbels*: Carla Shapreau, 'A Violin once Owned by Goebbels Keeps its Secrets', *The New York Times*, 21 September 2012. http://www.nytimes.com/2012/09/23/arts/music/nejiko-suwa-and-joseph-goebbelss-gift.html?pagewanted=all&_r=0.

p. 229   *The orchestra*: Carla Shapreau, 'The Loss of French Musical Property During World War II, Post-War Repatriations, Restitutions, and 21st Century Ramifications', *FBF Annual Report 2012–2013* (Berkeley, CA, 2014), p. 77.

p. 229   '*by order*': Ibid, p. 77.

p. 230   'has taken': Inter-Allied Declaration against Acts of Dispossession in Territories under Enemy Occupation and Control', 5 January 1943. http://www.lootedartcommission.com/inter-allied-declaration.

p. 231   *In 1939 Professor*: Halina Tchórzewska-Kabata, *More Precious than Gold: Treasures of the Polish National Library*, trans. Janina Dorosz (Warsaw, 2003), p. 189. http://bn.org.pl/download/document/1236004326.pdf.

p. 232   '*they gush*': Eric Hazan, *The Invention of Paris: A History in Footsteps*, trans. David Fernbach (London, 2010), p. 10.

p. 232   '*epic poet*': *Cahiers français*, no. 54 (April 1944), p. 29.

p. 233   '*Nostalgic but full*': WLDR, 180/17.

p. 234   '*Very fine*': Janet Flanner to Natalia Murray, 11 May 1944, in Natalia Danesi Murray, *Darlinghissima: Letters to a Friend* (London, 1988), p. 6.

p. 234   *Flanner wrote of*: Janet Flanner, *Paris Journal 1944–1965* (London, 1966), p. 5.

p. 235   '*For five years Europe*': Ibid., p. 4.

CHAPTER 19

p. 237   *On opening*: Hector Feliciano, *The Lost Museum: The Nazi Conspiracy to Steal the World's Greatest Works of Art* (New York, 1997), p. 165.

p. 237   *Rosenberg arrived*: Ibid., p. 170.

p. 238   *Anita Lasker-Wallfisch*: Anita Lasker-Wallfisch interview, 19 March 2014.

p. 238   '*I had once*': Anita Lasker-Wallfisch, *Inherit the Truth* (London, 1996), p. 150.

p. 238   '*I came*': Elisabeth de Waal, *The Exiles Return* (London, 2014), Kindle edition, ch. 15.

p. 239   '*These returning*': Ibid., ch. 4.

p. 239   *Her accounts*: Wanda Landowska, Income and Expenditure 1945, WLDR, 94/2.

p. 239   *the same year*: 'The Department of Commerce: Current Population Reports: Consumer Income', Series P. 60, no. 2 (2 March 1948), p. 11.

p. 241   *35,000 sets*: Harvey Sachs, *Virtuoso: The Life and Art of Niccolò Paganini, Franz Liszt, Anton Rubinstein, Ignace Jan Paderewski, Fritz Kreisler, Pablo Casals, Wanda Landowska, Vladimir Horowitz, Glenn Gould* (London, 1982), p. 161.

p. 241   '*It was totally*': Barbara Attie, Janet Goldwater and Diane Pontius (prods.), *Uncommon Visionary* (Bala Cynwyd, 1997).

p. 242   *He instructed*: Ibid.

p. 243   *Captain John Morey*: Doda Conrad to Landowska, 15 December 1945, WLDR, 175/8.

p. 243   *Nevertheless, he could*: Attie, Goldwater and Pontius, *Uncommon Visionary*.

p. 243   '*To describe*': Landowska to Doda Conrad, 4 January 1946, WLDR, 175/8.

p. 244   '*Do you remember*': Landowska to Marya Freund, 7 January 1946, WLDR, 64/8.

CHAPTER 20

p. 245   '*My dear boy*': Charles Vidor (dir.), *A Song to Remember* (Columbia Pictures, 1945).

p. 247   *It is the work*: In Roman Polanski's film adaptation he plays the far more difficult Ballade in G minor, Op. 23.

p. 248   *Nancy Mitford's words*: Nancy Mitford, *A Talent to Annoy: Essays, Journalism and Reviews* (London, 2013), p. 38.

p. 248   '*They emptied*': Arthur Rubinstein, *My Many Years* (London, 1980), p. 525.

p. 248   '*This Hall*': Arthur Rubinstein speech, http://www.msz.gov.pl/en/foreign_policy/international_organisations/united_nations/poland_and_the_un.

p. 249   '*a Chopin*': Alfred Cortot, *In Search of Chopin*, trans. Cyril and Rena Clarke (Mineola, NY, 2013), p. 209.

p. 249   '*I am the composer*': Alex Ross, 'Monument Man', *The New Yorker* (24 July 2014), http://www.newyorker.com/culture/cultural-comment/richard-strauss-and-the-american-army.

p. 249   '*Romanticism was impregnated*': Simon Kenway interview, 14 January 2016.

CHAPTER 21

p. 252   *over $65,000*: www.measuringworth.com.

p. 252   '*Piano Chopin*': Wanda Landowska to Dia Mathot, 20 April 1946, WLDR, 94/2.

p. 253   '*I hope to*': Rose Valland to Landowska, 15 July 1946, WLDR, 175/8.

p. 253   '*They are for me*': Landowska to Valland, 31 July 1946, WLDR, 175/8.

p. 254   '*My dear*': Mathot to Landowska, 6 July 1946, WLDR, 94/3.

p. 254   *In another letter*: Mathot to Landowska, 6 May 1946, WLDR, 94/3.

p. 254   *'I am unsure'*: Max Unger to Mathot, 27 July 1946, WLDR, 175/4.

p. 254   *No mention*: Willem de Vries, 'Wanda Landowska', WLDR, 175/8.

p. 254   *'All of the'*: Noel Strauss, 'Collection Found in Salt Mines', *The New York Times* (13 October 1946), p. X7.

p. 255   *The public imagination*: Janet Flanner, 'The Beautiful Spoils: Monuments Men', *The New Yorker* (8 March 1947), p. 47.

p. 255   *Allied troops*: Ibid., p. 48.

p. 256   *Göring reputedly*: Simon Goodman, *The Orpheus Clock: The Search for my Family's Art Treasures Stolen by the Nazis* (London, 2015), Kindle edition, ch. 6.

p. 256   *'organized plunder'*: The Avalon Project: Documents in Law, History and Diplomacy. www.avalon.law.yale.edu/imt/judrosen.org.

p. 257   *'How would you'*: Flanner, 'The Beautiful Spoils', p. 48.

p. 257   *Landowska's instruments*: Willem de Vries, *Sonderstab Musik: Music Confiscations by the Einsatzstab Reichsleiter Rosenberg under the Nazi Occupation of Western Europe* (Amsterdam, 1996), p. 225.

p. 258   *These moral questions*: See Carla Shapreau, *The Vienna Archives: Musical Expropriations During the Nazi Era and 21st Century Ramifications* (Berkeley, CA, 2014).

p. 259   *'I have long'*: Landowska to Mathot, 15 May 1946, WLDR, 94/3.

p. 260   *'of such tragic'*: *Exposition d'art Romantique: Chopin–George Sand et leurs amis* (Liège, 1947), p. 28.

CHAPTER 22

p. 261   *according to Prokofiev*: Arthur Rubinstein, *My Many Years* (London, 1980), p. 327.

p. 261   *Richter would later*: Bruno Monsaingeon, *Sviatoslav Richter: Notebooks and Conversations*, trans. Stewart Spencer (Princeton, NJ, 2001), p. 259.

p. 263   *'I could detect'*: Ibid., p. 265.

p. 263   *Liszt famously*: Oscar Bie, *A History of the Pianoforte and Pianoforte Players*, trans. E. E. Kellett and E. W. Naylor (London, 1899), p. 264.

p. 263   *'His playing'*: CPT, p. 272.

p. 263   *'In my opinion'*: Ibid.

p. 264   *Charles Hallé*: Ibid., p. 72.

p. 264   *An earlier*: Ibid., p. 73.

p. 264   *hair on end*: George Sand, *The Story of My Life*, trans. Dan Hofstadter (London, 1984), p. 240.

p. 264   *'Listening to'*: W. H. Auden, *Collected Poems* (London, 1991), p. 800.

CHAPTER 23

p. 266   *In 1953*: Doda Conrad to Wanda Landowska, 17 April 1953, WLDR, 64/12.

p. 266   *The buildings*: Summary document, 30 August 1945, WLDR, 94/1.

p. 266   *'Paris is sad'*: Conrad to Landowska, 11 April 1955, WLDR, 64/9.

p. 266   *'As for the Chopin'*: Landowska to Conrad, 1 August 1953, WLDR, 64/9.

p. 267   *'All but'*: Denise Restout to Willem de Vries, 28 September 1992, WLDR, 97/8; *in 1960*: Restout to Jack Pfeiffer, 4 November 1960, WLDR, 93/1.

p. 267   *'Although she is'*: 'Grandma Bachante', *Time* (20 June 1949), p. 42.

p. 268   *'red is for'*: 'Personality', *Time* (1 December 1952), p. 31.

p. 268   *'This small empress'*: Ibid.

p. 268   *One of these ghosts*: Conrad to Landowska, 16 January 1959, WLDR, 64/10.

p. 268   *But at seventy-nine*: Restout to Pfeiffer, 15 October 1994, WLDR, 175/2. At Landowska's behest, Conrad kept the volumes himself, later selling them to the University of Maryland when his financial situation was precarious.

p. 269   *'Several times'*: Restout to Conrad, 8/9 September 1959, WLDR, 64/10.

p. 269   *'When she held'*: Harold Schonberg, 'Landowska (1879–1959): Romantic Scholar', *The New York Times* (23 August 1959).

p. 270   *'If I am not'*: Denise Restout (ed.), *Landowska on Music* (London, 1965), p. 54.

p. 270   *'Let us not'*: Ibid., pp. 54–5.

p. 270   *'The twentieth'*: Malcolm Gillies interview, 18 November 2014.

p. 272   *Landowska's French assets*: WLDR, 202/1.

p. 272   *'which since'*: Restout to Rose Valland, 18 November 1964, draft, WLDR, 88/9.

p. 272   *'Do you think'*: Ibid.

p. 272   *Playboy magazine*: 'How to get Wanda Landowska to play in your car', *Playboy* (October 1968), p. 55.

p. 273   *'Given these conditions'*: Valland to Restout, 13 January 1965, WLDR, 175/8.

p. 274   *Restout responded*: Restout to Valland, 23 January 1965, draft, WLDR, 88/9.

CHAPTER 24

p. 274   *'Diese nahm'*: Martin Elste (ed.), *Die Dame mit dem Cembalo: Wanda Landowska und die Alte Musik* (Mainz, 2010), p. 28. Elste dates this photo to 1917–18, though Landowska or Restout wrote '1913' on the back of her surviving copy.

p. 275   *'But had I'*: Elste to Paul Kildea, 23 September 2014.

p. 275   *'I have not'*: Carla Shapreau to Kildea, 23 August 2015.

p. 275   *'About the'*: Skip Sempé to Kildea, 24 August 2015.

p. 276   *'My "gut reaction"'*: Teri Noel Towe to Kildea, 26 August 2015.

p. 276   *'In general'*: Denise Restout to Jack Pfeiffer, 4 July 1994, WLDR, 82/9.

p. 276   *'Elsa, of course'*: Pfeiffer to Restout, 11 October 1994, WLDR, 82/9.

p. 277   *'Je désire'*: Sue Hackett interview, 20 January 2016.

p. 278   *'They think'*: Barbara Attie, Janet Goldwater, and Diane Pontius (prods.), *Uncommon Visionary* (Bala Cynwyd, 1997).

p. 279   *But his sole focus*: Alain Kohler to Kildea, 26 February 2016.

p. 279   *'Unfortunately'*: Christophe Nebout to Kildea, 22 April 2016.

p. 279   *'Perhaps Willem'*: Shapreau to Kildea, 17 November 2015.

p. 280   *'His hands'*: Willem de Vries to Kildea, 26 December 2015.

p. 280   *assiduously recording*: de Vries to Kildea, 21 August 2016; *names like*: de Vries to Kildea, 26 December 2015.

p. 280   *At one point Schunicke*: Order Imposing Conditions and Directing the Taking of Evidence in the Restitution Matter of Schunicke et al. vs. German Reich, WLDR, 175/7.

p. 280   *'I can only'*: Herbert Gerigk witness statement, District Court 4 AR 8/71, 24 February 1971, WLDR, 175/6.

p. 281   *'For ten days'*: Willem de Vries, *Sonderstab Musik: Music Confiscations by the Einsatzstab Reichsleiter Rosenberg under the Nazi Occupation of Western Europe* (Amsterdam, 1996), p. 237.

p. 282   *The court's ruling*: Sentencia A. P. Palma de Mallorca 332/2011 de 19 de octubre. http://portaljuridico.lexnova.es/jurisprudencia/JURIDICO/115956/sentencia-ap-palma-de-mallorca-332-2011-de-19-de-octubre-publicidad-ilicita-doctrina-de-los-act.

p. 283   *Cedric telling me*: Cedric Tiberghien interview, 19 March 2015.

p. 285   '*Are they applauding*': Stuart Proffitt interview, 17 March 2015.

p. 285   *Jean-Jacques Eigeldinger*: Jean-Jacques Eigeldinger to Kildea, 6 August 2016.

p. 286   '*Unable to escape*': Graham Bowley and Carla Shapreau, 'German Panel Rules that a Rare Violin Was Looted by Nazis', *The New York Times* (9 December 2016).

p. 286   '*Until I next*': Shapreau to Kildea, 11 November 2015.

ENVOI

p. 287   '*Of course*': Ruth Kraus interview, 3 July 2013.

Index

Italic page numbers indicate illustrations.